Second Edition

Crime and Policing in Rural and Small-Town America

Second Edition

Crime and Policing in Rural and Small-Town America

Ralph A. Weisheit
David N. Falcone
L. Edward Wells
Illinois State University

WAVELAND
PRESS, INC.
Prospect Heights, Illinois

For information about this book, write or call:
Waveland Press, Inc.
P.O. Box 400
Prospect Heights, Illinois 60070
(847) 634-0081

Contents

3   Rural and Small-Town Police   95

4   Other Parts of the System   143

5   Where Do We Go from Here?   163

Appendix A: What Is Rural?   179

Appendix B: The Study   197

References   201

Index   223

Preface to the Second Edition

FROM THE DAY WE SENT THE MANUSCRIPT FOR THE FIRST EDITION of *Crime and Policing in Rural and Small-Town America* to the editor, we have continued to find new data, new analyses, and new areas of research related to rural crime and rural policing. This second edition comes only about three years after the first, but the amount of new material available since the first edition was so substantial that a new edition was deemed necessary. This edition updates many of the official figures presented in the first edition, adds new information to existing sections, and includes several areas not touched upon in the first edition. New sections to this edition include a discussion of "white trash and rednecks," crimes related to the environment, the use of deadly force by rural police, the training needs of rural police, rural prosecutors, and probation in rural areas.

This edition also includes substantially expanded discussions of guns and crime, rural poverty, gangs, violence, arson, small-town municipal police, rural jails, and prisons. Appendix A includes a more thorough discussion of the question "What is rural?", an issue we consider essential to any study of rural crime. Those who wish to use the book as a resource will find the references have been substantially expanded.

The population of America continues to grow and expand outward into the hinterlands, which may have some role in accounting for the continued interest in rural places and rural crime. This second edition reflects a maturing of our understanding of rural crime and justice issues. The subject continues to fascinate us, perhaps because we are only beginning to appreciate its complexity. It remains a puzzle that is never quite solved, an intellectual challenge that continues to reveal things about crime and American society that are quite unexpected. Although we believe this second edition is a substantial improvement and extension of our work in the first edition, our research on rural crime and justice will continue to be "work in progress" for many years. We continue to feel fortunate to be working in such an interesting subject area.

Preface

Rarely do researchers have the good fortune to examine an issue in which there is a continuing series of surprises and unexpected results and in which conducting the research is, for want of a better word, fun! Such has been the case with this study of rural crime and rural justice. The study formally began with a response to a request for proposals from the National Institute of Justice (NIJ) to study rural policing. The roots of this project, however, go back much further. Each of us has some connection to rural America. Dr. Weisheit grew up outside of a southern Indiana community of just over 7,000, the largest community in the county. Dr. Wells grew up on a small town in Oregon, a community of 2,500 people far from any large urban centers. Dr. Falcone grew up in suburban Chicago but lived for several years in a remote rural section of southeastern Missouri. While we each had our connections to rural environments, for much of our academic careers we set those personal experiences aside in our professional work.

Prior to this study, Dr. Weisheit was funded by NIJ to conduct a study of commercial marijuana growers. Most large-scale growers in his study were rural dwellers, as were most of the police who apprehended them. Traveling to rural areas to interview growers and police raised a variety of issues about rural crime and justice which were beyond the scope of the earlier study.

The present study was possible only because of the collaboration among Drs. Weisheit, Wells, and Falcone. From his earlier work, Dr. Weisheit had already gathered a variety of materials about rural crime and rural culture and had published an article on conducting research in rural areas. Dr. Wells contributed the insights of a methodologist, a necessity in a multi-method study such as this one. Dr. Wells also had the expertise to manage, merge, and analyze large data sets, allowing part of our research to include secondary analyses of existing data. Dr.

Falcone's expertise is in policing, something about which Drs. Weisheit and Wells are less well informed. His practical experience, combined with his scholarly understanding of the issue, proved invaluable. Dr. Falcone was also responsible for conducting all of the focus groups and most of the interviews for the study.

At first, the challenge was to find something to say about rural crime and rural justice. This changed as a general framework for understanding rural crime emerged, a framework in which the focus was on the role of relatively close social networks within the context of relatively greater physical isolation. What had appeared to be a variety of narrowly focused studies covering a broad range of disciplines began to take shape as parts of a coherent whole. As we continued to dig through the literature and the data, and as information from focus groups and interviews came in, the challenge shifted to one of deciding how to *stop* writing. Additions of new materials were made even as the book was being prepared for typesetting, and we have already begun collecting materials for a third edition. The study of rural issues has caused each of us to rethink many of our assumptions about crime and police work. We hope this book has the same impact on others.

While we assembled and wrote the information presented in this book, it would have not been possible without the assistance of many people. Marilyn Moses, our grant manager at NIJ, was tremendously supportive throughout. It was Ms. Moses who first recommended we work with the National Sheriffs' Association (NSA). The National Sheriffs' Association was a delight to work with, providing technical assistance and feedback from the very beginning. We were also pleased to have been invited to present our results at three annual meetings of the NSA. We are particularly grateful to our contact person at NSA, Ms. Theresa Mathews, who went out of her way to assist us. And, for their comments on earlier drafts of this document, we would like to thank Sheriff G. C. "Buck" Buchanan of Yavapai County, Arizona; Carl R. Harbaugh, former sheriff of Frederick County, Maryland; and Sheriff J. C. Bittick of Monroe County, Georgia. The manuscript has benefitted enormously from the comments of Dr. Joseph Donnermeyer, one of the leading researchers on rural crime issues. Dr. Mark Hamm's comments on the hate crimes section made it far more clear and readable, and Mr. Larry Heisner's experiences as a rural police chaplain prodded our thinking in a variety of areas. We also had the good fortune to interview and receive comments from David A. Armstrong of McNeese State University, who was generously willing to share his prior experiences in rural policing. His keen insights helped clarify our thinking on a variety of issues. We are also indebted to the support and feedback we received from Sheriff Steve Brienen of McLean County, Illinois. He is responsible for both rural and urban areas within McLean County and has had a long-standing interest in the issue of rural policing. His advice and observations were most helpful.

We are also indebted to the National Center for State and Local Law Enforcement at the Federal Law Enforcement Training Center (FLETC), which has used material from the project to develop a training program on rural drug enforcement. In the course of developing this program, Dr. Weisheit was invited to participate and to conduct a portion of the training for the pilot program. His involvement put him into contact with a variety of people whose comments were of great help. These include, but are not limited to: Special Agent Danny Ray of the Georgia Peace Officer Standards & Training Council; Lt. Tom Hargrave of the Cleburne, Texas, Police Department; and Thomas C. Durrett, Chief of Police of the Clarksburg, West Virginia, Police Department. From the National Center for State and Local Law Enforcement Training, we wish to thank Charlene Alentado, Senior Program Specialist; Steven T. Kernes, Chief of Program Management; and Hobart M. Henson, Director. While these have been our main contact people at FLETC, everyone there with whom we worked was extremely helpful and supportive. Our work has also benefited greatly from the comments and observations of Dr. Carl Hawkins, a captain with the Hillsborough County Florida's Sheriff's Office. His insights into community policing have been particularly helpful.

The authors also wish to thank the project staff. Mr. Michael Chitty provided assistance in locating and organizing much of the hard-to-find literature and undertook an interview study of conservation police. We wish to give particular thanks to Ms. Nancy Becker, who arranged interviews, transcribed tapes, and took care of a dozen other details to make this project possible.

We are also indebted to the staff at Waveland Press. Neil Rowe gave us encouragement and support throughout the project. We are also grateful to Jeni Ogilvie and Steve Dungan, who were instrumental in production of the book.

Finally, each of us would like to give a personal thanks to those near us who provided important emotional support throughout. Dr. Weisheit would like to thank his wife Carol for her continued support, and his son Ryan, who can always make him laugh. They both help keep everything in perspective. Dr. Wells wants to thank his wife Anna, along with Rachel and Loren, for their forbearance during the project, especially the busy times before meetings and deadlines. Dr. Falcone would like to thank his wife Joan for her support and understanding given his many absences from home while conducting field interviews.

Introduction

THE IMAGE OF AMERICA AS A "MELTING POT" IS AN IMAGE OF homogeneity with a single common culture arising from many different sources. This image is fostered by the "massification" of our society. Fast food restaurants and department store chains look pretty much the same everywhere in the United States. National television networks and even a national newspaper assure that major events in one part of the country will soon be known in all parts. Americans have more automobiles per capita than any country in the world, an extensive network of over two-and-one-quarter million miles of paved highways, and over 12,000 airports, making America a highly mobile society. Modern telecommunications have facilitated a continuous exchange of information among people across the country.

While America began as an agrarian society with a predominantly rural population, few people would characterize it as either agrarian or rural today. For many, the very idea of rural life seems like an historical concept with little relevance for a modern urban society. In short, contemporary American culture is considered not only homogenous, but an urban culture. Since most people have a television and a telephone, and most have access to some form of transportation, it is assumed that urban culture has permeated all parts of America, even those areas where the population is relatively sparse.

The focus on America as an urban society with a common set of problems seems particularly true in most current thinking about crime. In the minds of many, the crime problem is, by definition, an urban problem. It is assumed that rural crime is rare or nonexistent—that when it does occur, it is only a "small" version of the urban crime problem. The urban setting is seen as the true laboratory for studying crime problems that are universal to American society. Viewed in this way, it is easy to see how the study of rural crime might be viewed as esoteric and therefore less interesting and less informative. Also, given this general perspective, it is not surprising that the strategies suggested for dealing with rural crime are often those developed and implemented in urban areas. It is assumed that urban models can be used to teach rural citizens how best to deal with crime. Conversely, it is assumed that what goes on in rural areas is irrelevant and unimportant to those dealing with urban crime problems. Our findings directly challenge the assumption that crime and culture are identical in urban and rural areas. Rural crime and rural justice are not simply scaled-down versions of urban crime and justice. Rural crime and justice take place in a context that colors the process by which crime arises and by which justice is carried out.

This book will examine what is known about crime and policing in rural areas and small towns and how rural crime and justice are shaped by the rural environment. To place this discussion in a larger context, it is useful to discuss why a study of crime and the administration of justice in rural areas and small towns is important. Among the practical reasons are: (1) rural crime is a problem in itself, and some forms of rural crime may be increasing; (2) rural areas may have special crime problems, such as organized theft of livestock, equipment, and grain, for which urban police are poorly prepared, yet they are enormously costly to both the victim and to society. In addition to these issues, which are of direct concern to rural citizens, there are also ways in which rural crime and urban crime are interrelated: (3) rural areas are often used to produce drugs, such as marijuana and methamphetamines, for consumption in rural areas as well as for urban consumers; (4) rural areas are used as transshipment points for such illegal goods as drugs, stolen auto parts, and illegal cash; and (5) some have argued that urban crime networks, such as street gangs, are setting up "franchises" or "satellite operations" in rural areas. In addition to the practical benefits of studying rural crime and justice, there is the potential for advancing our understanding of the criminal justice system in society. If crime and justice are vastly different in rural and urban areas, an understanding of those differences might improve our understanding of crime and the administration of justice more generally.

This text, which resulted from a study undertaken with support from the National Institute of Justice, is designed to provide a better understanding of the rural crime problem and of issues facing rural and small-town police. The study was done by gathering and synthesizing information from a variety of sources (see Appendix B for details), including existing published literature, interviews with rural justice officials, focus groups, and a survey of rural and small-town police regarding their concerns. The nature of our study gives substantial attention to the police perspective. We recognize that by using this approach we have chosen to ignore other and perhaps very different views about rural crime and rural justice. However, we view this study as a first look at rural crime issues—not as the final word. A police perspective is not the only perspective, but it seems a reasonable starting point. In an area in which so little is known it is simply impossible to study more than a fraction of the issues and perspectives that are available. It is our hope that the findings reported here will encourage others to conduct more detailed examinations of particular issues and to do so from other perspectives.

One of the most difficult challenges in undertaking this study was defining the concept *rural*. While the term is very familiar, there are no definitions which are simultaneously precise, measurable, and widely agreed upon. Moreover, the meaning of rural has shifted somewhat over the past several decades (see Appendix A). Like such broad concepts as justice, truth, and beauty, the idea of "rural" is one that most people feel they readily understand but few can objectively measure. Among the studies we examined, a wide variety of definitions of rural were used, although the most common approach was to simply use the term without defining it. The interested reader will find a more elaborate discussion of the definition of the term rural in Appendix A. Throughout the discussion we will show some degree of flexibility in our definition of the term, often to make our discussion or data comparable to the work of others. Ultimately, the reader will observe that the elements of rurality that are most important for understanding rural crime and rural justice have less to do with population density and other objective measures than with networks of interpersonal relationships. This point will be emphasized in chapter 1, which discusses the rural setting of crime and justice. It is a theme, however, that runs throughout the book.

Our work began with an extensive review of the relevant literature, which gave clues to guide the content areas of our interviews and focus groups. The volume of literature on rural crime and rural policing is scant, particularly when compared to the amount of published work based on urban environments. To complicate matters, what literature is available is scattered across a variety of disciplines. Although there are many references to rural crime and justice, they are often only fragments of information or brief asides in discussions of other issues. The reader will forgive us if there are areas in which the discussion seems incomplete. Such is the state of knowledge about rural issues. Rural crime is worthy of further study, but for that study to be useful it must tie together these scattered pieces of information. The synthesis that follows begins to do just that, starting with what is known about the environment in which rural crime and rural justice take place.

Chapter 1

The Rural Setting
of Crime and Justice

'NOTHING TO DO' IS PLENTY
BY STEVE JAMISON

A common complaint about life in small town U.S.A. is that there is "nothing to do." That complaint is valid and here's a list to prove it, which consists primarily of things I didn't do during a recent holiday visit to my hometown, Winona, Minn. (pop. 24,632). While there:

1. I did not lock the car. Not once. No need to.
2. I locked the back door of my parents' house just once and was told not to do it again because somebody might get locked out.
3. I did not park in a parking lot or garage when I went to the bank. I parked on the street, directly in front of the bank, where there is usually plenty of space available.
4. I did not put money in the parking meter. There are no meters to put money in.
5. I did not need identification when cashing a check. I assured them that I was related to someone who lived in Winona.
6. I did not tip the bag boy at Randall's Market who carried our groceries out to the car in sub-zero weather. He was embarrassed that I even offered to give him money. . . .

These are just a few of the things I didn't do while home for the holidays. "Nothing to do" sounds pretty good, doesn't it?

Source: Excerpted by permission of Steve Jamison from the *Chicago Tribune*, February 5, 1995 (Downstate Edition), p. 23.

It is sometimes assumed that improved transportation systems and mass communication have homogenized our culture, have dissolved rural-urban differences, and have effectively destroyed what was once uniquely rural America. The above description suggests otherwise, expressing distinctive images of life in rural America that stand in stark contrast to the images of life in large cities. In this chapter we take issue with the assumption that rural life itself is not homogeneous across the United States. There remain many rural communities like the one described above, but there are also many rural areas which look nothing like this. There are four challenges in conducting a study of this sort. The first is to capture and summarize the essence of rural life, to identify those areas in which rural and urban are distinct and to recognize those areas they have in common. The second challenge is to appreciate the tremendous variations in rural settings from one part of the country to the next. Rural areas differ from each other in geography, economics, demographics, and culture, just as no two cities are exactly alike. The third challenge is to explore how the special features of the rural setting shape crime and justice. This will be our task in chapters 2, 3 and 4.

Finally, considering each of the first three challenges requires some appreciation of what is meant by the terms "rural" and "small town." This may be the most difficult challenge of all. These terms are part of our everyday discourse and their meanings are often taken for granted. It is assumed that everyone knows what the terms mean and that precise definitions are unnecessary. Consequently, the terms are not applied consistently across speakers or writers. We discuss the difficulties of defining rural more fully in Appendix A. For now, let us only say that a single definition of rural is not practical when drawing together the ideas of many writers. Further, as we argue in Appendix A, a single definition of rural may not even be desirable. As we discuss our own data, we will try to make clear what we mean by rural. However, when we discuss the research of others it will be too unwieldy to stop and provide a detailed accounting of how each study uses the term. We have chosen, instead, to include those studies that utilize the most commonly accepted meanings of the term rural, even if the writers never explicitly describe their work as focused on rural or small-town settings. At the same time, we have consciously left out studies which describe their setting or sample as rural but use that term in a questionable way. For example, we have read crime studies describing cities of 175,000 as rural or small town. These studies we have omitted from our discussion, except to periodically illustrate what we believe is a misuse of the term rural.

It is impossible to understand rural and small-town crime and justice without also understanding the rural environment. Unfortunately, policies and programs to deal with rural crime are often based on the assumption that what works in an urban area will also work in rural and small-town America. A 1977 conference on justice in rural areas reached a conclusion that still seems appropriate today.

> Generally, the participants believed that key decision-makers lack knowledge about the critical features and the great diversity of the rural environment. . . . Lacking its own data base, rural America often gets urban solutions for rural problems. . . . The conference participants expressed concern time and again for what they per-

ceived to be widespread imposition of the urban way of doing things on rural areas, and for the fact that too often the planning for rural areas takes place in urban centers. (Cronk, 1977, pp. 12–13)

More recently, Sampson (1986) found consistent and substantial rural-urban differences in national victimization data. He noted that rural crime rates were not only lower but may have been the result of different factors. For example, poverty was related to crime only in urban areas, whereas in rural areas the percentage of dwellings that were multiple-family structures was a more important predictor of crime rates. He concluded that:

> . . . to the extent that criminal justice programs and theoretical responses are based on the underlying assumption that the structural determinants of crime in suburban and rural areas are the same as those in central cities, then such policies and theoretical models may be misguided. (1986, p. 21)

In describing cultural and geographical features of the rural environment, this section will demonstrate why it is a mistake to apply urban definitions and urban policies to rural crime and rural justice. Crime and criminal justice do not exist in a vacuum. They are both a reflection of the communities in which they occur. The rural setting has several distinctive features that shape both crime and the exercise of justice. These include geographic isolation, the availability of guns, economic factors, race and ethnicity, and a distinctive social climate.

Geographic Isolation

The effects of geography alone pose serious problems for rural justice, having an impact on such things as response time and the speed with which support services can be provided. Mayhew and Levinger (1977), for example, contradict UCR data (to be discussed below) and suggest that the homicide rate in rural areas is higher, and that this "could easily be explained by the differential access to medical treatment in rural and urban areas, even if the actual violence is the same in both, or even higher in cities" (p. 457).

It is possible that geographic isolation increases the *lethality* of both accidents and violence by slowing the response of emergency medical services. Regarding automobile accidents, Brodsky (1990, p. 89) has observed:

What really matters most to the injured is the length of time it takes an ambulance to arrive after a crash.

In 1988, for the entire United States, rescue time in fatal road accidents in urban areas averaged about 12 minutes and in rural areas about 22 minutes. . . .

Given that a seriously injured person can go into an irremedial state of shock in 15 to 20 minutes, then the average rural rescue time of 22 minutes is still not fast enough.

As a New Mexico state trooper reported, "When I was in Vietnam, a medic was never more than 10 minutes away. Here you can wait by a wreck on the highway for 45 minutes before help gets there" (Applebome, 1987, p. 11). This can also be a problem in the Midwest, where one rural sheriff told us: "They [the instructors at the state training academy] always talk about responding to a call within two minutes. There are parts of my county that can take an hour to get to by car."

Long distances also mean that rural police officers can expect a longer wait for backup. Geographic isolation can be a particular problem for the many rural officers who patrol alone and whose interactions with suspects have no witnesses. The large geographic areas covered by some rural police make responding to calls more expensive and more time consuming than in urban areas. Long distances may not only slow the response time of criminal justice officials, but long distances and a lack of public transportation may make it more difficult for rural citizens to get to court to testify, to attend meetings with a probation officer, or to get to a shelter for battered women.

Those who believe that advances in technology have largely made geography irrelevant are laboring under a serious misperception. The majority of today's technological advances do more to facilitate the flow of information across great distances than to speed the direct delivery of human services across those same distances. Many of the problems that relate to geography, such as long response times to emergencies in rural areas, have not been solved by advances in technology. Further, even when technology can be of help it is not evenly distributed throughout society. For example, the U.S. Bureau of the Census (1993a, table 1) reports that households outside metropolitan areas are about twice as likely as those inside metropolitan areas to be without a telephone (8.7 percent versus 4.2 percent). And, as with most issues, variations among rural areas can be great. Take Kentucky as an example. Of the 108 counties in Kentucky which are nonmetropolitan, the percentage of houses without telephone service ranges from 2.5 percent to 29.3 percent, with

---

THE CODE OF THE WEST

Here are selected excerpts from a document prepared by John Clark for urban dwellers considering a move to his rural area of Larimer County, Colorado.

ACCESS

- Emergency response times (sheriff, fire suppression, medical care, etc.) cannot be guaranteed. Under some extreme conditions, you may find that emergency response is extremely slow and expensive.
- You can experience problems with the maintenance and cost of maintenance of your road. . . . many rural properties are served by private and public roads which are maintained by private road associations. There are even some county roads that are not maintained by the county—no grading or snow plowing. There are even some public roads that are not maintained by anyone!
- Mail delivery is not available to all areas of the county. . . . Newspaper delivery is similarly not always available to rural areas.

UTILITY SERVICES

- Telephone communications can be a problem, especially in the mountain areas of Larimer County. From time to time, the only phone service available has been a party line. If you have a private line, it may be difficult to obtain another line for FAX, computer, or modem uses. Even cellular phones will not work in all areas.
- If you have access to a supply of treated domestic water, the tap fees can be expensive. . . . If you do not have access to a supply of treated domestic water, you will have to locate an alternative supply.
- Electric service is not available to every area of Larimer County. It is important to determine the proximity of electrical power. . . . Power outages can occur in outlying areas with more frequency than in more developed areas. A loss of electric power can also interrupt your supply of water from a well.
- Trash removal can be much more expensive in a rural area than in a city. In some cases your trash dumpster may be several miles from your home.

Source: *The Code of the West.* Available: www.co.larimer.co.us/hot/codewest.htm (also reported in Possley, 1997).

22 counties having more than 20 percent of the homes without telephone service (U.S. Bureau of the Census, 1993b, table 1). In urban areas those without a phone often can find one next door or down the block when emergencies arise. In rural areas the nearest telephone may be some distance away. Similarly, in many parts of rural America there are no carriers of service for mobile telephones.

In the future the gap between rural and urban telephone subscriptions may widen as a result of changes in federal law. It costs much more to provide basic telephone service to rural areas, partly because of the distances involved and partly due to the diseconomies of scale from providing service to less populated areas. In the past a federal subsidy for rural telephone service kept the consumer's cost for rural service close to that of the urban dweller. Under the 1997 federal telecommunications law the federal government would shift responsibility for 75 percent of the subsidy to individual states (Van, 1998). Whether states will continue the subsidy remains to be seen, but without it the number of rural homes without telephone service will increase dramatically, particularly in economically depressed rural areas.

A parallel rural-urban discrepancy in the availability of technology has been noted for schools. While 27 percent of classrooms nationwide have the infrastructure to support computers, only 4 percent of rural schools have such an infrastructure in place (Rosenbush, 1998).

The impact of distance on the quantity and quality of service is not only an issue for the poorest and most remote rural areas. At the fringes of many large cities are upper-class residential developments in which homes are on large tracts of land, or in which homes are clustered but the clusters are scattered. One study found that emergency services, including police, took an average of six times longer to respond in these scattered site developments than in nearby communities. The study (Esseks, Dixon, Schmidt, & Sullivan, 1998, pp. 7–8) concluded that:

> . . . if you really needed help from the police, they might arrive up to 30 minutes after the call was placed. If you were having a heart attack, the ambulance could arrive two minutes to five minutes too late compared to a widely accepted standard. And if your house was burning down, the fire trucks could arrive up to six minutes too late relative to the national standard.

The study also concluded that while homes in these developments were very expensive, the tax revenues they generated did not compensate for the extra demands they placed on local government services. It was estimated that for every dollar of tax revenue generated by these developments, $1.11 was spent for services to the developments. Police services were particularly affected because many of the homes had expensive alarm systems that frequently sounded false alarms.

Geography is also likely to have different meanings in different parts of the country. A common unit of study for rural issues is the county, which is also a convenient unit regarding police agencies and the courts. As one moves from East to West, however, counties tend to be much larger in square miles. As a result of how counties were formed, they vary substantially in size. Arizona, for example, has only 15 counties that average over 7,500 square miles each—about the size of the state of New Jersey. By comparison, Georgia has 159 counties that average only 370 square miles each. Counties also differ in terrain, population density, and climate. For example, it periodically happens that hikers are lost in the mountains of Montana for a week or two before they find other people. Some Alaskan villages are so remote they are even difficult to reach by airplane (Marenin & Copus, 1991). In contrast, one would be hard pressed to find similar circumstances in the "wilds" of Delaware or New Jersey.

An example of how geographic perceptions vary, and of what Weisheit (1993) has called "urban ethnocentrism," can be found in the conviction and sentencing of Sheik Omar Abdel-Rahman. The sheik was convicted in federal court of conspiring to blow up the United Nations Building, the Lincoln and Holland Tunnels, the George Washington Bridge, and FBI headquarters in New York. Upon learning the sheik would be sent to the federal prison in Springfield, Missouri (in a county with a population of 240,000), the sheik and his lawyers were outraged. One lawyer complained that her client was being sent to "Middle America," to "Noplaceville" and "a particularly inaccessible part of the world." Another of the sheik's attorneys described the decision as a form of harassment, and the sheik himself viewed the selection of this "rural" site as an effort to break his spirit (Smith, 1995, p. 4). What would be rural to the sheik and his attorneys probably would not be rural to residents of Springfield, which was described in an article in *The Economist* as "the sleepy little town of Springfield, Missouri" (1996, p. 29). These descriptions tell us much about images of rural that persist among some urban residents.

Availability of Guns

The presence of guns is another area in which rural and urban populations differ, a difference that raises questions about assumptions often made regarding the link between guns and crime. Summarizing much of the literature on guns, Wright, Rossi, & Daly (1983) observed that gun ownership was much more prevalent in rural areas. As Figure 1 shows, in large cities about 27 percent of residents own some kind of gun, but in rural areas over 75 percent of citizens are gun owners (p. 106). While many of the rural gun owners are hunters who use rifles, the percent of citizens owning handguns is also higher in rural areas than in central cities (23 percent vs. 15 percent). Gun control legislation is often based on the assumption that the availability of guns is directly related to gun-related violence, but the case of rural areas shows that the relationship is far more complex. Ironically, rural residents may be more likely to own guns, but they are also *less* likely to use guns in the commission of crimes. Bordua and Lizotte (1979) found that crime was lowest in counties with the highest rates of legal firearm ownership. Similarly, a 1990 report by the Bureau of Justice Statistics found that rate of crimes committed with handguns was over three times as great in urban areas—5.9 per 100,000 in central cities versus 1.7 per 100,000 in non-metropolitan areas (Bureau of Justice Statistics, 1990a). Similarly, the *National Crime Victimization Survey* (NCVS) reports that in cities 37 percent of rapes are committed with a handgun, compared with only 14 percent of rapes in rural areas (Bachman, 1992a) (see Figure 2). Urban and rural areas are more similar regarding the use of handguns in robberies, but rural percentages are still lower (30 percent vs. 35 percent)—and with self-report data rural-urban comparisons on this crime are problematic because there are so few robberies in rural areas (see chapter 2).

Another source of information about gun use in crimes across geographic areas can be found in the *Uniform Crime Reports*, which indicate the weapons used for murders and robberies across jurisdictions of varying sizes. As Figures 3 and 4 show, guns are used less frequently in murder and robbery as the size of the community goes down, with an important exception. For both crimes, guns are least used in smaller towns, with suburban and rural areas showing higher rates. For murder, the highest rates of gun use are in cities of more than 100,000 people, although the differences among settings is not as great as would have been expected from the victimization data described above. For robbery, the greatest frequency of gun use is in suburban areas, with the rates in rural areas only slightly lower than those in the largest cities. These official police data generally support the view that guns are used less frequently in smaller communities, or at least that they are not used more frequently than in the largest cities. These data also suggest that the relationship is not a simple linear one—more guns do not automatically mean more gun-related crime. Figures 3 and 4 suggest the impor-

tance of being alert to differences between small towns and unincorporated rural areas. While we have no simple explanation for these patterns, they do challenge the assumption of a simple link between the
availability of guns and the use of guns in crime.

It is not simply that more guns are present in rural areas. In many
rural areas guns have a practical and symbolic importance that might

Figure 1.   Gun Ownership

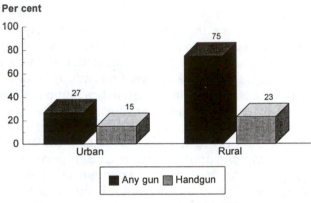

▪ Source: Created from data presented in Wright, Rossi & Daly, 1983

Figure 2.   Rapes Using Handguns.

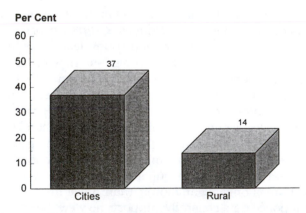

▪ Source: Created from data presented in Bachman, 1992b

Figure 3. Homicides Using Guns

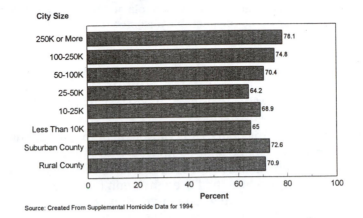

Source: Created From Supplemental Homicide Data for 1994

Figure 4. Robberies Using Guns

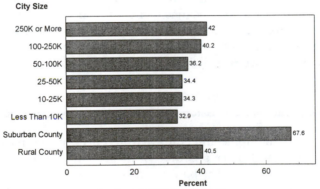

Source: Created from the Uniform Crime Reports for 1996, (FBI, 1997, Table 19)

be difficult for urban residents to understand. Kuhn (1995, p. 5) describes the context within which guns are viewed by probationers in Appalachia:

> The region was settled through the use of firearms. Often, the most cherished possession an offender owns is "grandaddy's shotgun." Even if it hasn't been fired in years, the firearm is such a part of the offender's history and identity that he or she may risk incarceration in order to keep it. Additionally, hunting and fishing seem to be almost universal interests in the region. It is not uncommon for

these activities to be the only formal type of recreation the offender knows, and they are passed down from parent to child as a way of life. In this writer's home county, schools are closed during deer season because of the considerable absentee rate among students and teachers alike.

Because firearms are so important to the Appalachian identity, offenders often request early termination of supervision so they can begin the process of "getting their rights back." Significantly, "rights" almost always means firearm possession instead of voting or being able to serve on a jury.

Finally, the 1995 School Crime Supplement to the National Crime Victimization Survey found that compared with students from urban schools, those from nonmetropolitan schools were significantly less likely to know someone who had brought a gun to school (11.1 percent versus 15.0 percent) (Chandler, Chapman, Rand & Taylor, 1998). While it may be obvious that kids cannot bring guns to school if they are not available, these findings suggest that availability itself is not a sufficient explanation, since guns are more available in rural areas but are less often taken to school.

It is quite likely that the link between guns and crime is different in rural and urban areas. Because these differences are not fully understood, their implications for public policy are as yet unclear. It is likely that the policies the public will most accept, and which will be most fully enforced, are not necessarily identical in rural and urban areas.

Economic Factors

In addition to geographic and cultural differences, economic conditions in rural communities are a source of important unappreciated divergence between rural and urban areas. In particular, three distinctive patterns in rural economies seem central for understanding the rural context of crime and criminal justice: (1) chronic poverty; (2) economic extremes, with wide diversity *between* rural areas; and (3) "thin economies," those which are based on a single industry or economic activity, with little diversity *within* rural areas.

Chronic Poverty

The first pattern refers to the substantial prevalence of profound and enduring levels of poverty in many rural areas. High rates of poverty have long been associated with high rates of crime, but studies of the link between poverty and crime are almost always conducted in urban areas. It is possible that the link between poverty and crime is different in rural and urban areas. For example, Sampson's (1986) analysis of national victimization survey data found that poverty was associated with victimization, but only in *central cities*.

Curiously, crime is less frequent in rural areas, although poverty is a common problem in rural America. Weinberg (1987), for example, has observed that of the 159 high-poverty counties in the United States in 1979, only six contained a city with a population of 25,000 or more. Further, Garkovich (1991) reports that the 1986 poverty rate in rural areas was 50 percent higher than in urban areas. While urban researchers express alarm over the rise of a "permanent underclass," this deep socioeconomic and cultural isolation "has been the experience of generations of the rural poor, especially in the South, where rigid social stratification has kept them out of the mainstream" (Tickamyer & Duncan, 1990). Unemployment is generally higher in rural areas; for those who are employed, wages are substantially lower. While housing is generally less expensive in rural areas, this savings is largely offset by higher transportation costs. In recent decades, the eroding economic base of many rural areas has encouraged high levels of out-migration by young educated and skilled workers (Garkovich, 1989), which makes future economic development more difficult.

Brown and Hirschl (1995) found that the highest levels of poverty were in rural areas, followed by central cities. They also examined the factors usually used to explain poverty, including such things as characteristics of households, the local economy, and the local labor market. They found that none of these factors, alone or in combination, could explain the difference between urban and rural poverty. They concluded that understanding the roots of rural poverty requires understanding the culture and structure of rural communities, and that purely urban models are inadequate for explaining rural poverty.

It is startling that the numerous studies of poverty and crime have so seriously neglected rural areas. Aside from rural-urban comparisons, some research has focused on the relationship between economic factors and crime among rural areas. Arthur (1991) found that such economic factors as unemployment, poverty level, and dependence on government assistance were related to both violent and property crime rates in rural counties, although the relationship was stronger for property crime. It is not clear why these findings differ from those of Sampson, noted above. Whatever the precise connection between crime and poverty in rural areas, it seems safe to conclude that the link is weaker than in large cities.

Of course, the economic problems facing rural areas can be expected to affect not only the nature and extent of crime, but the resources available to rural police. Where tax bases are small, rural police departments are likely to be seriously understaffed and to do without important resources. One of the authors of this review interviewed a local sheriff whose desk consisted of an old door stretched across two half-height filing cabinets, and who had a total of three officers (including himself) to patrol a large county seven days a week, 24 hours a day.

Economic Extremes

While poverty is common in many rural areas, some rural areas have experienced economic growth and development. As a general trend, this growth is selective—occurring strongly in some rural communities while leaving others even further behind. Strong growth is perhaps most evident in "collar counties" that surround major urban areas. Analysis of census data shows that the *highest* poverty levels are in rural nonmetropolitan areas (distant from urban centers), while the *lowest* poverty levels are in rural locations within (or immediately adjacent to) metropolitan areas (Fuguitt, Brown, & Beale, 1989). In addition, pockets of rural growth can be based on a variety of factors, such as tourism, retirement communities, industry, natural resources, or government services (Bradshaw & Blakely, 1982). This means that the economic health of different rural areas will be based on widely different economic bases. There is tremendous diversity across rural areas, which makes it difficult to provide general statements about rural conditions or to develop singular economic development policies for rural areas. What prompts growth and development of one community may be irrelevant and ineffective in another rural area.

Closely related to the economic conditions in rural areas are demographic trends that are driven by changes in economic opportunities. A study of population shifts over time shows a steady out-migration of young people from rural areas, combined with an influx of senior citizens, leading the population of rural America to be older, on average, than that of the country as a whole (Johnson, 1993). It also appears that two types of rural counties were most likely to experience population growth in the 1980s: those whose economies were based on tourism and those serving a large number of retirees (Johnson, 1993).

There is a body of research that concludes that rural areas experiencing rapid growth will also experience a disproportionately large increase in crime. In a meta-analysis of empirical studies, Freudenburg and Jones (1991) report that 21 of 23 studies found that in rural communities with rapid population growth, crime grew even faster; in fact, *crime increased at three to four times the speed at which the popula-*

tion increased. They speculate that "the accumulated findings may best be explained by narrowly focusing on changes in community social structure that accompany rapid growth and result in impairment of informal social controls, particularly the declines in a community's density of acquaintanceship" (p. 619).

Aside from the increase in crime that commonly accompanies rapid growth (Freudenburg & Jones, 1991), the basis of economic development may lead to unique crime problems. For example, a growing tourism industry not only requires local police to deal with victims and/or offenders who are transient, but the demands on police and the resources to pay for police services may fluctuate throughout the year, and from one year to the next. One police chief told us that his community's permanent population was about 4,000 people, but during the height of tourist season the population could reach as high as 70,000 people. It is likely that crime and justice in such communities are very different from that in rural areas with highly stable populations.

Unfortunately, efforts to spur economic growth in rural areas have sometimes increased crime-related problems while having little impact on the economic vitality of the area. Particularly discouraging is the trend for rural areas to pursue economic development through promoting tourism and by recruiting labor-intensive industries, such as meat and poultry processing plants. Leaders of rural communities are often taken by the idea of bringing such growth to their area and providing jobs to their residents. While it is assumed that an increase in employment will better the lives of residents, this is not always the case. Wages are often so low that full-time employees still have incomes well below the poverty level, so that when the area's unemployment rate drops it merely represents a shift from the unemployed poor to the working poor.

Gouveia and Stull (1995) provide a good example of this problem in their examination of the impact of two large meat packing plants near the small community of Garden City, Kansas. The first plant opened in December of 1980 and the second in 1983, and together they employed about 4,200 workers in a county (Finney County) with a population of about 33,000 people. In addition, a number of other jobs were created in the service industry as retail stores and restaurants opened. Because of technological advances in meat processing these new jobs were all unskilled. Consequently, wages in these plants were very low, and wages in the newly created service sector were even lower. As a result, county income dropped from 94 percent of the state average in 1980 to 91.5 percent of the state average in 1988—more than $1,300 below the state average and $2,111 below the national average (Gouveia & Stull, 1995). In addition to low pay, the work was demanding and injuries were frequent; as many as 4 in 10 meat processing workers were injured each year (Stull & Broadway, 1995). Since the local population was not large enough to supply the labor needs of the plants, workers were recruited from across the country. Mobile home parks sprang up to house the workers, and other social problems soon followed. School enrollment soared, particularly for minority and bilingual students. "In 1990, Garden City's school district had the highest dropout rate in Kansas, student turnover of almost one-third each year, and chronic absenteeism" (Gouveia & Stull, 1995, p. 91). Demands on temporary shelters increased two-and-a-half times in just six years and crime increased dramatically. "Both violent and property crime climbed throughout the decade in Finney County, while falling in the state. The incidence of child abuse more than tripled to exceed the state average by 50 percent" (Gouveia and Stull, 1995, p. 91).

Solving the problems described in the meat and poultry processing industries is complicated by the rise of a world economy in which cheap labor in the most underdeveloped countries competes directly with cheap labor in the United States. Harvey's (1996) discussion of the poultry industry in North Carolina notes that in rural areas with high unemployment, "Those living in relatively geographically isolated rural towns of this sort are, consequently, easy prey for an industry seeking a cheap, unorganized and easily disciplined labor force" (1996, p. 335). Such areas are also likely to have an inadequate tax base to fully support the increased demands placed on the criminal justice system, a problem compounded by the common practice of extending generous tax incentives to initially attract processing plants to the area. Certainly the experiences in these types of communities suggests that population growth and an improved standard of living are not necessarily synonymous.

The potential long-term impact of these low-wage, labor-intensive industries is particularly disturbing. As Hall (1995, p. 223) has noted, "What good is an economic development strategy that succeeds in attracting new investment but slowly overwhelms a community with environmental waste, crippled workers, and disenfranchised farmers?"

Another disturbing trend is that as meat processing operations grow increasingly large, they tend to locate in increasingly small rural communities (Hackenberg, 1995). Some of the largest operations, for example, are sited in communities of only 1,100 or 1,200. This means that residents could not possibly supply the labor needs of the industry. Consequently, companies make national efforts to recruit unskilled immigrants, particularly Asians and Hispanics, who are desperate for work. There are allegations that the companies also recruit directly in Mexico. The Immigration and Naturalization Service estimates that as many as 25 percent of the meat processing workers in the Midwest are illegal aliens (Heges, Hawkins, & Loeb, 1996). The potential for future crime problems is substantial. Taking economically dispossessed immigrants and putting them into culturally homogeneous small communities creates a high long-term potential for racial tensions and "hate crimes." In addition, it is unlikely that the justice system in these rural communities is prepared for handling culturally diverse populations or for responding to hate crimes.

Thin Economies

Understanding the economic influences on rural areas requires not only appreciating economic variability across rural areas, but also recognizing the "thin economies" that characterize most rural areas. That is, rural economies of particular areas are commonly based on or dominated by a single industry or occupational activity (such as farming, mining, logging, tourism) and lacking in economic diversity and depth. While there is wide diversity across rural areas, there is very little diversity within rural areas—a pattern which is the reverse of urban economies. This means that rural communities, even those currently undergoing economic growth, are more susceptible to boom-and-bust fluctuations, because they lack the buffer that economic diversity provides (see Browne, Skees, Swanson, Thompson, & Unnevehr, 1992).

Race and Ethnicity

Studies of the link between race and crime are common, and they almost exclusively draw on urban samples. There is no reason to assume that race and crime issues are similar across rural and urban areas, particularly since the minority population is not evenly distributed across rural and urban America. Before addressing the issue of race and crime, it will be useful to first look at rural-urban differences in the distribution of minorities in the United States.

Race in Rural Areas

U.S. Census data show that rural areas are substantially more homogeneous than are central cities on both race and ethnicity. While the U.S. population as a whole is 80 percent white, the population in central cities is 66 percent white. This contrasts sharply with the population in rural areas, which is 89 percent white. As with many other issues, these national averages mask large inter-state variations. While space precludes an analysis of each state, Table 1 shows those states with the greatest and the least rural-urban differences in the percent of the population that is white. It is worth noting that the difference between these two groups is mainly due to differences in the proportion of minorities in central cities, not to variations across rural areas.

Table 1.   States with the Highest and the Lowest Rural-Central City Differences in Percent of the Population which is White,1990

	State	Percent White Central Cities	Percent White Rural Areas	Difference (RA-CC)
Highest Difference	Delaware	42%	85%	43 points
	Illinois	56%	98%	42 points
	Michigan	50%	97%	47 points
	New York	56%	97%	41 points
Lowest Difference	Maine	97%	99%	2 points
	Utah	90%	93%	3 points
	Vermont	97%	99%	3 points
	Wyoming	93%	94%	1 point

Source: U.S. Bureau of the Census (1990), table 4.

It is also true that the national trend for minorities to be underrepresented in rural areas is not true for all states. In fact, there are seven states in which minorities are more represented in rural areas than in urban areas: Alaska, Arizona, Idaho, Montana, New Mexico, North Dakota, and South Dakota. In these states there are large Native American (or Eskimo) populations. Native Americans are among the only minority groups in America which are routinely more represented in rural areas than in central cities.

Ethnicity in Rural Areas

The Census Bureau makes a distinction between race and ethnicity. In particular, Hispanics are considered an *ethnic* group, not a racial category. In terms of race, Hispanic residents are categorized as white. While this distinction between race and ethnicity may not be recognized and used by most of the public, any discussion based on census data must, of necessity, use Census Bureau categories. The census data show that Hispanic citizens are much more represented in urban areas (14.8 percent) than in rural areas (2.6 percent). Further, only three states have a higher percentage of Hispanics in rural areas than in urban areas (Hawaii, Idaho, and Washington). In none of these states do Hispanics constitute more than 8 percent of the population. Several states do have rather large percentages of Hispanic residents in rural areas, including New Mexico (34 percent), Texas (16 percent), Arizona (14 percent), California (13 percent), and Colorado (11 percent). In each of these states, however, the percentage of Hispanics in urban areas is even greater than in rural areas.

Race, Ethnicity, and Crime

Although seldom explored, it appears that the links between race and crime differ across rural, suburban, and urban areas. Bachman's (1992a) examination of NCVS data reveals that blacks had higher victimization rates than whites for violent crimes in urban areas. In rural areas the violent crime victimization rate for whites was higher than that for blacks. For such property crimes as burglary and household larceny, blacks had higher rates of victimization across community sizes.

Using NCVS data, Laub (1983b) estimated personal crime offending rates for communities of varying sizes. He found that while crime rates did generally increase with community size, there were threshold sizes above which increases were small or nonexistent. For whites, this threshold was 2,500 residents or more, while for blacks, the threshold community size was 10,000 or more. Interestingly, race differences across community sizes varied by age. For juveniles ages 12 to 17, metro/nonmetro differences in offending rates are greater for blacks than for whites. Correspondingly, black/white differences in offending rates for juveniles are greater in central cities than outside central cities. For adults, these differences practically disappear.

Jensen, Stauss, and Harris (1977) used several data sources to study crimes by Native Americans. They found that crime rates for this group were higher than for white, black, or Asian Americans. They also found that white/Native American differences were smaller in rural than in urban areas. Native American crime rates in urban areas were four times those of whites, while in rural areas the crime rate was only about two and one-half times higher. While urban studies of the street-level drug trade reflect a high representation of minorities, Weisheit's (1992) study of rural marijuana cultivators found that blacks were almost completely absent. This was true even though marijuana cultivation required few resources and few specialized skills. Although the minority population may be smaller in rural areas, it is unclear why their *rates* relative to whites should be lower in rural areas, or why minorities have such a small role in marijuana cultivation. This pattern should be explored further, for it raises questions about assumed links between race and crime.

Related to the issue of race and crime is the way minorities are handled in the criminal justice system. Most studies find that minorities are overrepresented in the justice system compared with their numbers in the general population. However, nearly all such studies are conducted in urban areas. One examination of juvenile offenders in the state of Washington included both rural and urban counties (Bridges, 1993). Minority juveniles, particularly blacks, were overrepresented in the justice system across the state as a whole. However, there were substantial variations across counties. In some areas minorities were *underrepresented* in the justice system. Counties in which minorities were most overrepresented had three features in common: (1) most of their population was urban, (2) there was a large minority population, and (3) the violent crime rate was high. The study also considered disproportionality at each of eight stages in the system. While this was the general pattern, not every metropolitan county showed high disproportionality, and not every rural county showed low disproportionality. Further, interpreting these findings is complicated by the small minority populations in many rural counties. For example, in 1990, 23 of Washington's 34 counties had small minority populations and sentenced no minority youths to confinement.

While there is little research on the link between race and crime in rural areas, the link between ethnicity and crime in rural areas has been completely ignored. What fragmented evidence does exist suggests that urban assumptions about race and crime, and about race and justice, may not hold in rural areas—or that these relationships may be more complex than is sometimes assumed. Further, while racial and ethnic minorities tend to be underrepresented in rural areas, there are counties with large minority populations. This is particularly true for blacks in the South and Native Americans in the West. Filling this void in our knowledge should be given a high priority.

Hicks, Rednecks, and "White Trash"

The relative neglect of race and economic factors in rural crime is particularly evident in the absence of research on criminality among poor rural whites. This neglect is particularly surprising considering that stereotypes about these groups abound in popular culture. Terms such as white trash, rednecks, hillbillies, and trailer trash are much used in everyday language. Technically these terms are not equivalent, but are often treated as such. Originally most of these terms referred to poor rural whites from the South or Appalachia, but in recent years the terms have been applied more broadly to groups with a particular lifestyle or set of behaviors and attitudes (e.g., Murray, 1986; Friend, 1994; Wray & Newitz, 1997; Goad, 1997). Stereotypes portray white trash as slow witted and inbreeding, with high illegitimacy rates and frequent involvement in crime. These images are reflected in such popular films as *Deliverance* and *Sling Blade*, in which poor rural whites seem to have been drawn straight from the writings of Lombroso, portrayed as a brutish subspecies of humankind.

It has been argued that the social category of white trash is the only group in America for which public ridicule and scorn are considered acceptable. It is hard to imagine many jokes about rednecks or white trash being tolerated if some other group were substituted in the joke. When Paula Jones accused President Clinton of sexual harassment, comments about white trash were freely dispensed. James Carville, former adviser to the president, was quoted as saying, "Drag a hundred dollar bill through a trailer court and there's no telling what you'll find"; a reporter for *Newsweek* said on television that Jones had a reputation for being "just some sleazy woman with big hair coming out of the trailer parks"; and *U.S. News and World Report* described Paula Jones's home town as a "land of big hair and tight jeans and girls whose dreams soar no further than a stint at a hairdressers school" (Lee, 1997, p. 11; Thurman, 1997, p. 3). As a group, white trash may be more despised than other minorities. When people from the mountains of Virginia and West Virginia moved into Russell Baker's Baltimore community, he observed:

> "Hillbillies," I called them. Everybody called them "hillbillies," and everybody deplored them. The all-white police force of the era, among whom I worked, and whose racial bigotry was hair-raising, agreed to a man that the "hillbillies" were more deplorable than black people. (1997, p. 23)

Similarly, O'Brien (1996) notes in his description of the South that:

... land, as well as money, conferred status; lowest of all on the ladder were poor white men or women, white sharecroppers or migrant workers, with neither land nor money. There was less stigma attached to being black and poor, since less was expected of a race considered inherently inferior; blacks themselves looked down on poor whites, who lacked even the legacy of slavery and discrimination to blame for their condition. (p. 5)

Included in this image of poor white trash is the mobile home, where "trailer trash" reside. As one study of mobile homes observed (Hart & Morgan, 1995):

Few middle- and upper-class Americans have any first-hand experience of mobile homes, and ignorance begets prejudice. Most Americans, if they even think about them at all, perceive mobile homes as one of the social pathologies of rural areas, and they suspect that the kinds of people who dwell in them are short of cash, short of pride, and probably short of both. . . . critics complain that they foster child abuse, welfare fraud, theft, violence, and sensational crime, and the media have not been hesitant to capitalize on their unsavory reputation. (p. 36)

Over time mobile homes increasingly have become a rural phenomenon as metropolitan areas exclude them through zoning (Hart & Morgan, 1995). Geisler and Mitsuda (1987) note that in 1960 nearly half (48 percent) of mobile homes were in rural areas. By 1995, this figure had risen to nearly three quarters (72 percent) (U.S. Department of Commerce, 1997). Consistent with the idea that white trash is connected with the South, mobile homes are very much a southern phenomenon, with about half of all mobile homes in the United States located in the South (Finn & Kerr, 1991).

Our research did not specifically focus on the issue of white trash, but in our interviews with rural police and sheriffs, the issue of trailer parks did come up periodically. When asked if there were parts of their town or county which were particularly demanding of police services, there were a number of occasions when we were told that many of the town's problems were centered in trailer parks. This was not a universal response, and we are not prepared even to speculate about the extent to which there is a reality to public stereotypes about trailer courts, or about regional variations in this phenomenon. However, it is an issue worth further study.

As with the issues of poverty and handguns, studying the link between race-ethnicity and crime in rural areas may prove to challenge some of our long-held assumptions. Conventional wisdom about common causes and correlates of crime is based on data from urban populations, leading to different conclusions about the social causes of crime than when rural data are explicitly included. Further, a study of the rural context of race, ethnicity, and crime may be useful for understanding the link between these social characteristics and crime in other settings. At this point there is too little information to make any firm statements on this issue.

Social Climate

Precisely measuring and describing a local culture is extremely difficult. There are, however, several features of rural culture which distinguish it from urban culture and which have implications for rural crime and rural justice. Among these features of rural culture are informal control, a mistrust of government, and a reluctance to share internal problems.

Informal Control

It is commonly believed that rural areas are more governed by informal social control than are urban areas, and there is some empirical evidence to support this proposition. Lyerly and Skipper (1981), for example, found rural delinquency was less frequent than urban delinquency and concluded that "certain structural conditions in rural areas tend to foster conformity among the juvenile population" (p. 39). Similarly, Gardner and Shoemaker (1989) found that social bonding was a more important factor in protecting against rural delinquency than against urban delinquency. Smith (1980) found that in rural areas shoplifting and employee theft were rarely reported to the police. Instead, most cases were handled informally. He quotes one rural criminal justice official as saying:

> I simply can't get people to tell me things. I hear about them two or three weeks later, and when I ask them why they didn't come to me about it, they say, "Oh, I took care of it myself." We simply can't get people to take advantage of the services of this office. (p. 52)

Kowalski and Duffield's (1990) study of homicide concluded that "the traditional bond of group cohesion assumed to be associated with the rural environment and its residents continues to have an inhibiting effect on homicide for counties in the United States" (p. 76). A focus on informal control should not be confused with a tolerance of crime in rural areas. To the contrary, rural areas are often less tolerant of crime and of deviance in general (Wilson, 1991). For example, a national survey published by the Insurance Research Council (1993) found that rural citizens were less tolerant of insurance fraud than were urban residents. When given the statement, "It is all right to increase the amount of your insurance claim by a small amount to make up for the insurance premiums you have paid when you had no claims," 46 percent of large-city residents agreed, compared with only 12 percent of rural residents. Similarly, only 3 percent of rural residents agreed that "it is acceptable to receive treatment after an injury has healed." In contrast, 25 percent of large-city residents agreed with the statement.

Informal control is facilitated by the fact that many residents of rural communities, including the local police, know each other socially. As Salamon (1997) has noted:

> Everyone "knows everyone else" in small towns. Life there revolves around a core of social institutions: family, community, school, and church. Kin, neighbors, and friends meet one another at work, at church, on main street, at school, or leisure activities such as high school basketball games. Daily life thus takes place among a cast of familiars whose social networks are overlapping rather than segmented. Children are considered to belong to the whole community. If a child misbehaves, a neighbor will have notified a parent with the news before the child reaches home. High school sporting events are occasions when the entire community turns out. Everyone is related to or knows someone on the team, in the band, or on the cheerleading squad. (p. 172)

One factor which contributes to the familiarity of residents is the relative stability of the local population. Unless they have chosen to out-migrate, rural citizens less frequently change addresses, often staying in the same county or even the same house for several generations. In comparing urban and rural poverty, Auletta (1982) makes the following observation about Preston County, West Virginia:

> Unlike the cities of the North, where ghetto residents constantly shift addresses, almost 70 percent of Preston County's 25,000 residents have lived in the same house all their lives; another 20 percent of the people there have moved, but within the county. Upward mobility is relatively rare, . . . the average mother receiving Aid to Families with Dependent Children (AFDC) has been on welfare more than six years. (p. 159)

The mobility that does occur in these rural areas, as mentioned earlier, is often out-migration of younger skilled workers. All of these factors have implications for rural policing. The low levels of mobility and low population density mean that rural police officers, such as sheriffs, are likely to know most offenders and their families personally. If a victim can identify a thief, for example, the sheriff is likely to know where to find the offender and to know already quite a bit about the offender and his or her family. Given this, a greater reliance on informal control in rural areas should be of no surprise.

The term "density of acquaintanceship" has been used to describe the extent to which people in a community know one another. In general, smaller communities are high in density of acquaintanceships. Freudenburg (1986) studied four small towns in Colorado. Three of the towns had populations ranging from 1,000 to 5,000 people and were high in density of acquaintanceship. A fourth town had grown rapidly from 5,000 to 10,000 people and was now much lower in density of acquaintanceship. He found that residents of communities higher in density of acquaintanceships less often reported being the victims of crime. They were also half as likely to believe it was necessary to lock their doors when they left home for a few hours or less, and they were five times less likely to believe it necessary to lock their doors when they were gone for a day or more. Similarly, high school students in high-density acquaintanceship communities were half as likely to report having felt physically threatened in their school.

Density of acquaintanceship can influence crime in several ways. It can increase the watchfulness of citizens, make it more likely they will feel a responsibility to act, and may make it easier to identify suspects. As Freudenburg (1986) observed:

> In a smaller community, a high density of acquaintanceship can allow the watchfulness to extend to the entire community: if a resident sees a person entering a house even in another section of town, there is a relatively high likelihood that the resident will know whether the person entering the house has any right to do so, and if not, that the resident will take appropriate action. . . . When more of the faces in town are strange . . . a lawbreaker probably will find it easier to escape detection, and capture. He becomes a "white male, about 5 feet, 10 inches tall, between the ages of 16 and 19," instead of "Ruth Johnson's nephew, Frank." (p. 32)

A high density of acquaintanceship can also provide for monitoring and correcting early misbehavior and delinquency. As one youth in Freudenburg's study complained, "A guy can't get away with anything around here. It seems as though whenever I do anything wrong, my old man's found out about it before I even get home" (1986, p. 46).

Mistrust of Government

A greater reliance on informal social control is also consistent with a greater suspicion of government, particularly state and federal government, which are seen as insensitive to local needs. This suspicion of a strong central government is reflected by the attitudes of rural residents, who are generally less supportive than urban residents of government programs which provide welfare, housing, unemployment benefits, higher education, and Medicaid (Swanson, Cohen & Swanson, 1979). This rural attitude is why proponents of rural development warn against public policies dictated by a strong central government (Littrell & Littrell, 1991; Seroka & Subramaniam, 1991). In 1994 most police cooperated with provisions of the recently enacted federal Brady Act, which required local police to conduct background checks on potential gun buyers. However, five rural sheriffs went to court challenging the act. Their biggest concern was the federal government's attempt to coerce them into enforcing the federal law. As Sheriff J. R. Koog, of Val Verde County, Texas, remarked, "No, sir, Congress can't sit up there and tell this lowly little sheriff out here at the end of the world what to do" (Verhovek, 1994, p. A8). Another sheriff remarked, "The federal government does not have the power to conscript me to do a federal job" (Greenburg, 1996, p. 4). It is probably no coincidence that all five of these sheriffs were from rural areas and, as we will see in chapter 3, that all were sheriffs rather than municipal police chiefs.

Regarding the rural American West, Flynn and Gerhardt (1989) have observed that "the West's frontier roots still make it hostile to anything smelling of central authority, and the federal government reeks of it" (p. 10). One example of this mistrust of the federal government has been the rise of citizen militias in the West, where the movement has been spurred by federal actions to control private gun ownership and to restrict grazing, logging, and mining on public lands (deLama, 1994, October 27; 1994, October 31). Activists in the militia movement have armed themselves in the belief that it may soon be necessary for them to use force to protect their rights from being lost to the government. They have been described by George deLama (1994) as "an angry stew of libertarians, right-wing isolationists, constitutionalists, tax protesters and white supremacists, they are linked in a fervent fear, if not paranoia, about what they see as Uncle Sam's encroachment on their property rights and right to bear arms" (October 31, p. 10).

On April 19, 1995, a federal office building in Oklahoma City was bombed, killing dozens of people including children in the building's child-care center. Within a short time police arrested Timothy McVeigh, and news that he had attended militia meetings in Michigan set off a flood of stories about militias in the United States. At the time militias were operating in over 30 of the 50 states, and the media was quick to link these groups with the Christian Identity movement, the Ku Klux Klan, and other groups with hate-based philosophies. (The Christian

Identity movement and the assorted hate groups with which it has been affiliated are discussed in a later chapter.) While militias undoubtedly do attract some fringe elements, it would be a mistake simply to group most militias with violent hate groups. A June 1995 report by Klan-watch estimates there are at least 224 militias and their support groups in 39 states, but only 45 of these groups (20 percent) were thought to have ties to neo-Nazi and other white supremacist groups (Klanwatch Intelligence Report, 1995). In other words, the majority of these groups are driven primarily by anti-government sentiments, with racism and hatred aimed at some religious groups playing a secondary role.

The mistrust of government expressed by militia groups has a long history in America, dating back to the very origins of our country, and has long had ties to the countryside (Stock, 1996). It has been said that on the day of his arrest in the bombing of the federal building in Oklahoma City, Timothy McVeigh was wearing a t-shirt with a quote from Thomas Jefferson: "The tree of liberty shall be fertilized by the blood of tyrants and patriots."

Philip Jenkins has argued that current militia movements and anti-government activities have a striking similarity to events in the 1940s when such groups as the Christian Front were active. In January of 1940:

> The FBI smashes a dead-serious plot to overthrow the federal government and reveals that for more than a year the right-wing militias involved were undergoing army-style training, fired up by inflammatory talk radio. They planned to use their bombs, rifles, and machine guns to wage guerrilla warfare on American cities, and they claimed friends and allies in government and the military. . . . The goal: to remove all liberal and anti-Christian forces from government, not least the liberal President and his activist wife. (1995, September, pp. 38–39)

David DeLeon (1978) has argued that radicalism in the United States has historically been very different from that in Europe, Asia, or the Third World.

> Unlike Scandinavian social democracy, Fabian bureaucracy, and Soviet communism, our traditional critiques of the existing order have been pervaded by suspicion, if not hostility, toward any centralized discipline. . . . Our radicals have concentrated on emancipation, on breaking the prisons of authority, rather than on planning any reconstruction. They are abolitionists, not institution-builders . . . anarchists, not administrators. They generally presume that the free spirit will require little or no guidance. (p. 4)

The mistrust of government so openly expressed by many rural citizens is something with which many Americans can sympathize. In a national survey taken shortly after the Oklahoma City bombing, 39 percent answered yes to the question, "Do you think the federal government has become so large and powerful that it poses an immediate threat to the rights and freedoms of ordinary citizens?" (Urschel, 1995).

Anti-government sentiments appear particularly strong in the West, where the federal government controls or regulates vast areas of land and water. Government control of these resources is a particularly sensitive issue, since many residents earn their livelihood from agriculture or from such extracting industries as logging or mining. In some areas, threats of violence against federal authorities have caused federal agencies to stop performing some of their duties. As the *New York Times* has reported, "To wear a uniform of the Federal Government in some counties is now seen as wearing a target" (Egan, 1995, p. A1). However, threats against government officials cannot be narrowed to a few well-organized militias. The threats come from a variety of individuals, from weakly organized citizen groups, and even from local government officials—particularly in the Northwest.

While anti-government sentiments may be strongest in the rural West, they may be spreading to other regions of rural America. The concerns of these activists, and their responses, are exaggerated expressions of sentiments commonly held by rural citizens. It is not that they believe a centralized government is inefficient, as some conservatives might argue. To the contrary, they appear to believe that the government has been very efficient at eroding the principles upon which the country was founded. While frustration with the federal government may be felt by many citizens, these sentiments have a long history in rural areas and continue to be particularly strong there.

Reluctance to Share Internal Problems

One problem with studying rural areas and gaining insights into rural crime and criminal justice is the tendency of residents in some rural communities to keep community problems to themselves. This attitude, combined with a greater reliance on informal control, also sets the stage for a greater mistrust of government. In his study of marijuana growers, Weisheit (1993) cites a rural police officer who observed:

> People in rural areas tend to be pretty conservative generally and don't want government coming in, or an outsider coming in, or foreigners coming in. They want the status quo and that's it. And when they develop a cancer from within they don't want it going out. They

don't want people telling about it and they don't want people rock-
ing the boat. They are the same people who will ostracize members
of their society who get caught doing this [marijuana growing]. (p.
223)

A similar observation was made by Hafley (1994) in her study of
marijuana growers in Kentucky:

The rural central and eastern Kentucky resident relishes socializing
with others and discussing activities within the community. However, they will not discuss [with outsiders] illegal activities occurring
within the community. For an outsider it can be difficult to get the
rural resident to even admit such activities occur in their community.

Rural central and eastern Kentucky residents take pride in not
divulging the community's business to outsiders. Other residents
are aware of those within the community who are or have been participating in illegal activities. It is only the outsider who is deceived
by protestations of moral outrage. (pp. 140–141)

Informal control, keeping things in and showing a greater suspicion of government may also help account for rural-urban differences in
the willingness of local communities to cooperate fully with reporting to
the FBI's *Uniform Crime Reports.* Reporting to the UCR program in
1996 differed by population density, with reports covering 97 percent of
citizens living in metropolitan statistical areas but only 87 percent of
those living in rural areas (FBI, 1996). Similarly, Laub (1981) has found
that while the overall likelihood of reporting crime to the police is similar for rural and urban citizens, those in urban areas fail to report
because they think nothing can be done, while those in rural areas fail
to report because they consider the crime a private concern, even when
the offender is a stranger. As a New Mexico state police officer observed,
"In a lot of these [rural] areas, there's really no law enforcement—no
police, no sheriff, no state police station. People prefer to handle their
own affairs and disputes by themselves" (Applebome, 1987, p. 11). The
officer's comment should be taken as more figurative than literal,
although there are remote areas of Alaska where the statement could be
taken literally. The statement does reflect two dimensions of the issue
that are distinct but tend to reinforce each other. First, rural citizens
may less often choose to deal with a problem formally because they see
it as a local problem. Second, in some rural areas formal police authority is in fact physically distant and is not an immediate option.

Summary

It is important to remember that rural areas vary enormously both in the extent to which they are physically isolated and in their social environments. This description of rural culture has been, of necessity, a caricature. Particular rural areas will exhibit more or less of these features, and in varying combinations. As a group, however, these features suggest important differences between rural and urban areas—differences that have implications for rural crime and the response to rural crime. Two illustrations of the unique workings of crime in rural areas can be found in the role of poverty and the role of guns in crime. While rural areas contain some of the deepest pockets of poverty in the United States, crime in rural America is substantially less frequent than in urban areas. In addition, while gun ownership is much higher in rural areas than in cities, the percent of crimes involving guns is lower in rural areas. Poverty and guns may be connected to crime, but looking at rural areas suggests the relationship may be more complex than would be assumed by considering only urban settings.

There are several features of rural life that distinguish it from urban life and that may shape crime and justice. Most obvious is the issue of physical space and geographic isolation. Rural areas are also characterized by homogeneity, as illustrated by the relatively low level of racial diversity. That is, while there may be substantial variation from one rural area to another, people within a given rural area tend to be relatively homogenous on a variety of social characteristics. Rural areas are also characterized by a reliance on informal control, a mistrust of government (particularly the federal government), and a reluctance to share internal problems with others outside of the community. All of these factors would seem to have implications for crime, policing, and justice in rural areas. It will be argued throughout the following discussion that rural crime, policing, and justice have features that distinguish them from their urban counterparts, and these features are all a consequence of the unique character of the rural environment. Having described several key features of the rural environment, the focus now shifts to describing patterns of rural crime.

Chapter 2

Rural and Small-Town Crime

DRUGS IN THE HEARTLAND

Clarence Summerfield was dozing in his ranch-style farmhouse near Willow Springs, Mo., one day last month. Suddenly armed invaders, dressed in protective gear that made them look like spacemen, stormed into his home. They were cops, and they had good reason to be there. Tucked away in the Ozarks, the house functioned as a laboratory where Summerfield allegedly used highly flammable chemicals to "cook" illegal methamphetamine, a form of speed. The raiders say they found 25 pounds of powdered "crank." The street value is $1 million. . . .

Dangerous street drugs, once regarded as an urban plague, are now for sale in the nation's remotest country lanes. Drug rings in Eastern cities are supplying small-town contacts with increasing quantities of cocaine and crack, and business is booming. . . .

Many crank dealers moved their operations into the country to elude the law. The drug, made with ether and other chemicals, is relatively simple to produce. . . . But in the manufacturing process the drug emits a strong, unpleasant smell that makes labs detectable in crowded cities. . . .

But even as they're raking in illegal money, most rural drug dealers maintain a low profile, running a farm or holding down a regular job. The invisibility of dealers, and their customers, frustrates authorities.

Source: Baker, King, Murr, & Abbott 1989, April 3, pp. 20–21.

Information about rural crime can be drawn from a number of diverse areas. In this section, some of the better-known sources of information are used to demonstrate areas of concern, suggest topics that distinguish rural areas and merit further study, and identify emerging issues relevant to policing in rural areas. The discussion begins by examining fear of crime in rural areas and then shifts to a description of patterns of rural crime. Changes in rural crime over time are then considered, followed by a discussion of special issues and emerging problems.

Fear of Crime

Fear of crime has several implications for policing. It may affect community support for policies and budgets related to policing, and it may be important in mobilizing citizens to report crime, cooperate with investigations, and participate in anti-crime programs. Fear of crime is among the rural crime issues most frequently studied. Studies conducted in the 1970s generally concluded that urban residents were far more fearful of crime than were rural residents (e.g., DuBow, McCabe, & Kaplan, 1979; Baumer, 1978; Clemente & Kleiman, 1977; 1976; Conklin, 1976; 1971; Lebowitz, 1975; Erskine, 1974; Boggs, 1971). Studies in the 1980s and 1990s were more mixed in their conclusions. Some found rural citizens less fearful (e.g., Belyea & Zingraff, 1988; Smith & Huff, 1982; Ollenburger, 1981), while others found only minor rural-urban differences (Bankston, Jenkins, Quentin, Thayer-Doyle, & Thompson, 1987; Lee, 1982). Still another approach is used in the American Housing Survey, which asks citizens a more general question about what bothers them about their neighborhood. In 1991, 15 percent of central city residents specifically mentioned crime, compared with less than 2 percent of rural residents (DeFrances & Smith, 1994).

Lee's (1982) work demonstrates the problem of simply transporting methodologies developed for an urban population to a rural setting. For example, he showed that while general urban-rural concerns about victimization were similar, the two groups had very different perceptions about victimization on nearby streets, a question frequently used as the sole indicator of fear in early studies. Lee argued that because of differences in the physical environment this question was largely irrelevant for the rural population, for whom residential streets are often part of their private space rather than public access. In the most rural areas streets near homes may be little more than access roads with very little public use by strangers. For rural residents, fears were manifest in other types of crime, such as theft or vandalism. When other victimization concerns were considered, rural-urban differences faded.

Elaborating upon earlier work in urban settings, Austin, Woolever, & Baba (1994) surveyed residents of small communities regarding their feelings of safety. As in larger urban areas, they found that perceptions of safety in small towns were related to prior victimization and to participation in local organizations and associations. Those most involved in the community felt most safe. These findings mirror those in the discussion of density of acquaintanceships in chapter 1, again indicating the importance of social networks in small communities.

One response to concern about crime is to develop a prevention program, such as neighborhood watch. It has been found that similar factors motivate both rural and urban citizens to participate in crime prevention programs (Smith & Lab, 1991). It has also been suggested that the interpersonal bonds and patterns of social interaction in rural areas are positive factors which can facilitate the development of rural crime prevention programs (Donnermeyer & Mullen, 1987). Consistent with this, Mullen and Donnermeyer (1985) found that among rural citizens one of the most important factors related to fear of crime was the extent to which they viewed their neighbors as trustworthy and watchful against crime.

A study of popular images of rurality by Willits, Bealer, and Timbers (1990), though not specifically a study of fear, does provide interesting insights into perceptions of crime across rural and urban areas. In their survey of the public, they found overwhelming agreement with the statement, "There is less crime and violence in rural areas than in other areas." Over two-thirds of rural, suburban, and urban residents agreed with the statement. The authors also observed that crime was a topic that brought out anti-urban sentiments. For example, most respondents, including those from urban areas, agreed with the statement, "Crime and violence characterize city life in America."

Taken as a whole, these studies suggest the importance of considering the social and physical environment of rural areas before applying "urban definitions" to the crime problem and before conducting research on rural crime (see also Weisheit, 1993). It also appears that aside from violent street crime, rural citizens share many of the same concerns about crime as their urban counterparts. Unfortunately, research on rural crime seldom draws on knowledge about the unique features of rural culture and geography which are essential to understanding how to study fear in rural areas, how to interpret results, and how to develop programs responsive to community concerns.

Rural versus Urban Crime

In addition to considering fear of crime, several studies have examined rural crime itself, using either self-reports or official records. Many of these studies make rural-urban comparisons (Gardner & Shoemaker, 1989; Laub, 1983a; 1983b; Carter, 1982; Lyerly & Skipper, 1981). Most research concludes that crime is less frequent in rural areas, and it is often speculated that greater informal controls in rural areas protect against high crime rates (Smith, 1980).

Some rural-urban comparisons have tried to account for these differences by looking for correlates, i.e., factors which would seem to go along with the lower rates in rural areas. Kowalski and Duffield (1990), for example, conducted a county-level study of homicide and rurality and found that rural counties had lower rates and that counties with lower homicide rates were also those with lower divorce rates, lower poverty levels, less religious diversity, and lower percentages of minorities. They concluded, "In rural areas, individualism is reduced, group identification is strengthened, and the potential for violence is diminished" (p. 86). They also noted that rurality is a multidimensional phenomenon and that separate dimensions may impact crime rates differently.

Wilkinson (1984) also used county-level data but came to a very different conclusion. In contrast to other data, he found that homicide rates were higher in rural areas. He accounted for this by noting that in a geographically dispersed population, social interactions occur more frequently among family members and close acquaintances; both are groups at a relatively higher risk for homicide. Wilkinson also observed that when compared with large cities, homicide rates were higher in rural areas but lower in small cities. Taken together, these findings highlight the importance of crime-specific analyses and of using care in defining the term rural. Simply treating everything outside of major metropolitan areas as rural can mask important patterns.

The belief that crime is less frequent in rural areas is supported by recent *Uniform Crime Reports* (UCR) data (see Table 2) that presents crime by type and population group. Of particular interest is a comparison between crime in cities of 250,000 or more and that in rural counties. Studies of police departments commonly focus on departments serving cities of 250,000 or more people. In contrast to large cities, rural counties are outside of metropolitan statistical areas and cover areas not under the jurisdiction of city police departments. The data in Table 2 reveals several interesting patterns.

(1) Rates for urban areas are higher than for rural areas for *every* index offense, including homicide.

(2) The gap between rural and urban crime is greater for violent than for property crime.

(3) For property crime the rank order of offenses is roughly similar for urban and rural areas. That is, larceny is the most common crime and arson the least common in each area.

Table 2.   Crime Rates for Cities 250,000 or More Versus Rural Counties, 1996

Crime Type	Cities 250,000+	Rural Counties	City:Rural Ratio
Violent Crime			
Total	1,443.7	242.6	6.0:1
Murder	18.4	4.8	3.8:1
Rape	57.7	24.6	2.3:1
Robbery	609.7	18.0	33.9:1
Agg. assault	757.8	195.3	3.9:1
Property Crime			
Total	6,674.2	2,014.8	3.3:1
Burglary	1,375.9	680.0	2.0:1
Larceny	4,075.0	1,196.5	3.4:1
Vehicle theft	1,223.3	138.3	8.8:1
Arson	83.9	18.9	4.4:1

Note: Figures for arson are drawn from table 2.31 of the UCR and are not included in the row on total property crime.

Source: Federal Bureau of Investigation (1996), table 16.

(4) For violent crime, the rank order is thrown off by the very large rural-urban difference in robbery.

(5) Even for crimes with the most similar rates across areas, such as rape, the urban rate is much higher.

(6) The greatest difference is for robbery, which occurs over 34 times more often per 100,000 citizens in urban areas.

Official counts of crime are useful indicators but suffer from a number of shortcomings. Not all crimes are reported to the authorities, not all reported crimes are recorded, and not all recorded crimes are forwarded to the UCR. One alternative is to ask citizens whether they have been victims of crime. One of the most frequently used data sources for studying victimization is the National Crime Victimization

Survey (NCVS), an annual survey begun in 1973 which utilizes a randomly drawn national sample, and which includes information about the size of the respondent's community.

Substantial rural-urban differences are found from national household victimization surveys. The 1990 survey of households touched by crime, for example, reported the percent of households indicating any form of victimization in urban, suburban, and rural areas was 30 percent, 23 percent and 17 percent, respectively. Bachman (1992a; 1992b) noted that between 1973 and 1990 victimization was consistently highest in central cities and lowest in nonmetropolitan areas, and this was true whether the study focused on individuals or households. This pattern of differences appears to hold true for both violent and property crime. In his study of victimization, Smith (1980) found that about 25 percent of victimizations of rural residents took place while they were away from their communities, while this was true for only 10 percent of urban residents. He concluded that "rural residents are particularly vulnerable to personal theft crimes when visiting urban areas" (p. 51). This also means that the usual rural-urban comparisons of victimization rates probably *understate* the difference in victimization between the two areas.

Instead of comparing rural and urban areas, some studies have analyzed the variations within rural areas (e.g., Donnermeyer & Phillips, 1982; Miller, Hoiberg, & Ganey, 1982; Smith & Huff, 1982). This research generally focuses on patterns across rural areas and correlates of rural crime. Arthur (1991), for example, examined property and violent crime in 13 rural Georgia counties. He found that unemployment, poverty, public aid, and race were related to both property and violent crime rates, and the relationship was particularly strong for property crime. Bankston and Allen (1980) compared homicides among 10 social areas in rural Louisiana and found that both socioeconomic and cultural factors shaped homicide rates. Significantly, the relative importance of each varied from one social area to another, suggesting the importance of appreciating variations among rural areas. Thus, a good understanding of rural crime requires not only appreciating how it differs from urban crime, but how rural crime and rural justice vary across rural communities.

Trends in Rural Crime

There has been concern for some time that rural and urban crime rates are converging, and the issue has raised considerable debate. Some have argued that with modern communication and transportation, rural-urban differences are shrinking through what Fischer (1980) has called "massification."

   Carter (1982) used UCR data and found that between 1960 and 1979 the percent increase for index crimes in rural areas was greater than in urban areas. Similarly, Swanson (1981) found that between 1969 and 1978 the percent increase for rural crime was greater than for urban crime. However, because rural rates are much lower and the size of percent change depends heavily on the size of the rate at time 1, conclusions based on percentage change should be accepted with caution. In fact, using Carter's own table (his table 2.2), the difference between the rates in rural and urban areas in absolute magnitude actually *increased* over time. In 1960 there were 95 more violent crimes per 100,000 citizens in urban areas than in rural areas. By 1979 there were 411 more violent crimes per 100,000 citizens in urban areas than in rural areas. Extending the logic of Carter's work, by 1996 there were nearly 1,200 more violent crimes per 100,000 citizens in urban areas than in rural areas. That is, the absolute rural-urban gap grew substantially over time, despite his conclusion that rural crime had increased at a higher rate than urban crime. In other words, Carter's data suggest that rural and urban crime rates are *not* converging, providing little support for arguments that massification is leading to the end of rural-urban differences.

   Table 3 uses UCR data from 1980 through 1996 to make rural-urban comparisons over time for both violent and property offenses. Several findings revealed in this table are worth noting:

   (1) In large cities violent crime rose from 1980 to 1991 and by 1996 had declined to nearly 1980 numbers.

   (2) In rural counties violent crime followed a less clear path, declining some after 1980 and then rising, beginning in the early 1990s, during which time it was higher than in 1980.

   (3) Between 1980 and 1996, property crime fluctuated some but ended up somewhat lower in both urban and rural areas.

   (4) The ratio (gap) of city to rural violent crimes fluctuated between 1980 and 1993 but changed little overall. After 1993 the ratio is somewhat smaller.

   (5) The ratio (gap) of city to rural property crimes went up somewhat between 1980 and 1993 and then returned to the levels of the 1980s.

   (6) The ratios for both violent and property crime are relatively stable between 1986 and 1993.

   (7) In every year the gap between rural and urban areas is greater for violent crime than for property crime.

Table 3 should not be considered the definitive word on the matter, however. These data represent *reported crime*, not actual crime—and are as likely to express changes in reporting and record keeping practices as they are to express real changes or differences in the numbers of crime. There are two important areas not covered in the table. One

Table 3   Crime Rates for Cities 250,000 or More versus Rural Counties, 1980–1996

	VIOLENT CRIME			PROPERTY CRIME		
Year	Cities 250,000+	Rural Counties	City:Rural Ratio	Cities 250,000+	Rural Counties	City:Rural Ratio
1980	1414.2	185.9	7.6:1	7987.9	2215.8	3.6:1
1981	1440.9	179.4	8.0:1	8030.4	2119.1	3.8:1
1982	1353.9	184.2	7.4:1	7851.0	2041.2	3.9:1
1983	1294.0	165.0	7.8:1	7345.4	1824.8	4.0:1
1984	1288.3	159.8	8.1:1	7307.5	1740.5	4.2:1
1985	1344.5	176.9	7.6:1	7606.1	1743.8	4.4:1
1986	1645.5	192.8	8.5:1	7993.8	1791.1	4.5:1
1987	1603.8	193.9	8.3:1	8062.7	1887.5	4.3:1
1988	1540.4	180.7	8.5:1	8271.3	1882.3	4.4:1
1989	1641.1	198.2	8.3:1	8245.0	1923.3	4.4:1
1990	1813.0	209.0	8.7:1	8361.4	1923.1	4.4:1
1991	1890.3	213.6	8.9:1	8223.0	1978.0	4.2:1
1992	1802.1	226.2	8.0:1	7722.2	1927.6	4.0:1
1993	1711.9	233.1	7.3:1	7492.6	1883.3	4.0:1
1994	1657.4	255.9	6.5:1	7129.0	1936.5	3.7:1
1995	1564.3	253.0	6.2:1	6998.9	2011.8	3.5:1
1996	1443.7	242.6	6.0:1	6647.2	2014.8	3.3:1

Source: Federal Bureau of Investigation, *Uniform Crime Reports: Crime in the United States*, 1980 through 1996.

Table 4 Offense-Specific Index Crime Rates for Rural Counties, 1980–1996

	VIOLENT CRIME				PROPERTY CRIME		
Year	Murder	Rape	Robbery	Assault	Burglary	Larceny	MV Theft
1980	7.4	16.0	23.0	139.5	871.8	1202.6	141.4
1981	7.0	15.7	22.1	134.6	836.7	1157.7	124.7
1982	6.8	15.4	20.4	141.6	788.3	1132.9	119.9
1983	5.8	15.3	16.9	127.0	693.7	1027.6	103.6
1984	5.2	17.5	14.9	122.3	651.3	987.1	102.2
1985	5.6	18.5	15.0	137.7	668.2	967.2	108.4
1986	5.4	20.1	15.6	145.4	697.7	978.4	115.1
1987	5.7	19.6	15.6	146.7	728.1	1040.9	118.5
1988	5.4	19.6	14.8	140.9	711.1	1051.8	119.4
1989	5.4	22.8	16.4	153.6	719.9	1077.4	126.0
1990	5.7	23.7	15.8	163.8	708.1	1087.6	127.4
1991	5.6	25.4	17.0	165.6	741.0	1114.0	123.0
1992	5.3	27.3	17.0	176.7	701.4	1109.6	116.6
1993	5.5	26.6	17.1	183.8	675.5	1087.3	120.5
1994	5.2	28.4	18.6	203.6	679.9	1127.7	128.8
1995	5.3	26.2	18.6	203.0	687.4	1186.6	137.8
1996	4.8	24.6	18.0	195.3	680.0	1196.5	138.3

Source: Federal Bureau of Investigation, *Uniform Crime Reports: Crime in the United States*, 1980 through 1996.

problem is that it does not include crimes outside of the seven index categories. Some of these offenses may be of particular concern as emerging issues in rural areas, such as gang activity and drug trafficking. Non-index offenses are simply not reported in the UCR by population density, so these comparisons are not possible from published results.

Other rural-specific offenses, such as rustling and the theft of grain or farm machinery, are not separated from other more general crime categories. Some of these specific topics will be addressed in the next section.

A second problem with Table 3 is that it does not present changes for specific index offenses within the broad categories of violent and property offenses. For the sake of parsimony, the focus here will be on changes in specific index offenses only within rural counties. Table 4 shows that changes are not the same for all offenses. Among violent crimes both murder and robbery generally decline between 1980 and 1996, while rape and aggravated assault both increase. Among property crimes the pattern is less clear. Burglaries decline between 1980 and 1983 but do not change dramatically after that. Larceny fluctuates some but shows no clear pattern over time, while motor vehicle theft declines from 1980 through 1985 and then gradually rises from 1985 through 1996.

The *National Crime Victimization Survey* (NCVS) also permits considering changes over time by community size and provides an alternative data source where changes in official record keeping are not an issue. Figure 5 is based on NCVS data and shows that rural violent victimization is persistently lower than urban victimization. Where convergence has occurred it is between suburban and rural areas, and this has more to do with drops in suburban victimization than with increases in rural violent victimization. Rural crime changed less over time than either suburban or urban crime, with all three showing declines in the most recent years.

Fischer (1980) used data on violent crime in selected California counties to argue that the gap between rural and urban crime was less important than their relative patterns of change over time. He demonstrated that changes over time in urban counties were followed by changes in rural counties and concluded that "cultural change is continually generated in major urban centers, diffuses to smaller cities and then to the rural hinterland" (p. 416). Cultural cycles, whether they be of violent crime, fashion, or inventions, begin in urban areas and ripple out through the countryside. This argument is consistent with contemporary observations about the rise of drug trafficking and gangs in rural areas, an issue to be addressed in the next section. This seems to be particularly true of gangs, which appear to have little presence in rural areas outside of ties to gangs in larger communities. Although the processes are less explicit, to some extent the idea of diffusion into the countryside from the city is also true with drugs, including cocaine and perhaps even methamphetamine production.

Figure 5. Violent Victimization 1973–96

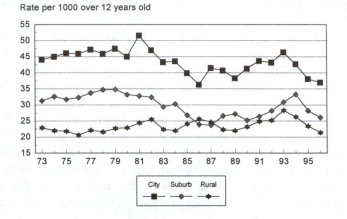

Rate per 1000 over 12 years old

Note: Because of changes in the instrument, post-1992 rates were adjusted to be comparable to pre-1992 rates. For violent crimes the multiplier is .671 times the post-1993 rates.

Sources: Bachman, 1992a; 1992b; Bastian, 1995; Perkins & Klaus, 1996; Taylor, 1997; Ringel, 1997; Rand, Lynch & Cantor, 1997

Special Issues

The focus on rural-urban comparisons has also meant a focus on particular categories of crime, often the street crimes listed in Part I of the *Uniform Crime Reports*—what are called the index crimes. Many issues relevant to rural policing, such as gang activity, do not neatly fit these categories or are emerging issues that have not been explored in the professional literature. What follows is a sampling of these topics, often based on reports in the popular press, but clarified where possible with systematic relevant data. Because many of these discussions are based on anecdotal evidence, the information should be interpreted with caution, as suggestive but not definitive. However, we argue that these are areas which merit scholarly research and which will be of increasing concern to rural police.

Gangs

Traditionally street gangs or "youth gangs" in the United States have been viewed as an urban, inner-city problem, associated only with large metropolitan centers such as Chicago, Los Angeles, New York, or Detroit. Most of the available research and other collected wisdom on gangs reflects this traditional view. For example, Huff's (1996) comprehensive collection of contemporary gang research includes no discussion of gangs in smaller cities and rural areas. However, many observers and scholars have recently noted the spread of urban street gangs to areas outside the inner city—in the rural countryside as well as in the suburban fringes. The popular press has provided numerous stories of cases where big-city gangs have appeared in unlikely non-urban locations. In addition, academic researchers have increasingly reported on the diffusion of urban street gangs into the hinterland as a well documented trend (e.g., Klein, 1995; Short, 1998). However, a critical question about any "crime wave," such as the spread of gangs, is whether it represents a real increase in actual crime versus an increase in public alarm and awareness of crime. Is the recent rural gang wave as real and pervasive as it seems?

Despite being regarded as a "proven fact," empirical documentation of this rural gang diffusion is surprisingly hard to find. Current knowledge is based largely on subjective impressions and some sketchy research reports, which, because they are repeatedly cited and frequently referenced, seem numerous and substantial. In fact, systematic and objective data on gangs and their activities in rural communities simply have not been available to verify or disconfirm these conclusions. The difficulty is that: (a) comprehensively collected official crime data such as the Uniform Crime Reports or National Crime Victim Surveys do not collect specific information on gangs or gang crimes; and (b) research specifically focused on gangs has been confined almost exclusively to larger urban areas and police departments. Almost all gang studies have been done in communities with populations over 100,000, usually well over a million. Studies of rural areas and smaller police departments have involved only a few isolated case studies using impressionistic, qualitative data of atypical communities. Further, it is not unusual for studies to include communities precisely because they are reported to have gang problems, thus creating skewed samples that overstate the prevalence of gangs in similar communities. This approach cannot provide representative, reliable estimates of rural gang activity.

How can we tell if gangs are really occurring in rural communities? While the data are only suggestive, some very recent surveys provide some concrete details. Specifically, in 1995 the National Youth Gang Crime Survey was collected to provide a more systematic assessment of gangs in communities throughout the United States by surveying 4,120 police departments and sheriff's agencies in the United States (Office of

Juvenile Justice and Delinquency Prevention [OJJDP], 1997). In addition to the usual assortment of large and medium-sized cities studied in prior surveys, the 1995 survey included a random sample of smaller cities and counties (of less than 100,000 population). While the questionnaire used is very brief, its gang measurements depend entirely on police records and definitions, and the overall sample is not really a random sample of U.S. communities, the NYGC Survey does provide a more representative sampling of smaller nonmetropolitan communities and the first systematic assessment of the presence of gangs in such communities. The survey only briefly asked police agencies about gang problems in their jurisdictions during 1995, as well as in the years prior to 1995. Keeping in mind the limitations of allowing respondents to define for themselves what counts as a gang, these items allow some general overall estimates of the prevalence of gangs in rural or small-town locations.

According to the 1995 National Youth Gang Crime Survey, how prevalent are street gangs in different kinds of community settings? Figure 6 shows the percentages of police agencies who reported having gangs in 1995, where communities have been divided into six rural/urban categories based on classification of the counties in which they are located, using a rural-urban typology developed by the U.S. Department of Agriculture (Cook & Mizer, 1994). These results confirm the common assertion that gangs are found in communities of all sizes and locations. According to the police, gangs were present in significant numbers in 1995 in every community category, although they are less prevalent in smaller, less urbanized locations. Almost three-fourths of the police agencies in large metropolitan counties report gangs in their communities. Almost two-thirds of the agencies in smaller metropolitan counties, as well as the "semi-metropolitan fringe" counties, reported gangs in 1995. These percentages are lower than the 90 percent figure reported in earlier surveys (e.g., Curry, Ball, & Fox, 1994), which focused selectively on communities already identified as having gang problems (communities without gangs being excluded as uninteresting and uninformative). This earlier approach resulted in a biased sampling of gang-affected communities that inflates estimates of gang prevalence.

Outside of officially designated metropolitan areas, gangs are still frequently reported by police agencies in the 1995 survey. Over half of agencies in nonmetropolitan-but-urban counties (i.e., containing cities of between 20,000 and 50,000 population) report gangs in their jurisdictions. In smaller and more rural communities, the percentages of reported gangs are noticeably lower but still appreciable. About 40 percent of police agencies in nonmetropolitan counties containing only

Figure 6. Reports of Gangs by County Size

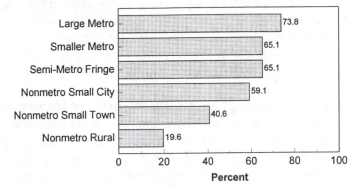

Source: see table 5

small towns (between 2,500 and 20,000 in population) reported gangs in their jurisdictions in 1995. About one in five of the agencies in completely rural counties (which contain no officially urban locations of at least 2,500 persons) reported gangs in 1995. Thus, gangs indeed may be found anywhere these days, but they are still far more likely (and far more numerous) in larger urban centers.

Is the appearance of gangs in small towns and outlying areas really a new development? How recently has this occurred? The data allowed us to consider the percentages of police agencies with gangs in 1995 who also reported gangs in the early 1990s and in the 1980s. These results confirm that the diffusion of gangs is a recent phenomenon taking place mainly in this decade; gang problems do not appear in most communities until after 1990. Most agencies who reported gangs in 1995 also reported that gangs were present in their communities during the prior five years. This percentage is remarkably consistent across different sizes of communities, hovering around an 80 percent rate for all categories. However, the percentages reporting gang problems *prior to 1990* are much lower and are clearly related to community size. About half of the large metropolitan jurisdictions with gangs in 1995 also had gangs during the 1980s, showing the substantial and well-known continuity of gangs in these largest urban settings. However only about a third of the smaller metropolitan locations reported gangs during the earlier decade. Or put another way, two-thirds of the agencies in metropolitan counties with populations between 100,000 and 1 million persons who had gangs in 1995 did not have them before 1990.

Looking at police agencies in semi-metropolitan or nonmetropolitan, smaller urban counties, the fraction of jurisdictions with gangs prior to 1990 drops to one-fifth, while in counties with only small towns, only one-eighth of police agencies reported gangs before 1990. None of the 37 completely rural police agencies who reported gangs in 1995 indicated any gang presence before 1990. These results confirm Klein's (1995) assertion that the growth and spread of street gangs has been recent and nonlinear, with a very rapid expansion of gang presence in the early 1990s, increasing both in numbers of gangs and in their geographic distribution.

Acknowledging that gangs are now common but far from universal in rural areas, what are the characteristics of rural communities associated with having gang problems? What are the conditions that put some communities at higher risk? Of special concern for gang migration is the *proximity* of rural areas to larger metropolitan centers that have highly developed, chronic gang problems. Table 5 reports the percentages of agencies in nonmetropolitan counties who reported gangs in 1995 classified by whether they are geographically adjacent to a metropolitan area (MSA county). All the comparisons in Table 5 show the effects on rural communities of being geographically accessible to larger cities with gangs. Prevalence rates of reported gangs are consistently higher for nonmetro counties that are adjacent to metropolitan areas than for those nonmetro counties that are more geographically distant.

Table 5   Police Agencies Reporting Gangs in 1995
(% of Survey Agencies in non-MSA Counties)

Non-MSA Counties	In Counties Not Adjacent to an MSA	In Counties Adjacent to an MSA
Contain small cities (20,000 to 50,000 population)	59.1%	66.8%
Contain only small towns (2,500 to 20,000 population)	37.9%	44.2%
Completely rural (contains no towns or cities)	13.6%	33.3%
All non-MSA counties (conbined total)	38.8%	50.4%

Source: Created from data provided by the National Youth Gang Center, Institute for Intergovernmental Research, Tallahassee, FL (OJJDP, 1997) and by the Economic Research Service, U.S. Department of Agriculture, Washington, DC (Cook & Mizer, 1994).

According to most explanations of gangs, *economic* conditions are a critical consideration in accounting for the development of gangs in a community. This is especially relevant since rural areas vary so widely in their economic circumstances and prospects. Table 6 separates nonmetropolitan communities into those located in "persistent poverty" counties and those located in more economically favorable counties. As these results show, economic conditions do have an impact, especially in counties geographically removed from metropolitan centers. The low risks for gang development of being located away from the large cities are offset by the higher risks for gang development due to chronic poverty. However, the nurturing of economic development by encouraging plants, factories, and production facilities to relocate into more rural areas does not seem to provide a simple answer for the effects of poverty, as Table 6 shows. In outlying areas (not adjacent to metropolitan centers) the presence of a dominant manufacturing economy is associated with *increased* prevalence of gangs. In contrast, communities in outlying areas with predominantly farming-based economies report the lowest risks of gang problems.

Table 6   Reported Gangs by Characteristics of Non-Metro Counties
(% of Agencies Reporting Gangs in 1995)

Nonmetro County Type	Not Adjacent to MSA	Adjacent to MSA
Persistent poverty counties	52.0%	59.8%
Nonpoverty counties	37.0%	49.0%
Manufacturing counties	50.0%	47.9%
Nonmanufacturing counties	36.9%	50.0%
Farming-based counties	28.8%	61.2%
Nonfarming counties	41.2%	48.7%
Retirement destination counties	41.3%	56.3%
Nonretirement counties	38.5%	49.6%
All non-MSA counties	38.8%	50.4%

Source: Created from data provided by the National Youth Gang Center, Institute for Intergovernmental Research, Tallahassee, FL (OJJDP, 1997) and by the Economic Research Service, U.S. Department of Agriculture, Washington, DC (Cook & Mizer, 1994).

Where do gangs in rural communities come from? Are rural gangs exported from large metropolitan areas (as urban gangs expand their territories), or are they home-grown (as expressions of local social conditions and networks)? This question is important since specific answers to it imply very different problems for rural communities and lead to very different gang control strategies. While no specific empirical data are available to definitively answer the question, a variety of qualitative studies of rural delinquency and crime have suggested the general outline of an answer. They suggest there are several distinctly different patterns of rural gang development that occur in different communities with different local situations. One common theme of several patterns is the deliberate migration of gang members from urban to rural locations who take the gang with them wherever they move. According to Donnermeyer (1994), two common patterns are: (1) displacement and (2) the branch office. *Displacement* occurs when urban police put too much pressure on urban gangs; members drift away from the city to outlying communities to find a location where they can set up their operations with lower enforcement pressures. The *branch office* pattern reflects the occasional case where an urban gang specifically targets a small town for criminal enterprise, either because the town is located on an important transportation hub or because the selling price of drugs in small towns is higher than in urban areas. When this occurs individuals from the gang move into an area for the express purpose of selling drugs and conducting other illegal activities. While some recruiting of locals into the gang may occur, such recruitment is of secondary interest to the exploitation of local markets and resources.

Alternatively, what may migrate is the gang as a set of ideas, behaviors, and organizational connections rather than as a set of specific persons. Donnermeyer (1994) described two additional ways in which this often occurs: (3) the franchise, and (4) social learning. The *franchise* occurs when small-town drug dealers seek to expand their business and their profits by linking up with an urban drug-dealing gang. It represents an alliance between local persons or groups and distant urban organizations to gain a competitive advantage in a local illegal market, using the urban gang connection as a supplier of illegal drugs or as a way to intimidate competitors. The *social learning* pattern refers to the way that correctional institutions often function as institutions of learning for criminal skills and values. Many rural and small-town areas have no detention facilities, and most states prohibit locking juveniles in adult jails, even for short periods. Consequently, it may be necessary to transport juveniles to centralized detention facilities located in urban areas. While incarcerated, the rural juvenile comes into contact with more hardened, gang-connected urban youths. These urban youths teach the rural juvenile the elements of gang culture, along with details of drug dealing, and provide opportunities for business connections. This knowledge and these connections are taken back to the rural community when the youths are released from detention. The process is even more likely in long-term correctional institutions for juveniles, since the period in which rural youths are exposed to urban gang influences is even longer. The actual frequency of social learning about gangs among rural youths has not been empirically documented for either short-term detention facilities or long-term institutions. However, both are possible avenues that have been noted by juvenile workers and deserve further study.

Our interviews with rural and small-town police suggested an additional and common scenario of gang diffusion that results paradoxically from attempts to reduce gang influence. The (5) *urban flight* pattern involves situations where urban families move into rural areas, either to get away from the higher crime of the city in general or to get their kids away from gang influences that are strong in urban neighborhoods. In other cases, the juvenile is an urban gang member sent to live with relatives in a rural community to remove him or her from gang influences. While this may spell the end of gang activity for some gang-involved youths, others may take the gang influence with them and try to establish a gang foothold in their new environment. This situation can also facilitate establishing a franchise or branch office.

The scant evidence available makes it difficult to say which of these patterns occurs most frequently, as well as which patterns occur in which types of rural communities. It is too early to tell if the current perceptions about the continued growth and diffusion of urban gangs will be correct. However, it seems clear that the combination of gangs, drugs, and crime in rural areas is an important development that bears careful monitoring and more attention to the collection of reliable, systematic data on gang-related crime.

Alcohol and Drugs

Another issue is the problem of substance use, including alcohol and illegal drugs. This issue has two dimensions, *use* by rural citizens and *criminal trafficking* by organizations in rural areas. The professional literature has discussed the issue of drug use, while the issue of rural trafficking organizations has more often been addressed in the popular press. Alcohol, among the most popular of the mind-altering drugs, is of particular concern in rural areas. Each year more people are arrested for DUI than for any other single offense, and DUI is more common in rural areas (Weisheit & Klofas, 1992; Jacobs, 1989). According to the *Uniform Crime Reports,* (see Figure 7) the rate of arrest for DUI in cities under 10,000 is more than double that in cities of 250,000 or more, and the rates for both suburban and rural counties are much higher than in the largest cities.

Figure 7. DUI Arrest Rate, 1996

(Rate per 100,000)

Community Size

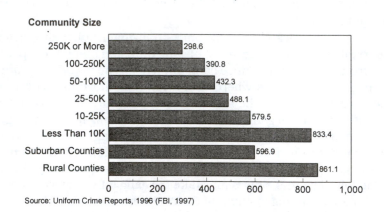

Source: Uniform Crime Reports, 1996 (FBI, 1997)

Studies commonly find that alcohol use by young people is more frequent in rural areas. Data from the Monitoring the Future annual surveys of high school seniors found that rural youths were more likely to use alcohol and to engage in binge drinking than were urban youths (Cronk & Sarvela, 1997). Even if urban and rural rates of alcohol use by young people were similar, the rural setting may be cause for greater concern:

> Similar rates of alcohol use, however, may be more of a problem for rural than for urban youth because rural youth must spend more time on the roads. The distances that must be traveled from homes to school and other entertainment events, or even to visit friends, are generally much greater for rural youth than for urban youth. The lack of availability of public transportation means that these youth spend a significant amount of time in cars. Most social use of alcohol by these rural teens is followed by driving or at least riding in a car where the driver has been drinking. The relative lack of traffic on rural roadways and the distances to be traversed often lead to driving at high rates of speed. With many rural roads in poor condition,

poorly marked for hazards, and poorly lit, these youth are already at higher risk of accidents leading to injury or death. (Peters, Oetting, & Edwards, 1992, pp. 25–26)

Regarding illegal drugs, one of the most common ways to compare rural and urban areas is to use self-report surveys. McIntosh, Fitch, Staggs, Nyberg, & Wilson (1979) found that rural youths began using both legal and illegal drugs at a younger age, but a higher percentage of urban youths were current users. Swaim, Beauvais, Edwards, & Oetting (1986) compared adolescent drug use in three rural communities with that in an urban community. They concluded that the differences in drug use *among* rural communities may have been greater than differences *between* rural and urban areas. They emphasized the importance of local variation and suggested that local policies and programs for rural areas *not* be based on aggregate national data.

In his summary and analysis of 65 research studies of drug use by rural youths, Donnermeyer (1992) concluded that for alcohol, rural and urban rates were similar. The use of marijuana in urban areas was higher, but these differences were shrinking over time. Rural youths generally reported greater use of inhalants and stimulants, but less use of cocaine and crack cocaine. Finally, Donnermeyer noted the relative paucity of research on rural drug issues, in particular the lack of information about how rural youths gain access to drugs. Cronk and Sarvela's (1997) analysis of the annual survey of high school seniors from 1976 through 1992 found that rural youths were less likely than urban youths to use marijuana, cocaine, or LSD, although marijuana and cocaine rates were converging by 1992.

An indirect way of comparing rural and urban drug use is to use arrest statistics. Belyea and Zingraff (1985) compared drug arrest data in North Carolina for urban and rural counties between 1976 and 1980 and concluded that rural arrest rates were consistently lower, and there was no evidence that rural and urban rates were converging. Castellano and Uchida (1990) estimate that the rate of drug arrests in urban areas is nearly four times that in rural counties. They speculate that because most drug enforcement is proactive, variations in arrest rates among jurisdictions are more the result of differences in enforcement efforts than due to differences in consumption patterns.

A 1990 report to Congress by the General Accounting Office (GAO) examined rural drug abuse using data from a variety of sources. The report found that the rate of total drug use, including alcohol, was similar across rural and urban areas, but there were differences in the types of drugs used. Cocaine use was lower in rural areas, but the use of inhalants was higher. Further, while total drug arrest rates were sim-

ilar across areas, alcohol arrests were higher and drug arrests correspondingly lower in rural areas. The report also found that anti-drug
programs in rural areas faced special problems:

> Rural programs can have greater per-client costs because of their
> "diseconomies of scale." These areas may find it difficult to attract
> and hold trained and experienced staff. Clients must travel farther to
> reach programs and program staff must travel farther to reach cli-
> ents. The programs may lack acceptance by the community, com-
> munity agencies, and the local school system. (General Accounting
> Office, 1990, pp. 6–7)

Where rural drug treatment programs do exist, the nature of their
services may be different:

> Rural substance abuse programs tend to offer a wider array of out-
> reach and acute response services, such as hot lines and crisis inter-
> vention. Outpatient services tend to be heavily utilized with respect to
> staff availability. Rural hospitals are less likely to provide inpatient
> services and the need for inpatient services is filled by sending the
> patients to the closest urban treatment facility. (Leukefeld, Clayton,
> & Myers, 1992, pp. 100–101)

Institutions and programs for juvenile offenders have a long history of operating in the rural setting, which is seen as purifying and less
criminogenic. An interesting case study by Milofsky, Butto, Gross, &
Baumohl (1993) documents another example in which the rural setting
is seen as therapeutic for drug abusers. They document the movement
of addicts from urban New York City into a small city in northeast Pennsylvania that had a number of treatment facilities and shelters for
addicts. About 300 addicts from New York City entered programs or
"sobriety houses" in this rural community each year. Many found the
safety and atmosphere of the small city a refreshing change from the
urban neighborhoods from which they came, and many of these addicts
eventually became permanent residents. In addition to problems that
ordinarily accompany population growth and the stigma that accompanies being an addict or an alcoholic, several characteristics of this immigrant group led to tension and even overt hostility from the host community. These characteristics include: (1) most of these immigrants (86
percent) reported an arrest history, and many were encouraged to go
there by probation and parole officers. Some came to the community
directly from prison; (2) the average immigrant was younger than the
average established citizen; (3) most of the established residents were
white, but most of the immigrants were minority; (4) most immigrants
applied for public assistance when they arrived; and (5) behaviors that
were common among urban residents were not considered civil in a

small community with a slower pace of life. These factors combined to create tensions between the immigrants and the host community.

Despite these tensions, many features of the rural environment made it ideal for drug and alcohol rehabilitation clients, and so the programs were highly successful. At the same time, the movement of urban residents into the rural community was destroying many of the very features that made the environment so therapeutic—both because the community was growing in population and because the immigrants brought in values and styles of interaction that changed the atmosphere of the community. As Milofsky et al. (1993) put it, the community was being destroyed by its own hospitality.

Whether this example represents an anomaly or a developing trend is yet to be seen. It is likely that rural environments provide therapeutic benefits for recovering addicts, but this needs to be analyzed and documented more fully. At the same time, there are reasons to be concerned about the impact of such programs on the rural communities in which they operate, an area about which we have only anecdotal data. Recent reports in the press suggest that patterns of urban drug use, including crack cocaine, are spreading to rural areas (Treaster, 1991; McConnell, 1989; Pope, 1996; Weingarten & Coates, 1989b). We simply cannot say with the existing data whether these reports anticipate emerging trends or are merely isolated cases. They do signal another area that should be monitored closely.

The issue of drug trafficking and production in rural areas is less understood than drug use patterns but seems to represent a growing cause for concern. Although there is a tendency to think that the illegal production of alcohol is an historical curiosity, there are many parts of rural America where illicit alcohol production continues to be a lucrative business. In rural Virginia alone, for example, it is estimated that about 500,000 gallons of moonshine are distilled there each year, with a street value of $25 or more per gallon (Verde, 1998). Similar problems are likely in other rural states, particularly those with a strong history of moonshining.

Regarding illegal drugs other than alcohol, reports suggest that rural areas may serve as production sites for methamphetamine, designer drugs, crack, and marijuana (Bai, 1997; McCormick & O'Donnell, 1993; Weisheit, 1993; 1992; Baker, et al., 1989; Weingarten, 1989; Clayton, 1995; Tyson, 1996; Howlett, 1997). Regarding methamphetamine laboratories:

> Although an increasing number of these laboratories are confiscated in urban and suburban neighborhoods, the majority are seized in rural sections throughout the country. Because of the chemical odors and toxic wastes associated with the manufacturing process,

isolation is often the best defense against detection. Therefore, operators commonly establish their laboratories in sparsely populated
areas as a way to conceal their activities while minimizing their risk
of discovery. Their operations are typically larger and more sophisticated than laboratories operating in more densely populated communities. (O'Dea, Murphy, & Balzer, 1997, p. 80)

In 1997 the state with the largest number of detected methamphetamine laboratories was Missouri, and most of the laboratories identified there were in rural areas (Stewart & Sitaramiah, 1997; Howlett,
1997; Wren, 1997). It has also been suggested that the dangers involved
in handling these chemicals and the complexity of the laws regulating
them make it important that rural police be trained in identifying and
responding to clandestine labs and the shipment of precursor chemicals (National Institute of Justice, 1993, p. 5).

Weisheit's (1993; 1992) studies of commercial marijuana growers
found they were almost exclusively rural operations. In addition, knowledge about marijuana growing was particularly easy to learn for those
who grew up in farm communities.

Other reports argue that rural areas have become important transshipment points for drugs destined for urban areas (Weingarten &
Coates, 1989a; *Chicago Tribune,* "Illegal Drug Trade Spreads," 1989).
The problem is exacerbated by an improved highway system and by the
large number of isolated airstrips set up for corporate farms and for
crop dusters serving rural farmlands.

As one response to the issue of drugs, about 70 percent of the
police agencies in the United States are currently part of multijurisdictional task forces (Schlegel & McGarrell, 1991). However, participation
in these groups varies by population density, with rural agencies underrepresented. For example, about 80 percent of the agencies that serve
populations from 25,000 to 99,999 are in task forces, but only 40 percent of agencies serving fewer than 10,000 citizens are in task forces
(Bureau of Justice Statistics, 1992). This low participation rate does
not mean, however, that rural agencies tend to minimize or dismiss the
drug problem. To the contrary, the issue of drugs consistently arose as
a major crime concern among the rural police officials with whom we
spoke (see chapter 3). They also believed that drug use was connected
to many of their other crime problems, such as theft and burglary. As
one sheriff put it, "I think the citizens are more concerned about burglaries and breaking and entering. However, the burglaries and breaking and entering are caused by drugs and alcohol. . . . if you concentrate
on drugs and make those arrests, you will put your burglars in jail also,
because the addict is usually the burglar."

Rural officers also expressed widespread and enthusiastic support for such drug prevention programs as DARE. Of course, such programs not only address the issue of drugs but also facilitate communication between the police and school-aged children; they are excellent public relations with the rest of the community. As one sheriff reported, "We have found the DARE program has been a great tool in helping us get things done in the community. The kids go home and say, 'Hey, those cops are OK, they're doing things for us.' It kind of rubs off on the parents a little bit."

Rural Schools

School safety and related issues are of concern in many communities. In several cases the issue has been examined across urban and rural areas. In *School Crime: A National Crime Victimization Survey Report,* students aged 12 through 19 in central city, suburban, and nonmetropolitan areas were asked about a variety of issues related to school safety (Bastian & Taylor, 1991). Students in central city schools were only slightly more likely than students in nonmetropolitan schools to report having been a crime victim in or around the school in the previous six months (10 percent vs. 8 percent). Students in nonmetropolitan schools were more likely to report that drugs were available in their schools (71 percent vs. 66 percent for central cities), but they also more often reported having attended drug education classes within the prior six months (44 percent vs. 35 percent). Compared with central city school students, nonmetropolitan students were more likely to report that alcohol was available in school (67 percent vs. 58 percent). Central city students were more likely to report a gang presence in their school (25 percent vs. 8 percent) and to report having taken a weapon to school for protection (3 percent vs. 1 percent). Finally, nonmetropolitan students were less likely than central city students to avoid places at school out of fear, to fear being attacked at school, or to fear attack while going to and from school.

This survey was repeated in 1995, although not all of the survey questions were identical (Chandler et al., 1995). In 1995, central city and nonmetropolitan students were about as likely to report any victimization (14 percent), and the two groups were not significantly different in the reported availability of drugs. Reports of gangs increased in both settings by a substantial amount, but gangs were still less often reported in nonmetropolitan schools (40.7 percent vs. 19.9 percent). Finally, as noted in chapter 1, students in nonmetropolitan schools were significantly less likely to know someone who had brought a gun to school

(15.0 percent vs. 11.1 percent). Thus, according to student reports, overall levels of crime in rural and urban schools are not substantially different, with rural schools higher in drug availability and urban schools higher in gang and weapon prevalence.

Teachers provide another perspective on school safety. A 1991 survey of 1,350 public school teachers reflected a number of urban-rural differences in concerns about school safety among adults (Tabs, 1991). Some of the results of this survey are presented in Table 7. Consistent with student reports, teachers from rural schools reported more problems with student alcohol use in the school. Reported levels of student drug use in school were similar for teachers from urban and rural schools. For all other areas, however, reported problem levels were higher in urban schools than in rural schools. When teachers were asked more specific questions about injury or abuse at the hands of students, urban teachers reported significantly higher levels of injury or abuse for each of the six specific measures of verbal and physical abuse.

Table 7   Percent of Teachers Reporting That Particular Problems in Their Schools were Serious or Moderate, by Location of School

Problem Area	City	Rural
Physical conflicts among students	37	18
Robbery or theft of items over $10	15	8
Vandalism of school property	30	16
Student alcohol use	16	29
Student drug use	17	17
Sale of drugs on school grounds	8	4
Student possession of weapons	10	1
Verbal abuse of teachers	41	21
Physical abuse of teachers	6	0
Racial tensions	20	6

N=1,350
Source: Constructed from table 2 of Tabs (1991).

As noted earlier, drugs are likely to be equally available in rural and urban schools, while alcohol is more likely to be an issue in rural than in urban schools. Beyond alcohol and drug issues, surveys of both students and teachers report greater problems in urban schools. However, the rural-urban differences are quite large in the study of teachers, but much smaller in the survey of students. It is interesting that drugs are equally available in rural and urban schools, but that urban schools seem to have more problems with violence. While the issue requires more careful study, it is possible that school violence and aggressive behavior have no simple, direct and invariant relationship to the availability of drugs in the school.

Two additional studies deserve mention, although limitations in their design make them less directly relevant. The Metropolitan Life Insurance Company (1993) conducted a large-scale survey of teachers and students concerning violence in school. Unfortunately, the results combine suburban and rural schools into one group, which is then compared with an urban school sample. Even though there is no purely rural group, urban respondents generally reported more violence and related problems than did respondents from the suburban/rural group. Another study by the National League of Cities (1994) included communities of varying sizes but sent the surveys to the community, where they usually were filled out by the local police chief or the mayor—neither of whom necessarily had firsthand knowledge about school safety issues in their community. Urban community officials were much more likely than rural respondents to believe that school violence had escalated in recent years. Urban respondents were also more likely than rural respondents to see gangs as a factor in school violence and to report serious injuries in school in the past five years.

Thus, while they agree on the urban problem of gangs, students, teachers and community leaders have differing perceptions about the amount of crime in rural (compared with urban) schools. Student reports suggest that rural and urban schools are not as different as community leaders believe.

Vice and Organized Crime

Aside from Abadinsky's (1986) passing reference to the "Dixie Mafia," little has been written about vice and organized crime in rural areas. Despite this, there is good reason to believe that vice and organized crime are features of the rural environment (Potter & Gaines, 1990). For example, small communities near major highways often have problems with prostitution set up for truck drivers. Also, areas which were traditionally involved in moonshining and bootlegging can use some of the same routes and expertise to transport drugs, stolen auto parts, and other illegal merchandise. In 1989, the so-called "Cornbread Mafia," operating out of Kentucky, was discovered to have marijuana operations in at least nine states. By April of 1990, 86 people were arrested as part of the operation, and the government had confiscated 475,000 pounds of marijuana on 33 farms (Coates & Weingarten, 1990; Yetter, 1989). At the same time, a group of over 30 people operating out of the Southwest who called themselves "The Company" ran an elaborate indoor marijuana operation. At the time of the group's arrest, about $1 million in growing equipment was seized by authorities (Coates & Weingarten, 1990).

Potter and Gaines (1992) used local newspapers, official records, and participant observation to identify 28 crime networks operating in 5 counties in rural Kentucky. A major activity of these networks was marijuana cultivation and the transshipment of cocaine, but they were also involved in the illegal sale of liquor, prostitution, and gambling. Of the 28 networks studied, 25 utilized corrupt relationships with public officials and local law enforcement officers. Further, 5 of these 25 corrupt relationships were based on kinship ties between law enforcement and members of the crime network.

While anecdotal evidence suggests that vice and organized crime are a rural problem, there is simply too little information to make general statements or even to speculate on the similarities and differences with urban organized crime groups.

Violence

There is an image of rural America as peaceful and bucolic, and as we will see below there is an element of truth to this image. Historically, however, rural areas have not always been so peaceful. Historical research suggests that in pre-colonial England and early colonial America, rural areas were often dangerous places inhabited by violent outcasts from more populated areas (Lane, 1997; Johnson & Monkkonen, 1996). In fact, the earliest form of robbery was highway robbery, which was predominantly a rural crime. While violence is not generally part of contemporary images of rural areas, historical studies remind us not to blindly accept these images as immutable facts. As will be shown below, rural violence is a complex phenomenon, with some forms occurring less often and other forms occurring just as often as in cities.

In previous sections, data from the *Uniform Crime Reports* were used to compare rural and urban levels of violence. Much of the focus in the UCR is on "street crime" involving strangers, an aspect of crime which may be less salient in rural areas where social interaction is more likely to be among acquaintances. For example, among index violent offenses, the crime most likely to involve strangers is robbery, and it is robbery for which there is the greatest rural-urban discrepancy. While the homicide rate in urban areas is about four times that in rural areas, the robbery rate in urban areas is almost 34 times that of rural areas. However, rural-versus-urban risks of harm from violence involve more than Part I street crimes.

Greenberg, Carey, and Popper (1987) used data from the National Center for Health Statistics (NCHS) to study violent deaths among young people aged 15 to 24, including deaths due to: homicide, suicide, highway automobile accidents, and such accidents as drowning, falling, and fires. The highest rates of such violent deaths were in four western states, and within these states rates were highest in *rural counties*. In these counties the violent death rate for young whites was even higher than for young inner-city blacks in the six most violent cities.

> Indeed, the white male violent death rate in the six most dangerous Western counties is 13 percent higher than the comparable black rate in the six inner cities. To be sure, black inner-city homicide rates are high, but rural Western violent death rates from auto and other accidents as well as for suicide more than offset their lower homicide rates. *The rural areas of the West, rather than the American urban ghetto, is where youth is far more likely to suffer violent death* [italics added]. (Greenberg, Carey, & Popper, 1987, p. 43)

Regarding criminal violence, as opposed to violence more generally, the data provided by the UCR are important starting points but also are incomplete in several respects. First, they tell little about differences in the character of urban and rural violence, as it relates to both the offense itself and to the manner in which police and prosecutors respond. Second, some forms of violence are not included, such as family violence.

Bachman's (1992a; 1992b) analysis of NCVS victimization data found that "on average, individuals residing in central cities experienced nearly twice as many crimes of violence as those in nonmetro areas and approximately 40 percent more than those residing in other metro areas . . ." (1992a, p. 551). Rural violence was more often among acquaintances—and among family members in particular.

Some of these issues can be illustrated using the few studies available on domestic violence in rural areas. In her observational study of families in a rural Appalachian community, given the fictitious name Raven Ridge, Gagne (1992) noted that both the police and prosecutor were reluctant to act in abuse cases, and, as a consequence, women were reluctant to call them for assistance.

> Most people I met agreed that police protection in Raven Ridge was inadequate. John explained that it took at least an hour for an officer to arrive after a call was placed, and that once the cruiser arrived, the officers would sit in the car and beep the horn rather than come to the door. His explanation for this behavior was that so many officers had been shot responding to domestic calls that few were willing to risk going to the door. . . . Acceptance of a man's authority over his wife and the belief in the sanctity of the home, together with officers' belief that they would be in danger if they responded to domestic calls, resulted in the failure of the legal system to provide protection for physically battered women. . . . Given the geographic isolation, lack of protection, and lack of economic opportunities available to them, women acquiesced to control in the short term while thinking about ways to improve their situation over time. (pp. 410–412)

Websdale's ethnographic study of battered women in Kentucky (1995; 1998) echos and expands upon many of Gagne's observations. For battered women in rural Kentucky, abuse was facilitated by physical isolation, an ideology of patriarchy, and isolation from potentially supportive institutions, including child care, health care, schooling, and other social services (Websdale, 1995). As Websdale observed in his research (1998, p. 5):

> One of the most common complaints of rural battered women concerns the physical and geographical isolation they experience. Some battered women who live up what is locally called a "hollow" (a secluded dirt road cul-de-sac with a small number of houses on it) seem to live extraordinarily isolated lives. Several of the women report not having any friends for years. With no public transportation and large distances between houses, they report that it is often physically difficult to engage in community life. Even if battered women live in small towns and work outside the home, they still report great isolation and loneliness. The irony here is that rural areas are often assumed to be more cohesive and neighborly, and to have a social climate that is more friendly.

> It is important to bear in mind that the geographic isolation experienced by battered women may stem from their batterers' calculated decision to reside in the country. In other words, the isolation may be a product of abuse, as well as a physical setting conductive to abuse.

The involvement of police in these settings is shaped by their own integration into the community. In some cases, where the officer is related to or friends with the woman, domestic violence laws may be aggressively enforced. More commonly, however, the officer is acquainted with the husband or is sympathetic to the husband's position (Websdale, 1998):

> Susan reported that nearly the whole community knew that her husband beat her brutally on a regular basis. However, the local police officer in the small town where they lived in western Kentucky did not offer her any protection. She told me the local constable was her husband's brother and refused to arrest her husband. Susan also noted it was common knowledge that the constable beat his own wife and confronting domestic violence was not part of his "calling" as a law enforcement officer. . . . (p. 103)

> Paradoxically, the more detached the police are from the community, the more likely they are to enforce domestic violence laws. Rural women mentioned that state police are more likely to make arrests, remove men from the home as opposed to removing women from the home, and inform battered women of their rights under the law. In general, the state police are also more likely to take battered women seriously and not collude, or appear to collude, with batterers. (p. 123)

The conclusions of these case studies receive some support from the few existing quantitative studies. In his study of police jurisdictions in Ohio, Bell (1986; 1989) found the highest rates for domestic violence disputes were in the least populated jurisdictions. In neither cities nor rural areas were the police likely to make an arrest following a domestic violence complaint, although arrest was somewhat more likely in urban areas.

The response of rural police to domestic violence may be changing. In our conversations with rural officers this issue arose frequently, usually reflecting a heightened sensitivity to the issue. Based on what we have heard, it is possible that rural police are increasingly willing to intervene in domestic violence cases—both because research suggests that arrest might be an effective deterrent and out of concern for lawsuits that might result from inaction, as a growing number of states pass legislation mandating a police response and an arrest in domestic violence calls. However, further study is needed to determine if and how the rural police response is shaped by these legislative and social changes in the way that domestic violence is perceived.

Even less is known about rural-urban differences in child abuse, but two studies by the National Center on Child Abuse and Neglect (1981; 1988) suggest the issue is worth further examination. The first study was conducted in 1980 and the second in 1986. The studies differed in one important respect: In the 1980 version abuse was defined as "demonstrated harm as a result of maltreatment" (1988, p. ix); the 1986 study included a definition of abuse which mirrored that of 1980 but also included children "placed at risk for harm," such as being left alone. When the first definition was used, abuse rates were higher in rural than in major urban counties. However, when the broader definition was used, urban rates of abuse were higher. The studies were based on a relatively small number of counties and could not address contextual issues which would explain these differences. Other research suggests that compared with doctors in larger cities, physicians in small towns detect more child abuse but are *less* likely to report cases to the authorities (Badger, 1989).

Another source of information about both spouse abuse and child abuse is the *National Family Violence Survey* (NFVS). This self-report national survey was conducted first in 1975 (Straus, Gelles, & Steinmetz, 1980) and then again in 1985 (Straus & Gelles, 1990); it measures violence using the Conflict Tactics Scales (CTS). These scales tap a range of behaviors from verbal aggression to inflicting serious physical harm and are considered the most thorough and sensitive measures of family violence currently available. Important for current purposes is that both surveys were specifically designed to include substantial numbers of rural respondents.

Regarding child abuse, the 1975 NFVS found that large cities (population of one million or more) had the highest rates, while rural, suburban, and small-city rates were similar. The 1985 survey found no differences in child abuse rates across communities of different sizes (Wolfner & Gelles, 1993). Regarding spouse abuse, the 1975 survey found that rates were highest in large cities and rural areas and were lowest in small cities and suburbs. However, the differences were rather small. Curiously, although the 1985 study was designed specifically to include urban, suburban, and rural respondents, the major book describing the 1985 findings (Straus & Gelles, 1990) makes no mention of differences in spouse abuse by community size. If domestic violence in rural areas is as frequent as in urban areas, this is particularly interesting in light of the substantially lower general crime rate in rural areas. This means that the justice system in rural areas may have a larger proportion of its caseload made up of domestic violence cases.

Some rural areas have a long history of violence, including lynching, labor unrest, and blood feuds (e.g., Angle, 1980; Littlewood, 1969). Lynching seldom occurs today, and labor unrest is comparatively nonviolent. While there are still pockets of rural America with clan violence (e.g., Bukro, 1991; Burrough, 1989), this, too, seems less common than in the past. Further, the nature of rural interactions means that such crimes as homicide, rape, and assault are more likely to be among acquaintances than is true in urban areas. This, combined with the greater distrust of government and the tendency previously noted to keep issues private, may also mean that the police are less likely to be called when such crimes occur. Consequently, preventing violent interpersonal crimes in rural areas may require different strategies than in urban areas.

In an earlier section it was noted that rural violence may be more lethal, because the distances involved may slow emergency response time. Scarce resources and close social networks may also influence the investigation of violent incidents. For example, there is evidence that a child's death is less often investigated with an autopsy in rural areas than in cities (Unnithan, 1994; Lundstrom & Sharpe, 1991). Part of this difference may be explained by the fact that urban areas are more likely to have medical examiners or forensic pathologists—trained medical professionals who exclusively focus on crime and who can conduct their own autopsies. In contrast, rural areas more often rely on coroners who are usually elected and for whom no medical training is required. In many rural areas coroners are part-time officials. They are often funeral directors but could just as easily be farmers or shop keepers. In many areas the pay is so low that the coroner must have another occupation:

> Missouri, for instance, pays its rural coroners an average of $1,200 a year to be on call 24 hours, seven days a week. At those wages it is often only the local funeral director who is eager to moonlight as a coroner—an arrangement that is good for business but potentially bad for autopsies. (Lundstrom & Sharpe, 1991, p. 24)

Within the close social confines of a rural community, and given that the funeral director's business depends on good relationships with members of the community, a family's objections to an autopsy on their child may often be respected.

In jurisdictions covered by coroners with no experience in forensic pathology, conducting an autopsy may require sending the body to a medical examiner in another jurisdiction, and paying a high price for the service. This can place a substantial hardship on a financially strapped rural county. These conditions effectively discourage autopsies in cases where there is nothing immediately suspicious about a death.

While most attention has focused on general rural-urban differences, an important but relatively neglected issue concerns large variations in violence *among* rural areas. One example of why a study of these variations might be useful is in the work of Nisbett and Cohen (1996), who argue that high homicide rates in the South reflect a "culture of honor" in which it is more acceptable than in the North to respond to threats to one's honor and reputation with violence. Nisbett and Cohen argue that higher rates of violence in the South are almost entirely explained by the substantially higher rates for white rural males, and that studies must simultaneously consider race, gender, and community size to understand Southern violence. The authors argue that Southerners are not more approving of violence in general, but they are more likely to endorse violence in cases of an affront to one's home, family, or person. Using multiple research methods they systematically examine the relatively higher levels of violence, especially homicide, in the South. They also argue that these regional differences are most substantial in rural areas, while urban areas show much less regional and subcultural variation. Carefully ruling out such factors as gun ownership and a history of oppression through slavery, Nisbett and Cohen argue that the culture of honor is a product of the type of agricultural activity in which the ancestors of current residents engaged. Those with a background in herding animals and a relatively nomadic lifestyle were much more violent than those with a background in the cultivation and tending of crops. Nisbett and Cohen, and others (e.g., Fischer, 1989), make a powerful case for incorporating community size and regional history, as well as race and gender, in subsequent analyses of violence in America.

It is clear that rural violence is poorly understood but potentially very serious. This is particularly true for family violence, which may occur as frequently as in urban areas. It is likely that the lethality of rural violence is greater because the distances that emergency teams must travel slows their response. Further, the poverty that characterizes so many rural areas may mean that advanced health services are less available. Rural areas also may be limited in the resources and expertise available to conduct thorough medical investigations in cases where the cause of death is in doubt. Finally, just as an understanding of differences between urban and rural violence may contribute to our understanding of the dynamics of violence in general, it is also important to understand variations in violence among rural areas.

Hate Crimes and Anti-Government Groups

Related to the issue of violence, although less well documented, is the use of rural areas by so-called "hate groups" and related extremist organizations. Some have argued that the terms "hate groups" and "hate crimes" lack scientific precision, are emotionally loaded, and serve to incense rather than inform (e.g., Jacobs, 1993). The discussion that follows maintains the label "hate crime" because it is familiar to most readers. While the discussion includes several groups under this definition, the focus is on groups that combine hatred—whether based on race, religion, or sexual orientation—with an ideology that fosters violence.

Before we discuss specific groups it is important to clarify that we do not argue that such individuals or such groups represent a numerical majority in rural America or even that rural citizens who show sympathy for these groups are necessarily involved in violence themselves. We would argue, however, that when compared with the urban environment, rural areas are more tolerant of antigovernment groups and talk of antigovernment violence. While most rural citizens would never join the violent activities of the extremist few, the latter are likely to receive a surprising level of support and sympathy from the rural community—surprising at least from an urban perspective. We had the occasion to interview a state highway patrolman from the Midwest who had been shot by an antigovernment extremist in his rural jurisdiction. The trooper had lived in the area for many years and reported that the most discouraging outcome of the incident was the unwillingness of members of the trooper's own church to condemn the shooting. These were people he considered personal friends. In his preliminary study of 26 rural Illinois prosecutors, Maroules (1998 reports that:

> . . . many have had legal experiences dealing with some type of militiamen, freemen, or other anti-government group. Many state's attorneys feel that such groups enjoy considerable ideological support in their counties. At the same time, they point out that any active cells include very few individuals, the majority of whom do not represent serious law enforcement problems. (p. 16)

For us, given the rhetoric and general environment in many of these areas, the surprise has not been the periodic eruption of violence, but the extent to which violence is not more frequent.

Aside from the physical isolation and privacy afforded by rural settings, rural culture has elements consistent with the mindset underlying some right-wing extremist groups. Flynn and Gerhardt (1989) make this argument regarding the rural American West:

> It is no accident that the Silent Brotherhood was spawned in the American West. It is a land of huge proportions, its vast emptiness alluring to the frontier spirit. . . . It is that frontier spirit that produced the Posse Comitatus, American Agriculture Movement, Sagebrush Rebellion, Aryan Nation, and other far-right groups. It also produced individuals steeped in the mountain man mystique of individualism and survivalism. (pp. 9–10)

> Over the last two decades, America's backwoods became dotted with survivalist training camps. A Klan-run camp at Anahuac, Texas, taught guerrilla warfare techniques. A Christian survival school deep in the Arkansas Ozarks taught urban warfare . . . The leader of the Carolina Knights of the KKK, Frazier Glenn Miller, claimed a thousand men would answer his trumpet call at Angler, North Carolina. . . . And farmers, the veritable salt of America's earth, put a "face" on their plight by blaming Jewish bankers for bringing them to the brink of economic collapse. (pp. 9–10)

In his discussion of the rise and spread of survivalist movements, James Coates (1987) addressed the question of where these survivalists come from:

> They come from the high pine forests of Montana and the coastal plains of Texas. They come from the hills and hollows of North Carolina and the rugged Ozark Mountains along the Missouri-Arkansas border. They labor in downstate Illinois and press the good fight in Wisconsin's dairy land. They clamor for what they deem to be righteousness on the Nebraska-Kansas-Missouri border and in the bayous of Louisiana. (p. 18)

Survivalists in particular eschew urban life and seek to return to simpler times in a world they can create and control, something much easier to accomplish in remote rural areas.

Some of these far-right groups have targeted farmers as potential members, particularly in the Midwest, with a combination of anti-Semitism, racism, fundamentalist Christianity, and a deep suspicion of government. In economically troubled farm-belt communities these groups have a particularly sympathetic audience (Zeskind, 1985).

Davidson (1990) describes the literature published by one group, the Iowa Society for Educated Citizens (ISEC):

> The literature decries race mixing, gun registration, the liberal (i.e., Jewish) media, the IRS, homosexuality, the Council on Foreign Relations, and driver's licenses—the last because by accepting them citizens are, in effect, legitimizing what the self-proclaimed patriots consider illegitimate authority. But the target of choice for ISEC members . . . is the Federal Reserve Bank: root of farmers' problems and the front organization for the international Jewish bankers. (p. 103)

> Many—especially members of the Posse Comitatus—refuse to recognize any government authority higher than county sheriff. (p. 109)

Dyer (1997) has specifically focused on the rural dimensions of the modern antigovernment movement through interviews with hundreds of farmers facing foreclosure, attending anti-government group meetings, and interviewing antigovernment group leaders and rural crisis hotline counselors. Although his research and writing took place well after the farm crisis of the 1980s, he makes a strong case for the impact of that crisis on the perceptions of rural Americans, including those having no direct involvement in agriculture. Whether the farm crisis of the 1980s was real, as some have debated, is secondary to the perceptions about the crisis, that decisions arising from urban areas are at best indifferent to the consequences for rural citizens and, at worst, are designed to destroy the rural economy. Dyer offers little hope that the situation will improve. As he observes:

> The more globally minded and urban-conscious Washington becomes, the more out of step it gets with rural places (p. 148). . . . The federal government continues to offer rural America no solutions to take the place of the pseudo-solutions being concocted by the [anti-government] movement. It has offered no hope that rural people's lives will improve. Washington's policy is to destroy the anti-government movement without ever trying to understand why it exists. (p. 192)

Sometimes the beliefs of these rural groups lead directly to violence, as when members of the Posse Comitatus fight paying taxes and farm foreclosures, or when they commit robbery and theft to fund their activities. In perhaps the most famous incident, Gordon Kahl killed two U.S. marshals in North Dakota in February of 1983, before being killed himself in a shootout with law enforcement officials in Arkansas four months later. Kahl avoided arrest for four months with the help of a loose network of sympathizers (Corcoran, 1990).

Many of these groups weave together violence and religion, believing that Armageddon is near and that they must be heavily armed for self-protection. As Colvin (1992) notes, the rural setting plays a role in these beliefs:

> The most fervent members of the Posse [Comitatus] were armed survivalists whose stated goal was to be prepared for an eventual, and inevitable, catastrophe—a war or economic depression. Fundamental to the beliefs of the Posse was that only rural dwellers would survive a war and that unprepared urban individuals seeking food and shelter would become enemies. Accordingly, followers were instructed to collect arms and stockpile food. (p. 20)

While it may seem ironic, many of these groups see themselves as highly patriotic and deeply religious. They believe that the U.S. Constitution and the Bill of Rights were divinely inspired, but that subsequent amendments and laws have undercut these documents to serve special (i.e., Jewish) interests. Religion not only underlies their patriotism but is also used to justify racism.

Among the most visible religious forces behind these hate groups is the Christian Identity movement. Identity is not a formal religious organization but a loosely structured set of beliefs (Barkun, 1994). As such, people from very different perspectives are able to borrow those aspects of Identity they find most appealing. In this way Identity provides a loose fabric connecting right-wing groups that might otherwise have no connection. Identity followers believe that descendants of Northern European stock are the true lost tribes of Israel and that the United States is their promised land. They also believe that Jews are descendants of Cain, who was fathered by the devil in the form of the serpent in the Garden of Eden. "Nine months after eating the apple, Eve bore two sons. Adam's son was Abel. Satan's was Cain. Cain killed Abel. Cain's descendants killed Jesus. Now, under the banner of world Jewry, they're trying to kill all white Christians" (Coates, 1987, p. 82).

The Identity movement also decries race mixing, believing that people of color were mistakes by God in the process of creating man, "false starts before God made the perfect—read white—Adam and Eve" (Corcoran, 1990, p. 39). Viewing them as less than fully human, Identity followers commonly refer to people of color as "mud people." The Identity movement's focus on a literal interpretation of the Bible makes it appear, at least on the surface, to have much in common with traditional fundamentalist Christian groups. In rural areas this has considerable appeal to many people. While such groups may be on the fringe in their beliefs, these beliefs are only an exaggerated and distorted version of existing rural values emphasizing religion, patriotism, and independence from government tyranny.

The number of active members of these fringe groups is unknown, but they probably number no more than ten or twenty thousand. However, these groups have a high potential for crime, particularly violent crime. Unlike young urban skinheads, whose dress and behavior cry out for public attention, members of rural hate groups blend perfectly into the surrounding community and actively avoid saying or doing things in public that would draw the attention of authorities or the press. Rural hate group members do not generally look like rebels and are often longtime residents of their communities. As Hamm (1993) has observed, American hate groups have found they are best served by secrecy and an unwillingness to share information about their groups with outsiders:

> Evidence of a politics of silence among members of the far right is well documented. . . . withholding information (or silence) becomes a political tool: The less outsiders know about the individual and organizational features of extremist groups, the safer the group becomes from outside threats to control them through public policy (regardless of their criminal exploits). Silence, therefore, serves to "harden the target" of right-wing extremism by providing a paramilitary umbrella over the individual and organizational interests of such groups. (pp. 99–100)

Our conversations with rural police indicate these groups are widely scattered and, where they are known to exist, keep a relatively low profile. While secrecy and maintaining a low profile are the rule, there are several notable exceptions, including Tom Metzger in California and Gary Rex Lauk in Nebraska. Neo-Nazi literature, newsletters, electronic bulletin boards, telephone message services, hate-based music, and even public access cable television programs have been attributed to one or both of these men (Bjorgo & Witte, 1993; Dees, 1993; Hamm, 1993).

Rather than highly visible public demonstrations intended to attract national attention, some antigovernment groups have taken a more local approach. In the West and Midwest a number of small-town and county governments have had key elected positions filled by antigovernment supporters. These community leaders have sought to eliminate all local government regulation, including building inspections, road repair, and zoning enforcement. They have succeeded in abolishing local building and sanitation departments, and in several counties they have won the sheriff's office. Other county officials who attempt to thwart their plans have received anonymous death threats, and the counties have seen their insurance premiums skyrocket (Southern Poverty Law Center, 1998).

The groups described here are distinct from a host of other "fringe" groups attracted to rural areas. Many religious cults that find rural areas appealing have no organized involvement in crime. The Amana colonies in Iowa have historically provided one example. Other groups may be involved in crime, but neither the group nor the crimes of its members are driven by an ideology of hate that also connects them to other groups. This category is illustrated by David Koresh's Branch Davidian compound outside of Waco, Texas. The compound was burned to the ground on April 19, 1993, killing most of its members, after a 51-day standoff with federal authorities. While Koresh stockpiled (illegal) weapons and explosives in preparation for a coming Armageddon, there was no evidence that the group's philosophy was driven by racial or ethnic hatred, that the group planned such crimes as murder or robbery against people outside the group, or that the group was connected ideologically or organizationally with other hate groups (Gibbs, 1993; Linedecker, 1993). Ironically, the heavy-handed actions of federal agents in the Waco case, and several others, might be interpreted by survivalists as evidence for their worst fears about the federal government.

There will always be groups and leaders driven by individual pathology. The concern in this section has been with groups connected by a criminogenic ideology that combines religion, politics, and racism, and is based on institutionalized hatred. Ultimately, such groups have a greater potential for crime and violence and will be more difficult to control. We have suggested that features of the rural environment make it easier for hate-based groups to operate there. The secrecy with which they operate, and the lack of empirical evidence about their numbers and operations, makes it difficult to determine whether such groups are a greater problem in rural areas than in urban areas. This is an important issue that merits careful scrutiny and more systematic documentation.

Satanic Cults

The issue of satanic cults is also relevant to rural areas. Sensational stories about devil worship and satanic cult activity periodically arise and lead to great public concern, particularly when juveniles are thought to be involved. These sensational stories sometimes portray satanic cult activities as coordinated by a loosely structured national network. Usually the stories emphasize either the kidnapping and brainwashing of young people, or the idea of luring disaffected youths into their ranks.

In addition, they frequently emphasize criminal activities, including drug use, sexual perversity, torture, animal mutilation, or even murder (Bromley, 1991). As Jeffrey S. Victor (1993) has noted:

> Perhaps the most widely accepted claims about Satanism are claims about teenage involvement in Satanic cult activity. . . . Local police spread claims about teenage ritualistic crime in police conferences, in lectures to community groups, and in police magazines. Child protection social workers spread the claims in conferences about the problems of youth. Anti-cult organizations spread the claims at conferences about teenage involvement in religious cults. A host of religious evangelists spread the claims at church and community meetings about teenage Satanism. (p. 133)

A number of authors, including Victor, have questioned the extent to which satanic cults are organized, pervasive, and extensively involved in crime (deYoung, 1994; Victor, 1993; 1991; 1990; 1989; Hicks, 1991; Richardson, Best & Bromley, 1991; Lanning, 1989). Evidence of national conspiracies is thin, and when individual "satanic crimes" are investigated closely, they are usually found to have little direct connection to Satanism but rather are found to be part of a larger pattern of delinquency and misbehavior.

Given the level of public concern and the perceived link between Satanism and crime, it is not surprising that police are often called and that some police officers have become experts, sharing their knowledge and experiences with others. A survey of 153 "cult cops" found that "many were raised in small-town settings; two-thirds grew up in a town of 50,000 people or less" (Crouch & Damphouse, 1991, p. 195). Also, the smaller the responding officer's agency, the more likely the officer was to see Satanism as "a clear and present danger in need of immediate attention" (p. 198). Finally, the longer an officer had worked in the area of Satanism, the *less* likely that officer was to see Satanism as a clear and present danger.

Perhaps the work on Satanism most relevant to rural issues is that by Jeffrey Victor (1993; 1991; 1990; 1989). Victor (1991) has focused on instances of satanic cult rumor-panics. In particular:

> A rumor-panic in a community is identified by the existence of widely occurring, fear-provoked behavior, indicated by numerous incidents of extraordinary fight-flight reaction. This collective behavior may include protective behavior, such as the widespread buying of guns, or preventing children from being in public places. It may also include aggressive behavior, such as group attacks on people perceived to be sources of threat, or destruction of property. It may also include agitated information seeking for "news" about the threat, and intensified surveillance of the community by authorities. (p. 222)

Victor examined the rise and spread of 31 satanic cult rumor-panics in the United States. Several of his findings are worth noting here. First:

> In none of these cases was any group found which resembled the stereotype of a Satanic cult, that is, a well-organized group committing crimes and justifying their actions with a "Satanic" ideology. In a few cases, authorities found groups of juvenile delinquents who had engaged in vandalism and proclaimed themselves "Satanists" but even that was unusual. (1993, p. 61)

Second, and most relevant to this review, all but one of these 31 rumor-panics occurred in small towns and rural areas. Where these communities were near large cities, the rumor-panic did not spread into the city. Thus, *panics* about satanic cults are primarily a rural phenomenon. More specifically, satanic cult rumor-panics were more likely in rural areas under economic stress in which there was the perception of a rapid decline in traditional moral values. According to Victor, what fueled these rumors was not mass communication but the kinds of personal networks through which information often flows in rural areas. In many cases rural police also played a role in helping these rumor-panics spread and persist:

> Certain groups in American society are more ideologically receptive to the symbolism of Satanic cult rumors and are more likely to actively disseminate them. These groups include small town police and fundamentalist churches. When such stories are spread on the local level, in face-to-face relations and through personal communication networks, these bizarre claims attain greater credibility than they ever could through the mass media alone. There is no more powerful way of being exposed to an outrageous or frightening story than learning about it from "a-friend-of-a-friend" who "really knows." (1993, pp. 69–70)

Thus, it is important for rural police to be sensitive to the public's concern about satanic cults but to respond without causing unnecessary alarm. Satanic panics are infrequent events, but when they do happen they can be traumatic for the community.

Arson

The Insurance Committee for Arson Control reports that although urban arson receives the most media attention, rural arson has been increasing. "Unlike arson in cities, which for the most part is confined to a limited site, whether a building or an entire block, rural arsons can cover vast acres of forest and wildlands as well as structures and machinery. With the depressed condition of the farm economy, some observers fear rural arsons could be on the upswing" (*Security Systems Digest*, 1985).

In contrast, the 1991 annual report of the National Fire Prevention Association (1992) reflects relatively stable arson rates in rural counties between 1983 and 1991. Table 8, based on 1996 UCR data, shows that as the size of the community goes down the rate of arson offenses also goes down, from a rate of 84 per 100,000 people in cities of 250,000 or more to a rate of only 19 per 100,000 in rural counties (FBI, 1997, table 2.31).

Table 8   Rate of Arson Reported in the UCR by
Population Size, 1996

Area	Rate per 100,000
Cities of 250,000 or more	83.9
Cities 100K–250K	50.4
Cities 50K–100K	40.6
Cities 25K–49K	36.0
Cities 10K–25K	26.5
Cities under 10,000	29.5
Suburban counties	33.3
Rural counties	18.9
Source: FBI, *Uniform Crime Reports: Crime in the United States*, 1997, (table 2.31).	

These official FBI figures must be regarded with caution, because there may be substantial differences in the quality of these data across communities of differing sizes. Jackson (1988) surveyed fire departments in the United States, asking about the number of arsons in the prior year and the number of those reported to the UCR. He found that in communities of under 25,000 people, only 32 percent of the arsons were reported to the UCR, compared with 95 percent of those occurring in communities of 70,000 or more (see Figure 8). When calculating the actual arson rate, based on arsons known to fire departments rather than the rate reported to the FBI, Jackson found no significant differences in the arson rate by community size. Jackson did find that the rate of arson known to fire departments was nearly double the official rate reported in the UCR.

Figure 8. Arsons Reported to the U.C.R.

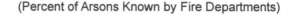

(Percent of Arsons Known by Fire Departments)

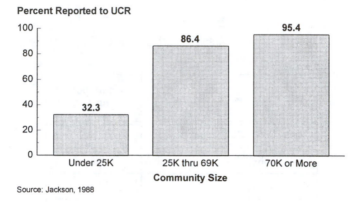

Source: Jackson, 1988

Whether rural arson rates have increased or have remained relatively stable over time, and whether the differences across community size are real or a product of reporting practices, there are important differences between arson problems in rural and urban areas. Compared with urban areas rural communities more often lack the resources and staff to fully investigate arsons. In its *Rural Arson Control* report (1989), the International Association of Fire Chiefs, Inc. (IAFC) noted that: "Rural arson control efforts are hindered by constraints and requirements specific to rural areas. These special conditions make rural arson prevention, detection, and control different from and more difficult than urban arson problems" (p. i). Small staffs and substantial travel distances can slow response time and impede rural arson investigations. The problem is compounded by a lack of resources and technical equipment for conducting thorough investigations. Further complicating investigations, rural fires more often advance to the "total burn" syndrome, in which the structure is completely destroyed. In fact, "fire damage in rural areas runs at least three times urban rates" (p. 17). Total-burn arson fires often require additional firefighting personnel and equipment to sort through the debris. Consequently, rural fires are often not investigated for arson unless the preliminary evidence is particularly compelling.

Among the recommendations of the IAFC report is that it is particularly important for rural arson investigators to cultivate good working relationships with local and state police and with the insurance industry. These relationships can somewhat offset the shortage of personnel and resources. Further, the absence of explicitly worked-out cooperative procedures for reporting arson fire incidents contributes to the mix-reporting of arson data to the UCR system (IAFC, 1989).

Existing evidence suggests that the problems of rural arson and its investigation are not identical to those in urban areas. It appears that some of those problems can be minimized by greater cooperation between arson investigators and rural police, but this merits further study.

Agricultural Crimes

Most of the crimes discussed to this point (e.g., homicide, child abuse) take place in both urban and rural areas. Some crimes, however, are peculiar to the rural setting. These include such offenses as poaching and agricultural crime, neither of which has been extensively studied. The focus here is on agricultural crime because some literature is readily available and because of its impact on the country as a whole through escalating food and insurance prices.

The *Uniform Crime Reports* does not separate agricultural crime from other offenses. However, each year the UCR does list specific items of theft and the rate at which these items are recovered. Among the listed items is livestock, which accounts for losses of about $37 million in 1993, only about 12 percent of which was recovered (FBI, 1993, table 24). Charles Swanson (1981), along with Leonard Territo (Swanson & Territo, 1980), assembled selected incidents of agricultural crime which illustrate its scope and seriousness. These include:

- $1 million in annual thefts of avocado, lime, and mango fruit in Florida
- $1 million in annual losses to timber thieves and vandals in western Washington alone
- $2 million in annual losses from pesticide thefts
- $30 million in annual thefts from California farmers

Eighty percent of surveyed Iowa farmers had been victims of theft in the prior three years.

Further, Swanson and Territo (1980) note that single offenses can be enormously costly. They cite embezzlement at an Iowa grain elevator that produced a loss of $10 million. They also cite anecdotal evidence that organized crime is active in agricultural crime in several states. Much of Swanson and Territo's information came from a variety of sources, but primarily from state Farm Bureau offices. Although not a conventional source of crime data, the Farm Bureau may be a good source of data specifically on agricultural crime.

In Collier County, Florida, where harvested tomatoes can be sold for as much as $20 a box, the sheriff's department has established an Agricultural Crime Unit (Johnson, 1994). This unit investigates stolen produce, as well as cattle theft, trespassing, and a variety of other crimes affecting farmers.

The problem of agricultural crime illustrates the importance of accounting for the considerable variation across rural areas when addressing the crime problem. Most discussions of rural crime focus on the close and relatively informal nature of rural life, and this is true in many rural communities. However, many farmers, particularly those with large farms, are physically isolated from their neighbors and their community. In their study of Montana ranchers and farmers, for example, Saltiel, Gilchrist, and Harvie (1992) included respondents who lived as far as 78 miles from the nearest emergency services. In addition, the average distance to the nearest neighbor was four miles. Those most isolated were most concerned about sufficient police patrols, but these were the very areas in which increased patrol activity was impractical. Saltiel et al. (1992) observed:

> Although those living closer to population centers may face greater risks, those who live farther away are more isolated from potential sources of help when problems arise . . . Those who live farther from the police appear to be particularly sensitive to the ability of law enforcement to patrol effectively. . . . Those who live farthest from law enforcement are more sensitive to the lack of available help from their neighbors which in turn increases concern about the sufficiency of police patrols. . . . The greater the isolation of farm residents, the greater the reliance on police. (p. 542)

While police services are often thinly spread across these remote rural areas, the importance of these services is magnified by the isolation of residents from each other and from other service agencies.

Crime prevention in farm communities has been the focus of some research. The theft of livestock, grain, and expensive farm machinery is facilitated by the trend toward larger farms. As farms increase in size, farmers more often live away from storage sheds, machinery, and livestock, frequently leaving them unattended. This not only makes theft and vandalism easier to commit but also means that the crime may go undetected for some time, making apprehension more difficult.

In our conversations with rural police in farming areas, a common complaint was that farmers were too casual about marking expensive equipment and about leaving it unattended near roadways where the temptation for theft would be greater. As one sheriff told us, "People in a rural community have a tendency to trust everybody and they get real sloppy about leaving their stuff laying around. Especially the farmers. They'll have an implement set out in the field and thieves will steal part of it." Some of these casual attitudes reflect the reality that theft and vandalism are not everyday occurrences for the typical farmer. For example, a survey of victimization among 428 Alabama farmers found that in the prior 12 months, a relatively small percentage had experienced vandalism (13 percent), burglary (8 percent), or theft (9 percent) (Dunkelberger, Clayton, Myrick, & Lyles, 1992). Just over half (58 percent) of the farmers reported any of these victimizations over their years of farming. Most farmers in the study either did not have such simple security devices as locks on storage sheds, or they had them but did not use them. Perhaps the study's most interesting finding was that theft, vandalism, or burglary were not the crimes about which these farmers were most concerned. Their greatest concerns were about what the study's authors describe as "nuisance" crimes—poaching, trespassing, and dumping trash on farmland.

It was also found that victimization and crime prevention were related to the size of the farm operation. Large farms were more likely to be victimized. The operators of large farms were twice as likely to leave machinery unattended overnight in fields but were more likely to take other crime prevention measures, such as marking cattle and locking farm gates. Interesting within the context of the earlier discussion of rural crime, the most widely practiced security measure was: "Have a neighbor watch the farm when out of town," which was reported by over 80 percent of the farmers in the study.

The importance of farm size in the Alabama study has implications for the study of farm crime in other parts of the country. The size of the average farm varies substantially from one state to another. For example, in 1990, the average farm in Kentucky was 152 acres, while the average farm in Arizona was over 4,600 acres (U.S. Bureau of the Census, 1993). This wide inter-state variation in farm sizes again highlights the importance of recognizing and considering regional variations across rural America.

In the future the problems associated with agricultural crime are likely to be compounded by urban growth. Continued population growth and urban sprawl will mean a steady reduction in the number of rural areas, and a continuous supply of places in transition from rural to suburban or urban. "Across the nation, one million acres of farmland are being converted to urban or suburban uses each year, a rate of two acres per minute" (Brandon, 1996). In California's Central Valley, for example, it is estimated that by the year 2040 the population will triple and housing will use more than one million acres of irrigated farmland (Goldberg, 1996). At least one study has concluded that the loss of farmland to suburban sprawl will reduce agricultural production to the point that the United States will have difficulty feeding itself. The study predicts that within 60 years, there will be a reduction in food variety available to typical consumers and an increase in food prices of 300 to 500 percent (Pimentel & Pimentel, 1997). As discussed above, this rapid growth is likely to be accompanied by an even more rapid increase in crime in the newly suburbanized areas. It is also likely to lead to an increase in such agricultural crimes as the theft of crops, already a serious crime problem in some sections of the United States (e.g., Johnson, 1994).

As fertile farmland is taken out of production, farmers increasingly will be pressured to maximize yields on the land that remains. This will mean an even greater reliance on pesticides, herbicides, and concentrated fertilizers. The theft of farm chemicals is already a problem and is likely to become more serious in the near future. Sold in highly concentrated forms and difficult to tag with identifying markers, the theft of farm chemicals may become simpler and more lucrative than the theft of livestock or farm machinery. In California, for example, a 1992 report indicated that pesticide thefts were becoming more frequent and more expensive, with a single theft's typical replacement value between $30,000 and $70,000 ("California Pesticide Thefts on the Rise," 1992). More recently, California officials brought charges against a man for fencing $1.5 million worth of stolen herbicide ("Farm Thieves Reaping Big Profits From Agricultural Chemicals," 1995). Commonly used varieties can sell for $175 for a five-gallon case. The most expensive types of herbicide can sell for as much as $115 for only 7.5 ounces, which will cover nearly five acres. It is possible to carry more than $500,000 of this concentrated herbicide in the back of a pickup truck (Smith, 1996). Given these prices, the profits for thieves can be substantial, with correspondingly large losses for farmers. Despite the magnitude of annual losses, little is known about the larger structure of these theft operations. "It has been suggested that at least some of the black market for these stolen pesticides is international" (California Pesticide Thefts on the Rise, 1992). Farmers who legally purchase these powerful chemicals are generally required to be trained in their application. For stolen chemicals, however, there is no way to know if they are being applied in a way that is safe for either the user or the environment.

As a closing comment about agriculture-related crime, it is striking that so little is known about crime and victimization of migrant workers. This group is interesting for practical as well as theoretical reasons. Migrant workers can be found in nearly every state, and their labor is often integral to the rural environment. At the same time they remain outsiders in most communities where they work. Consequently, they may experience the informality of the rural justice process without the benefit of the personal familiarity with criminal justice authorities that is common for most permanent rural citizens. They sometimes suffer from abuse and in some cases have been subjected to outright slavery (Kelley, 1993).

Wildlife Crimes

Similar to agricultural crimes, wildlife crimes are almost exclusively a rural phenomenon. In recent years, wildlife crimes, especially poaching, have become a major concern for conservation police officers (i.e., game wardens, wildlife officers, etc.). According to the U.S. Fish & Wildlife Service, "wildlife shipments entering and leaving the United States during Fiscal Year 1990 had a declared value of over $1 billion" (U.S. Department of the Interior, 1991, p. 3). In a 1986 publication, the estimated replacement costs of illegally harvested fish and wildlife exceeded $45 million in Illinois, while the poaching of deer alone was estimated to cost Pennsylvania over $93 million a year in replacement costs (Pash, 1986). The numbers of animals poached, as well as their replacement costs, are difficult to calculate and may vary from one state to another and over time. Whatever the formula, however, these costs are likely to be quite high.

While poaching may impose costs on the state, particularly replacement costs for poached game, it can be quite lucrative for the poacher.

> A poacher might get $1000 to $2000 for a mule deer scoring 190 Boone and Crockett points [scoring system for trophy deer and elk]—double that for a 350 [point] or better elk. It's not uncommon to hear prices of up to $1000 per inch [of horn] for a Rocky Mountain bighorn, and $50,000 or more for a full-curl desert bighorn. A gyrfalcon illegally captured alive in Alaska and smuggled into Saudi Arabia recently sold for more than $100,000. (Hanaback, 1992, as cited in Chitty, 1994, pp. 25–26)

Poachers operating at this level have a great deal to gain from poaching, but they also have a great deal to lose by being caught and having their catch confiscated. In reality, the odds are against their being caught. Working in sparsely populated areas, poachers can be particularly difficult to apprehend. According to Lt. Don Hastings of the Illinois Department of Conservation's Law Enforcement Division, "It is estimated that the conservation officer learns of one out of every fifty [poaching] violations" (Hastings, 1985).

Not all poaching is done for big money; some poachers are trying to put food on their table. At one time, this was probably the most common reason for poachers to take game illegally. This appears to be less true today than in the past. As a conservation officer put it:

> . . . a lot of these people want you to believe that they're just poor folks out here trying to feed their families. That's just not the case. That's a misconception I want to clear up. These people are cruising in four wheel drive trucks that are newer than the one I drive. They're out there for kicks, for fun, and trophy hunting for big antlers. These are the slob hunters. In nine years, and I've made scads of deer cases, I can say out of all those confrontations, I can't think of one case where an individual was truly destitute for food. (as cited in Chitty, 1994, p. 72)

Today poaching is frequently for thrills, or simply to kill a wildlife "trophy" (Bristow, 1982). In their study of poachers in the rural South, Forsyth and Marckese (1993) found that poaching was exciting and was seen as a test of wit and skill between the poacher and the game warden. Many poachers were proud that they could easily outmaneuver the technology and complex modern strategies of the game warden. "The conflict is similar to the city slicker versus the country rube. Although game wardens are not representative of sophisticated urbanites, they are in the same position" (p. 169). In addition, poaching may reinforce the rural mistrust of outsiders and of government. "They [poachers] are constantly in contact with others who support an 'us' and 'them' orientation toward the larger society. Both game wardens and the laws they enforce represent outsiders" (p. 169). As one poacher put it, "I outlaw because nobody is gonna tell me what to hunt, where to hunt, or when to hunt. My daddy hunted like that and his daddy before him" (Forsyth and Marckese, 1993, p. 168). Poachers may recognize that the nature of their activities, and the large-calibre weapons carried by game wardens, can lead to violent confrontations, but for some the inherent danger only adds to the excitement. As Forsyth and Marckese (1993) observed, "In essence, these men saw poaching as a very rough game.

They took pride in being tough enough to participate in it and being successful in evading the law" (p. 167).

Finally, when illegal harvesting of wildlife takes place on the hunter's own land, there is sometimes an attitude of "my land, my game"—a philosophy that fits well with the general distrust of government in many rural areas. This attitude may make it difficult for poachers to define their behavior as criminal. Gathering food, collecting trophies, and a sense of "my land, my game" all reduce the likelihood that citizens will cooperate with the investigation of wildlife crimes, and all undermine the perceived legitimacy of the wildlife officer.

There is a tendency to speak of poaching and poachers as distinct from other types of crime and offenders. Conservation officers, however, report a great deal of overlap between the two groups. The most common scenario is for the poacher to be using alcohol and/or drugs while poaching. As one conservation officer put it, "I've run a lot of drugs, cannabis type things. That's almost a common occurrence. You get a deer poacher, they're going to be smoking pot or drinking beer. You ask, 'Where's the deer, where's the pot, where's the beer?'" (as cited in Chitty, 1994, p. 89).

Aside from the use of illegal drugs while poaching, it is not unusual for poachers to have other criminal offenses in their backgrounds, as these three conservation officers observe (as cited in Chitty, 1994, pp. 89-91):

> A lot of the guys we arrest, we run a criminal history background on them. It's not uncommon for over fifty percent of the guys that I run a check on [to] come back with some type of criminal history: drugs, battery, alcohol charges.

> A true poacher, not the guy who makes a mistake or has done it once or twice, but the guy who continually does it is probably the guy that every deputy in the county knows, and he's been arrested before for burglary or something else.

> If we catch somebody wrong on a conservation violation, sixty to seventy percent of the time they have a criminal or traffic problem also.

The problem of poaching is difficult to solve, in part because of the lucrative nature of poaching, the difficulty of catching people whose crimes occur in remote areas, and the thrill that some poachers receive from avoiding arrest. Controlling the problem is further complicated by the mindset of "my land, my game" and by a rural hostility to a centralized government authority, as represented in the state conservation officer. Further, it appears that people who most actively engage in poaching are also likely to have had other problems with the law.

Borders

The contiguous United States has 10,913 miles of border. Alaska and Hawaii account for an additional 8,928 miles, making a total of almost 20,000 miles. It is often forgotten that the land along border areas is frequently in rural areas. Of the 316 counties in the continental United States which are located on a border, 151 (48 percent) are counties with populations of fewer than 50,000 people—that is, nonmetropolitan counties (constructed from data in *Worldmark Encyclopedia of the United States* and U.S. Census Data).

Drug smuggling and illegal immigration are only two of the issues raised when talking about the borders of the United States. Other crime problems are common, depending on the particular region. For example, along the Texas border auto theft is a common problem, with stolen cars taken across the border into Mexico. In the Northeast, a more common problem is the smuggling of tobacco and alcohol across the border between Canada and the United States.

Environment and Ecology

This section will focus on one broad category of crime, sometimes known as ecological crime or environmental crime. This category includes a range of activities, from illegally dumping hazardous wastes to the militant activities of those seeking to preserve the environment.

The extent to which rural areas are used to illegally dump hazardous waste is not known, but the relative isolation of many rural areas would make such dumping relatively easy to do. As the problem of disposing of hazardous waste grows and as the cost of disposing of that waste legally climbs, it can be expected that illegal dumping in rural areas will increase, as will the risk to the health and welfare of rural residents.

In addition to illegal dumping, impoverished rural areas may be under great financial pressure to serve as legal dumping sites for urban centers, often from other states (*Rachel's Hazardous Waste News*, 1988; Fritchen, 1991). There are thousands of landfills and similar in-ground storage sites which are contaminated and leaking. As Setterberg and Shavelson (1993) have noted:

> The U.S. government estimates that over sixteen thousand active landfills have been sopped with industrial and agricultural hazardous wastes. Most are located near small towns and farming communities—and the contents of them, according to the Environmental Protection Agency (EPA), will eventually breach their linings and penetrate the soil, as many already have done. Underground chemical

and petroleum storage tanks scattered throughout cities, suburbs, and rural America number between three and five million; 30 percent already leak. (p. 4)

We can expect a thriving illicit industry to arise in response to this problem. This illicit industry will include everything from clean-up scams that defraud rural residents, to conducting fraudulent tests for toxins in the ground and water, to the legitimate excavation of these sites followed by illegally dumping the contaminated excavated material.

Surprisingly, discussions of "environmental justice" or "environmental victimology" have not generally considered the rural setting, except when including underdeveloped countries. This is a serious oversight, since both preventing and investigating environmental crimes may be more difficult in rural areas where there may be fewer resources for responding to the problem.

More has been said about militant environmentalists. Perhaps the most extreme and famous such extremist is Theodore Kaczynski, also known as the Unabomber. It has been speculated that this mathematician-turned-hermit not only targeted people with connections to advanced technology, but did so in sympathy with a larger movement to protect wilderness areas (Chavez, 1996). Some of the most visible activities of radical environmentalists have been observed in the West, where efforts to save forests have in some instances involved sabotage, and in others threats to loggers and government officials who support logging. St. Clair and Cockburn (1997) have reported that the Idaho National Guard considers environmentalists among the groups posing a "hostile threat" to the state of Idaho. Throughout the country nuclear power plants generally are located in rural areas and would be logical targets for terrorists, domestic or otherwise, wishing to draw attention to their cause.

Another probable source of environmental crime will likely be related to the treatment of animals in modern farms, which might more accurately be described as factories. Driven by small profit margins, poultry, beef and pork producers have built larger facilities into which the animals are more tightly packed than ever. Animal rights activists have increasingly focused on these large operations, in which the animals may be born and live most of their lives within a few square feet of space.

> To people whose image of raising pigs evokes Old McDonald's farm, the sight of big confinement operations would conjure up something more from George Orwell. For example, every steel building at a Premium Standard plant near Harris, Mo., houses 1,150 hogs—48 pens 20 feet long and 9 feet wide, each holding about 25 pigs. The

pigs are genetically designed to produce an identical cut of meat. They are inseminated artificially, and their hooves never leave concrete (Johnson, 1998).

As an industry agriculture has been slow to recognize the potential problems of these so-called mega-farms. In late 1997 the Council for Agricultural Science and Technology issued a report in which it admitted there was no scientific knowledge about the impact of these facilities on animal welfare, and called for the study of "animal well-being" in these facilities (cited in Orr, 1997). The report was partly in response to the objections of animal rights activists.

There are also concerns about potential damage to air, land, and groundwater from some of these modern facilities. Operating in rural areas sometimes means that regulations are less strict or are less strictly enforced. The waste water from poultry processing plants, leaks in the "lagoons" that hold the raw sewage from large hog farms, and the eye-watering odor of some operations have raised concerns among many rural residents. In one small Iowa town, for example, the issue of "mega hog farms" has divided the community, with emotions running high on both sides (Kilman, 1995):

> The issue has turned meetings here of the county Board of Supervisors into such heated affairs that a panic button was installed so supervisors could summon the sheriff's office. Vandals have struck the construction sites of some corporate hog complexes. The sheriff's department patrols them, and it tracks their sprawl with pins on its wall map (p. A1).

The largest of these facilities gravitate to the most rural areas where zoning laws are lax, property taxes are low, and weak economies undercut resistance from area residents. As Schildgen (1996) has observed, "Like its liquefied manure, the hog industry flows downhill, to wherever it finds the fewest regulations and the lowest wages" (p. 29).

As beef, hog, and poultry facilities grow larger, they will increasingly become highly visible targets of vandalism and sabotage. A related type of sabotage has already happened and appears to be on the increase in the mink industry. In Mt. Angel, Oregon, in the summer of 1997, for example:

> An estimated 8,000 to 9,000 animals were freed in what may have been the largest "eco-terrorism" attack on the U.S. mink industry, said a spokeswoman for Fur Commission U.S.A., an industry group for mink and fox farmers. "The number of incidents seems to be escalating," she said. (*Chicago Tribune*, 1997, p. 6)

In 1997 there was a series of similar releases in Wisconsin and other areas of the Midwest totaling more than 22,000 animals for 1997 (Frisch, 1997a; 1997b). The first incidents were thought to be the acts of isolated individuals, but as the number of releases increased authorities became suspicious that the acts represented a coordinated effort. Between 1995 and late 1997 there were a total of 43 releases of minks in the U.S. and Canada, involving approximately 75,000 animals (Frisch, 1997a). The FBI investigates these crimes as "animal-enterprise terrorism" (Frisch, 1997b). The activities of these groups appears to be intensifying and spreading:

> Animal-rights activists also have changed course in attacking other industries, such as biomedical research and agriculture. They now target everyone involved in food production, from farmers to restaurants (Frisch, 1997b, p. 8).

America's continuous population growth will mean that the physical size of rural America will continue to shrink, and the battles over what to do with land and natural resources will become more heated. On the one hand, there is a growing need for the products of industries generally located in rural areas, such as meat processing and nuclear power, which will be producing an increasing volume of waste, some of it hazardous, that must be disposed of. On the other hand, as rural America shrinks, efforts to protect what remains are likely to increase. It is from the clash of these contradictory tendencies that ecological crimes and civil unrest will emerge and intensify. Technological fixes may delay the most serious clashes. For example, resistance to large hog farms may be diminished if systems were developed to substantially reduce the odor and the environmental damage from leaking lagoons. However, such fixes are likely to be short-term at best and to deal with only a few aspects of the problem.

Emerging Issues

In addition to traditional wildlife and agricultural crimes, it is clear that rural crime is assuming new forms to which many rural areas may be ill-equipped to respond. For example, modern telecommunications makes it easier to victimize rural residents with telephone scams and fraud involving credit cards. Similarly, the rise of interstate highways through rural areas has led to increasing problems with crime at rest stops and with crimes against people and businesses adjacent to the highway (McDowell, 1992). It has also created a situation in which rural areas find themselves situated along key transshipment routes for drugs and other illegal items. One sheriff commented to us, "You have to remember how many people we have incarcerated because of the interstate system. Our biggest drug population within the jail is from the pounds of cocaine or marijuana coming off the interstate." One study, using official police data from Oklahoma, found that index offenses were highest in rural counties intersected by an interstate, followed by rural counties bordering those counties intersected by an interstate, and then by noninterstate rural counties (Martin, 1995). Unfortunately, it was impossible to determine whether the crime was the result of visitors passing by on the interstate or the result of population growth and economic development facilitated by the presence of an interstate highway.

The growing elderly population in rural areas will also present the police with new sets of problems related to victimization. From our conversations with rural police, senior citizens may also expect police to provide a wider range of services, particularly in rural areas where other service providers may not be available. Several rural police commented to us about how a large population of senior citizens shapes what is expected of the police, requiring them to provide a wide range of services:

> We get a lot of calls from elderly people about checking on somebody. "Would you go over and check on Marge? Would you do this, would you do that?" Last winter I got a call from this woman who says, "I think I got somebody in my basement, would you come over?" She has a clothes chute, opened it and there was a light on down there. She "always" turned the light off, but this time she didn't!

Another sheriff used seniors as citizen volunteers to keep tabs on and provide assistance to other senior citizens:

> We can tell you about every widow or widower that lives in the county. A couple of times a week they [volunteers] will call just to see how they are doing. A lot of them are lonely, old, and by themselves. We check to see how they are doing, if everything is all right, if there are any problems, and are they feeling well. Just good basic conversations. Along with that, if they can't make it to town to buy groceries or medicine or make a doctor's appointment, we will actually send somebody out, whether it's a volunteer or a deputy, to make sure they make it to the doctor. We have made arrangements with the local grocery store so we can charge on their behalf. We have bought basic necessities to get somebody through a blizzard and had deputies deliver it on snowmobiles.

While senior citizens often demanded a great deal from the police, in return they often served as watchful eyes, noticing when things were not right and bringing it to the attention of the police. One sheriff reported that the largest marijuana seizure in his county was the result of a tip from watchful senior citizens.

In addition to the specific crime issues just discussed, little is known about how the features of rural culture may shape the incidence and reporting of a variety of offenses, particularly those outside of traditional index crimes. In their study of the caseloads of rural courts in four states, Fahnestock and Geiger (1990) observed:

> The criminal caseload profile reveals that certain criminal activity is seldom prosecuted in rural areas. There were no cases in the sample relating to illegal waste dumping or environmental offenses such as illegal use of pesticides, yet fish and game violations are frequently prosecuted. Banking law violations and other illegal business practices did not appear in this caseload. Few embezzlement, incest, and aggravated sexual assault cases were prosecuted, although it is common knowledge that these crimes are widespread. (p. 46)

As is demonstrated in the next chapter, responding to new forms of crime and to changes in the importance the public attaches to some existing crimes will require more than simply applying urban responses to rural settings.

Summary

Although findings are inconsistent, it is probably true that rural residents are less fearful of crime than are residents of central cities. It is hard to know, however, how much of the difference is a product of using questions that do not fit the rural setting—such as questions about crime on the respondents' streets or in their neighborhoods. In addition, some differences across studies may reflect real variations across the particular rural areas included in each study.

Rural-urban differences in fear of crime fit public stereotypes and are consistent with available data on rural and urban crime patterns. Official police data, as reported in the *Uniform Crime Reports*, show a pattern of higher crime in urban areas across a variety of crime types. Violent crime per capita is six times more prevalent in urban areas, and property crime is three times more prevalent in urban areas. Self-report studies of victimization also show rural-urban differences, with rural citizens reporting about half the victimization rate of urban citizens. This difference is large, but not as great as the differences observed in official reports.

Examining trends in rural and urban crime since 1980 suggests that rural and urban crime rates generally follow parallel paths. Official records show that violent crime in both rural and urban areas has drifted up slightly since 1980. A modest increase in the rural-urban gap in violent crime is due primarily to changes in the rate of robbery, which increased in urban areas and declined in rural areas. Since 1980 the rate of property crime has changed little in either setting. Self-reported victimization studies also suggest that rural and urban crime rates follow parallel trends over time, but according to victimization reports crime has rather steadily declined over time in both rural and urban settings.

In addition to these general patterns of crime, there are several specific issues that merit discussion. Gang activity was a frequently voiced concern among the rural police we interviewed but is rarely discussed in the professional literature. Documenting the nature and extent of gang activity in rural areas is a difficult but important task.

Drugs appear to be as available in rural areas as they are in urban areas, although rural drug users are less likely to use cocaine and more likely to use inhalants. Alcohol use, particularly DUI, is a greater concern in rural areas, where the distances travelled while intoxicated may be greater, public transportation is not an option, and roads may be narrow and poorly lit. Drug production, particularly of marijuana and synthetic drugs, is a rural issue about which relatively little is known. Finally, the distances involved and the lack of anonymity in rural areas may raise special concerns regarding the delivery of drug treatment services.

Vice and organized crime are also rural issues about which little is known. Rural areas may be directly involved, or they may be used as transshipment points. Some historical writers address this, particularly regarding the prohibition era, but there is relatively little written about the current status of either vice or organized crime in rural areas.

While violence among strangers is less common in rural areas, rural-urban differences in child abuse and domestic violence are not consistently found in the research. Earlier studies suggested that rural police were more reluctant to intervene in domestic violence cases than were urban police. Our interviews suggest this is changing rapidly. A growing sensitivity to domestic violence, combined with revisions in state laws requiring a more active police response, appear to make rural police increasingly likely to intervene formally.

Rural areas sometimes house groups that are loosely organized according to philosophies of race-based hatred, anti-Semitism, and/or a disdain for the federal government. A variety of factors make rural settings more hospitable to the establishment of enclaves for these groups.

The distances that must be served by emergency crews and the lack of technical staff complicate detecting and investigating rural arson. Buildings are more likely to be totally consumed because of the longer response time for firefighters. This not only increases the loss from fire but may destroy evidence that could be used by arson investigators.

Agricultural crimes are a rural concern. Each year there are substantial losses from theft and vandalism of farm equipment and from the theft of livestock and harvested crops. A major concern is motivating farm operators to become more actively involved in crime prevention.

Other rural crime issues include poaching, telephone fraud, dumping toxic waste, and crimes linked to traffic on interstate highways. Another issue, not addressed in the literature but a concern among some of the interviewed police, was crime linked to the operation of casinos and legalized gambling.

Many, perhaps most, aspects of rural crime are poorly understood. This is unfortunate because not only is rural crime a problem in itself, but it can also impact urban areas, as when drugs are produced in or transshipped through rural communities. It is likely that the social environment of rural areas shapes the types of crimes committed in these areas, as well as the relationship between victims and offenders. It is also likely that the rural environment shapes police work, an issue to which we now turn.

Chapter 3

Rural and Small-Town Police

BEING A COP IN THE COUNTRY

In Kersey, Colorado, police chief Rik Clark makes up 50 percent of his police force. He and his partner, Pat, provide 24-hour law enforcement duty for this tiny town of 1,200 by individually working 84-hour weeks of combined patrol and on-call duty.

Like other rural towns, Kersey has seen signs of gang and drug activity. When Clark hears from a high school student that a kid in a red Escort is flashing gang signs, he acts swiftly.

Since there's only one boy in Kersey who fits that description, Clark hunts him down.

"You were just seen cruising by the gym, so don't tell me you weren't there," he presses the teen.

Clark spends several hours a day at the high school. He knows all the gangbangers, their names, nicknames, and cars.

"If they're out driving, we pull in behind. We'll stop them to check for weapons. We tell them to get out of town (if they're not from Kersey), and they do, because they're not anonymous anymore," said Clark.

Clark's story reveals aspects common to many rural peace officers. Because of his familiarity with the townspeople, he has a network of information at hand to act proactively and prevent crime. Clark uses techniques that work based on real-world experience, not necessarily what a procedural manual instructs him to do. Clark realizes that he must be effective in his efforts. He may be the only obstacle between Kersey and the rampant infections of urban disease.

Source: Benson, 1995, March, pp. 46–47.

As noted earlier, the issues of rural crime and rural justice have received scant attention. For example, the distinction between rural and urban policing is acknowledged in a brief one-page section in the International City Management Association's (ICMA) 447-page book, *Local Government Police Management* (Garmire, 1982). Many consider this book the definitive reference on municipal police administration. The distinctions between urban and rural policing are considered nominal.

In fact, the authors state: "The historic distinctions between urban and rural police services are rapidly disappearing" (p. 21). This implies that rural policing is fundamentally the same as urban policing. It is reasonable to seriously question this assumption. Further, as evidence of an increasing trend discounting the importance of rural policing, the one-page acknowledgement cited in the 1982 edition is totally absent in the latest edition of ICMA's book (Geller, 1991). Clearly, there is an urban bias in research efforts concerning police organizations, management, operations, and methods in America.

Further evidence of the overall lack of knowledge about police agencies (especially rural departments) in the United States is revealed in the apparent inability to calculate the precise number of agencies. This issue has been a matter of much controversy for many years. For instance, the 1967 President's Commission on Law Enforcement estimated that the United States had approximately 40,000 separate police agencies (U.S. Department of Justice, 1977). By the early 1980s the estimated number of police agencies was greatly reduced; one scholar placed the number at 19,691 (Walker, 1983). That same scholar later placed that estimate at approximately 15,000 (Walker, 1992), while the Bureau of Justice Statistics estimated the number of police agencies at approximately 17,000 (Reaves, 1992a).

How do we account for this disparity? It is likely that the confusion results from the numerous special policing districts/agencies and the many, very small rural police departments which sometimes have no full-time officers. How should these agencies be counted, and who would keep records of their existence? Adding to the problem, it is only recently that state criminal justice information authorities have been in existence—obviously affecting the ability to gather any data. In short, those who would study rural policing must not only decide what is rural, but what is a rural police agency.

Who Are Rural Police?

In urban settings, any reference to "the police" invariably means the city police department. Various urban policing functions are carried out almost entirely by municipal-level police agencies, while state- and county-level agencies have more peripheral roles—ancillary or specialized tasks such as operating the jail, providing security for the courthouse, or ad hoc investigative task forces.

In rural settings, however, the picture changes. While municipal police departments are still the primary agencies in many small cities and towns that dot the rural landscape, county and state policing agencies become much more important outside urban areas. State police officers may be stationed to provide general policing functions in remote areas not well covered by other police agencies. In addition, they routinely provide highway patrol coverage of the open roads in rural areas. State conservation officers are responsible for enforcing fish and wildlife laws—especially relevant in rural areas where fishing, hunting, and outdoor recreation are major economic activities. They also have broader police powers in most states that are relevant in the outlying rural areas where they patrol.

A number of federal enforcement agencies also operate, to varying degrees, in rural areas. A brief sampling of these federal agencies includes: the Immigration and Naturalization Service, the Border Patrol, DEA, FBI, and the U.S. Forest Service. Unlike local sheriffs or municipal police, these federal agencies are ultimately responsible to the federal government, not to local citizens. In addition, federal agents are not generally from the areas they police, nor are they likely to develop long-term social attachments and commitments to the local communities in which they operate. While a number of state and federal police operate in rural areas, the key enforcement agencies are sheriffs and municipal police, to which our attention now turns.

Sheriffs versus Municipal Police

The major difference between rural and urban settings is the far greater importance of the county sheriff's office in the administration of rural policing and law enforcement (Falcone & Wells, 1995). In rural areas, the sheriff often becomes the central organization of policing rather than a peripheral or support agency (as in urban settings). Where "rural" necessarily includes all unincorporated areas outside of municipal units, these are by statute the primary jurisdiction of the county sheriff. Also, even incorporated places in rural areas may depend on the county sheriff for basic policing services. Where many small villages, towns, or small cities cannot afford full-time police coverage, the county sheriff's office may provide many basic policing services; the sheriff may also serve as a central agency to coordinate resources among the small local departments.

A clear understanding of the differences between rural and urban policing is closely related to recognizing the basic distinction between the municipal police department and the county sheriff's office as distinctive forms of police agencies. Because of its historical evolution, the sheriff's office has a different political structure and character from local, municipal police agencies. Correspondingly, the legal authority of sheriffs diverges from that of local police chiefs. The authority of the sheriff is grounded by centuries of legal evolution, not specifically delimited by statutory law, and includes a range of implied responsibilities and powers. In contrast, the authority of the municipal police is a relatively recent statutory creation, being expressly limited in power and function, and dating only to the nineteenth century.

Unlike most municipal chiefs, the sheriff is an *elected* official in all but two states—Rhode Island and Hawaii (National Sheriffs' Association, 1979). This expresses the independence of the sheriff from other political offices or executives within local governmental structure. It also means that the sheriff is directly subject to the community and to the power of public opinion. Since terms of office are often fairly short—usually two or four years—the sheriff depends on good relationships with voting members of the community. In these terms, the sheriff is less insulated from the public than is the police chief, lacking the administrative buffer that most municipal departments have in the mayor, police commission, or city board. The difference between sheriffs and municipal chiefs is well illustrated by a local sheriff who told about working with a local municipal chief. The chief pointed out to the sheriff that when they were together in public, e.g., having lunch in a restaurant, people introduced them to others as *the* police chief and *our* sheriff. We have heard comments like this from other sheriffs and can speculate that being elected changes the relationship between the police and the public.

The employees of the sheriff's office also depend on the sheriff's reelection, since they "serve at the sheriff's pleasure" in many jurisdictions. Slightly less than half of the sheriffs' offices in the United States have formal merit procedures for personnel decisions; the majority rely on discretionary administrative appointments. Since the election of a new sheriff can result in a new set of appointed deputies and supervisors in the office, personnel in a sheriff's office have a more symbiotic relationship with the sheriff than do police officers with their chief. Indeed, the latter often seem to have rather antagonistic relationships built into the bureaucratic structure of police organizations.

The sheriff's need to always think ahead to the next election makes the office political, but this does not mean that small-town municipal chiefs are free of political influences. The political pressures small-town chiefs face are different from those of sheriffs, and those pressures can often be more intense and less predictable. One sheriff, comparing his job with that of the local chief, commented, "At least I know I'll have my job until the next election; he [the chief] can be fired at any time." For municipal chiefs the pressure is less from the electorate than from local political and business leaders. We are familiar with a chief who began targeting DUIs in his community. Local tavern owners complained to the mayor and city council, with one bar owner complaining that a squad car had driven past his bar at least twice on New Year's Eve. Rather than commend the chief for combating DUI, the mayor and city council threatened to fire him for possibly discouraging outsiders from coming into the community to drink. As Bass (1995) has observed about these small-town chiefs:

> . . . while rural police are equipped to perform the duties of general law enforcement, they are strongly discouraged from doing so by governing authorities. They are instead encouraged to neglect enforcement, or compelled to enforce the laws selectively as pre-scribed by city fathers. (p. 72)

As one chief told Bass (1995):

> Being a small town chief is a political job, not a police job. They only want you there to keep watch at night–during the day you'll get fired if you write tickets. They don't want you to upset the community–just be seen. They just want to say they have a *cop*. [italics in original] (p. 71)

In contrast, sheriffs are relatively independent of local political leaders; often they themselves can be considered leaders of the community with concomitant political muscle.

By virtue of its historical evolution, the legal responsibility and authority of the sheriff is much greater than that of local police chiefs. In most states, the sheriff is responsible for providing any (or all) of the following: (1) criminal law enforcement and other general police ser-vices; (2) custodial and correctional services, involving the transporta-tion of prisoners and the management of the county jail; (3) the process-ing of judicial writs and court orders, both criminal and civil; (4) security of the court via bailiffs; (5) miscellaneous services, such as the transportation and commitment of the mentally ill; (6) seizure of prop-erty claimed by the county; (7) collection of county fees and taxes; and (8) sale of licenses and permits; plus other services that do not fall neatly under the statutory responsibilities of other law enforcement or social service agencies. A unique expression of the sheriff's greater legal mandate is the doctrine of *posse comitatus*, under which the sheriff may compel the assistance of any citizen.

As a result, the sheriff's efforts are more divided across multiple, competing administrative concerns. Even though the public image of the sheriff's office may be based mostly on law enforcement activities, the sheriff cannot afford to concentrate on that task. The funding of the office may depend heavily on doing other tasks that generate important revenues for the county (such as serving court writs and warrants or collecting taxes and license fees) or tasks which involve substantial legal liabilities to the sheriff and the county (such as holding unconvicted defendants in jail pre-trial). In relatively small sheriffs' offices, generalist road deputies find that a large portion of their shifts are taken up with the processing of court writs, either criminal or civil. Since most writs are for civil matters, deputies are left with little time for proactive criminal law enforcement, unlike their municipal counterparts.

Generally associated with county-level government, some sheriffs provide services for independent cities; however, this occurs less than 1 percent of the time (Reaves, 1992b). The geographic area of jurisdiction for most sheriffs is the county or parish; however, it is the unincorporated regions within those areas that are of special concern to sheriffs. Sheriffs have criminal and civil jurisdiction throughout their counties, but it is the unincorporated areas for which they are primarily responsible. In contrast, municipal police are responsible for police services only within their incorporated areas.

As a countywide police agency, the sheriff's office holds the potential for coordinating police efforts throughout the county. In fact, in rural settings the county sheriff is seen as not only a coordinating office, but as a higher law enforcement authority with better-trained criminal investigators and technicians (most of whom are generalist officers) than municipal officers in small rural police agencies. Where local agencies do not provide full-time police coverage, the sheriff's deputies often provide services upon request to incorporated areas in the county.

The sheriff's office is generally more personalized in the way in which tasks are accomplished and in the way in which the office is organized. For example, deputies and civilian employees tend to work "for the sheriff" rather than for the organization *per se*. There is less distance and impersonal separation between the sheriff's office and the community it serves. In most offices, the sheriff's deputies are required to be members of the community in which they serve. According to the 1990 *Law Enforcement Management and Administrative Statistics* survey (Bureau of Justice Statistics, 1990b), 87 percent of sheriffs require deputies to be residents of their legal jurisdiction, while just under 50 percent of municipal police make such requirements of their officers.

The preceding discussion has treated both rural sheriffs' departments and small-town municipal police departments as if they were uniform across the United States. Variations in department size will be discussed below. There are also important differences across states in the authority given rural police. These variations in authority are particularly marked for sheriffs' agencies. Some of the variation is the result of constitutional or statutory differences in the authority granted the sheriff. Other differences are the result of custom and budgetary issues at the state and county level. In some states, the sheriff has extensive power and is among the most powerful police officers in the state. In other states, such as Pennsylvania, the authority of the sheriff is much more limited. In rural areas, it is not a matter of striking a balance between the power of the sheriff and that of the municipality, as it might be in an urban county. Instead, authority is shared between the sheriff and the state police. In most states, the state police have authority and are actively involved in local law enforcement to the extent that the sheriff's authority is limited. Where sheriffs have greater power, the activities of the state police are more circumscribed. For example, there are several states in which the state-level policing organization is the "highway patrol" with limited investigative powers. Thus, a good understanding of police organizations in rural areas must include not only an understanding of small municipal departments, but also an understanding of how police powers are balanced between county sheriffs and state-level police organizations.

Federal, State, and Local Cooperation

Our work focused primarily on municipal and county police, with only secondary attention given to federal authorities or state police. Both federal and state police may work *in* rural areas, but they are not generally *of* those areas. It is often necessary, however, for federal, state, and local police to join efforts. We can make several observations about how well these cooperative efforts seem to work and the circumstances under which problems tend to arise.

In chapter 1 it was noted that rural citizens often have a mistrust of a strong centralized government. Similar concerns have been expressed by rural sheriffs. In California, for example, a contingent of 200 Army soldiers, National Guardsmen and federal agents spent two weeks clearing out marijuana growing operations in the King Range

National Conservation Area in northern California. As a result of their efforts 1,200 plants were destroyed, but not everyone was satisfied.

> "This is so frustrating when the Federal Government comes in and spends enough money that would keep my operation going for three or four years," said Sheriff David Renner of Humboldt County. His team of five deputies, cooperating with the state's seven-year-old Campaign Against Marijuana Planting, destroyed over 3,000 plants in one day this week.

> "If the Feds have the money for this kind of operation," Sheriff Renner said, "they ought to give it to local law enforcement that is more effective and is truly responsible to local citizens. Their results speak for themselves and they are not good." (Bishop, 1990, p. A11)

A rural sheriff interviewed by Weisheit was asked why, if his department was chronically understaffed, he did not call in the DEA to assist in raids on marijuana-growing operations. The sheriff responded:

> I did call the feds in a couple of times. Then I quit. I have no confidence in them. In the first place, they are ego-maniacs. They think they are really something on a stick. They come into an area like this, of which they know nothing. They don't know the history of it, the people, the terrain. They can mess up an investigation faster than you can shake a stick at it. I had two unfortunate experiences. One was with this two-and-a-half-million-dollar patch we had. I could see it was quite an important thing; I mean we really needed to catch somebody. So I called the DEA. You would have thought they were a SWAT team. They came in with all this fancy stuff. You can't imagine the equipment and stuff they had with them. I'm sure, just by the way they approached the plot, they scared the people off. [He said that by their approach the growers probably saw them well before they arrived at the patch.] And eventually, all we did was pull all the plants and burn them. I decided after that we would handle it ourselves, because we knew more about the territory than any of them did. (as cited in Weisheit, 1992, p. 138)

In many cases the objections are not to federal or state assistance *per se*, but to the attitudes displayed by state and federal agents. Where there was a sensitivity to the local area and a general show of respect for local police, local authorities seemed to be far more positive in their descriptions, frequently encouraging federal and state involvement. All of this suggests that local authorities can work effectively with state and national police. The rise of multijurisdictional task forces demonstrates that local authorities can work very effectively with others (Schlegel & McGarrell, 1991). Some of these task forces combine federal, state, and local police agencies to target a particular type of crime or a particular type of offender. The point is that state and federal authorities need to appreciate rural culture to make these relationships work effectively. Although we did not study this directly, it is possible that task forces have played a role in breaking down barriers among these different levels of police and law enforcement agencies.

Department Size

Nationally, most local police departments are small; over half of the nation's local departments employ less than 10 commissioned officers (see Figure 9). Ninety percent of all local police agencies maintain fewer than 50 sworn officers (Reaves, 1993), and 90 percent of the nation's police departments serve a population of under 25,000 (Reaves, 1992a). Perhaps the most interesting group is the 4.9 percent of all departments with no full-time officers. These departments have been almost completely ignored in research, although they outnumber departments with more than 100 officers.

Illinois provides one example of how small departments predominate. The state has nearly 35,000 combined state and local officers in approximately 1,008 separate and distinct police agencies (Illinois State

Figure 9. Sizes of Police Departments

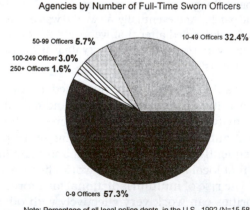

Agencies by Number of Full-Time Sworn Officers

50-99 Officers **5.7%**

100-249 Officer **3.0%**
250+ Officers **1.6%**

10-49 Officers **32.4%**

0-9 Officers **57.3%**

Note: Percentage of all local police depts. in the U.S., 1992 (N=15,588)
Source: Created from data in Reaves, 1993

Police, 1994). Although Illinois as a whole is heavily populated and is included in the enumeration of the 11 industrialized states, very small rural (municipal) police departments dominate the landscape. Most of Illinois' police departments have fewer than five full-time officers (59 percent), and approximately 32 percent have no full-time officers, i.e., only part-time officers. Further, relatively few Illinois municipalities (only 17 percent) have police departments with more than 20 officers (Falcone, Wells, & Charles, 1992).

Precisely what is meant by a small department? In their study of the organizational structure of police departments, Crank and Wells (1991) found it was misleading to assume that small police departments were rural or that rural departments were necessarily small. The truth is, ". . . no typology of police departments by size exists. Therefore no common definition of small town and rural police exists" (Sims, 1988, p. 15). One could forcefully argue that typing police departments by size (manpower allocation) is not reasonable, given that different contextual considerations might account for those numerical differences. A rural county, a bedroom community, a retirement community, and an industrial community, each with the same sized population, may have different manpower requirements (Sims, 1988), and even departments of the same size may have different missions. To complicate matters, some agencies policing rural America are not necessarily located in rural areas. Included in this category are investigative agencies at both the state and federal levels. The potential for conflicts between local citizens and "outsiders" who enforce the law is substantial, as described in earlier chapters.

With these complexities in mind, a sense of the relative size of rural and urban departments can be gained by comparing the average department size in metropolitan (i.e., a population of more than 50,000) and nonmetropolitan counties. Table 9 shows these differences, while also highlighting the differences between municipal departments and county-level sheriffs' offices.

Another reality for rural policing, especially for rural sheriffs' departments, is that these agencies are responsible for dealing with generalized police services for a given and nonshrinkable geographic area despite shrinking populations and thus resources. Current budgetary realities, along with the fact that many of the nation's worst roads exist in rural areas, present special problems for rural sheriffs. An article in *Rural Missouri* (1992) reported that 80 percent of that state's fatal vehicular accidents happen on rural roadways—often policed by sheriffs' departments and augmented by the State Highway Patrol. According to the National Safety Council (1992), motor vehicle deaths per

Table 9 Department Size by County Population Size

County Size	No. of Depts.	Media Size	% w/less than 10 Officers
Municipal Departments			
Metropolitan	6,145	10	48.7%
Nonmetropolitan	6,267	3	79.4%
County Agencies (Sheriffs)			
Metropolitan	745	48	9.0%
Nonmetropolitan	2,361	8	57.6%
Source: Data drawn from the Bureau of Justice Statistics, 1990b.			

100,000 vehicle miles are over two and one-half times *higher* in rural areas than in urban areas.

The combined loss of population and tax base is a critical factor for local rural police agencies, at both the municipal and county levels. The Bureau of Justice Statistics (BJS) estimates that the per-officer expenditure for police agencies serving populations of fewer than 2,500 is $31,500, while in urban areas it is nearly double that at $62,600 per officer (see Figure 10). Similarly, departments serving a population of under 2,500 (the smallest they cited) spent about $95 per resident per year for local police expenditures, compared with $144 per resident per year in areas of 1,000,000 citizens or more (Reaves, 1992b).

Figure 10. Expenditures Per Officer

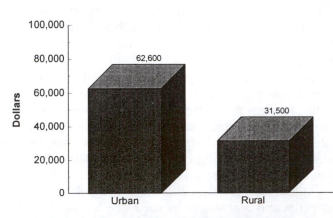

Source: Created from data presented in Reaves, 1992b

In the past, national and state commissions, among others, have operated under the presumption that the size of a police department is related to the quality of its performance. In particular, it has been presumed that departments with 10 or fewer officers are less efficient, less forward thinking, poorly organized and staffed by poorly trained officers. John Crank, in evaluating the trend toward civilianization in medium and small police departments, noted that rural agencies are civilianizing at nearly twice the rate of large urban departments (Crank, 1989). The *Uniform Crime Reports* (FBI, 1992, table 75) indicates that civilians constitute 22.4 percent of employees in the largest cities, but 34.4 percent of employees in agencies in rural counties. If civilianization is viewed as a progressive change, then Crank's findings and UCR data appear to contradict common perceptions that rural agencies are seldom in the vanguard of change.

One proposed solution is to do away with small programs by consolidation. The 1973 report by the National Advisory Commission on Criminal Justice Standards and Goals, for example, recommended that departments with 10 or fewer officers be consolidated. Ostrom and Smith (1976) have noted, however, that these assumptions and the policy recommendations that are drawn from them are generally without empirical foundation. Their study, based on interviews with police officials, police activity reports, and a survey of 4,000 residents in 29 jurisdictions of varying sizes, reached very different conclusions. They found that citizens in the jurisdiction of small departments reported less victimization, were less likely to believe crime was rising, and reported more positive police-community relations. Small departments fared less well than medium-sized departments in the speed with which they responded to citizen complaints, but small departments still outperformed large departments in this regard. On a variety of other concerns differences were small or nonexistent. They concluded that consolidation made sense for some small departments but was ill-advised as a blanket policy. More recent analyses of police consolidation suggest it is not necessarily cost-effective (DeBoer & Mann, n.d.; Gyimah-Brempong, 1987). Further, the community policing movement has been defined by some as a move away from consolidation and toward decentralization (Staley, 1992). These studies of agency size and police performance show that small departments can be quite effective and that small and rural are not interchangeable terms when describing police departments.

The Effectiveness of Rural Departments

It has been argued that small and rural are not synonymous, though there may be substantial overlap. It has also been argued that small departments may be more effective. The issue of effectiveness of rural departments has not yet been addressed. Additional evidence comes from the *Uniform Crime Reports,* which report the percent of crimes cleared by arrest by size of the community served. As Table 10 shows, agencies in rural counties have consistently higher clearance rates than departments in cities of 250,000 or more people. This pattern holds for every index crime, and the gap in clearance rates between rural and urban areas shown in Table 10 is particularly marked for violent crimes. Some of the rural-urban differences might be attributable to differences in reporting practices. Rural agencies might, for example, be less likely to write up a report on a larceny if there are no suspects. However, this argument cannot explain the very large rural-urban difference in clearance rates for homicide, which will almost certainly be recorded regardless of whether there are suspects. It is also possible that the close social networks in rural areas make it easier to solve crimes. One police chief told us:

> You've got a specific number of kids who are committing things and it's very easy after a crime to determine who did it here. The closeness of the community and the wide variety of MOs, when something happens they usually leave enough of a tell-tale sign that we know exactly who committed it. We only have one school that we have to listen to for rumors and things. We've got a lot of law-abiding kids that let us know what they are hearing. We solved almost every one of our crimes here. For every one of our thefts, burglaries, we know who has done it.

A county sheriff echoed this view by noting:

> For example, my secretary's husband owns the tire store. His tire store got burglarized. People know him and they know her, so they come and tell me "I know who did it." All we have to do is prove it. In some place like Fort Worth [Texas], that's not going to happen—ever. The people on the street don't know the cop, the cop doesn't know the person on the street. They don't intermix too much.

Expanding on the work of Ostrom and Smith, research by Cordner (1989) examined police jurisdictions of varying sizes in Maryland, with a focus on investigative effectiveness. He found that *neither* police agency size *nor* the size of the jurisdiction were among the most important determinants of investigative effectiveness. Instead, he concluded

Table 10   Percent of Index Crimes Cleared by Arrest, 1996

Crime Type	Cities 250,000+	Rural Counties
Violent	**40.9**	**62.3**
Murder	60.5	79.3
Rape	52.7	52.6
Robbery	24.3	42.1
Aggravated assault	53.3	65.0
Property	**14.4**	**19.8**
Burglary	11.4	17.7
Larceny	16.7	19.6
Vehicle theft	10.1	31.7
Arson	12.0	26.3
All Index Crimes	**19.0**	**24.3**
Source: Uniform Crime Reports (FBI, 1996), table 25.		

that "regional scale and community complexity" were more important, with greater investigative effectiveness in the more rural departments—that is, departments with the least complex community structures. He illustrates why complexity may be more important than size per se:

> Consider two small police departments, one located in a rural area and the other in a metropolitan area. Although the residential populations served by the two agencies may be the same size, the investigators in the rural departments have some natural advantages. They actually know, by name, by sight, and/or by reputation, a much greater proportion of the people in their jurisdiction and its surrounding area than the metropolitan agency investigators know of theirs. The witnesses that they deal with are much more likely to have recognized suspects they observed. Also, the rural investigator has only a few neighboring jurisdictions to keep in contact with, whereas the metropolitan investigator may have a dizzying array of other police departments in close proximity. (Cordner, 1989, p. 153)

Styles of Policing in Rural Areas

Given the differences between rural and urban crime and culture, it should be expected that police in rural and urban areas would approach police work differently. In his study of tasks regularly performed by police in 249 municipal agencies of differing sizes, Meagher (1985) found that small agencies were more concerned with crime prevention; medium-sized agencies showed the greatest concern for providing noncrime services; and large agencies focused on enforcing criminal laws and controlling crime through arrests. Similarly, Flanagan (1985) examined public opinion data about the police role. He found that the larger the community, the more likely citizens were to believe that police should limit their role to enforcing criminal laws. Conversely, people from smaller communities were more likely to want police to perform a wide variety of functions. In the sheriff's department in rural "Pine County" (a pseudonym), Decker (1979) observed that:

> The police were called upon and expected to render services for a wide variety of irregular occurrences, only a few of which were statutorily defined as law enforcement responsibilities. For example, the deputies complied with a request to inspect a boundary line between two farmers' property that was only accessible by tractor. In a related incident the same mode of transportation was used to check on a foundered cow. Many instances required the symbolic presence of a sheriff's deputy to legitimate its occurrence in the citizen's eyes. (p. 104)

In many rural areas, police *must* provide a wide range of services because other social services are either nonexistent or are more remote than the police. Marenin and Copus (1991) observed that in rural Alaska, where all types of social services are scarce, traditional law enforcement is a relatively small part of the service police are expected to perform. "Village policing is not normal policing, in the sense of law enforcement or crime control, but is much more of a social work kind of job" (p. 16), which includes firefighting, emergency medical services, and rescue operations.

Styles of policing are partly a reflection of the relationship between police and the community. While police in many urban areas may be viewed as outsiders, in rural areas they are an integral part of the community (Decker, 1979). In interviews with officers from one rural department and several urban departments, Kowalewski et al. (1984) found that officers in rural and urban departments had many similar concerns but differed in several interesting respects. Urban officers thought they were less respected by citizens. At the same time, police in rural communities felt more public support for being tough, particularly with juveniles. Dealing with juveniles is an important function for rural police, because this is often a major concern for rural community members (Decker, 1979).

Consistent with the greater informality of rural areas, rural and urban officers believed they were given public respect for different reasons. In urban areas, respect went to the *position,* and it was believed that a *good* way to improve public respect was through professionalizing the department. In contrast, respect was thought to be given to rural officers as *individuals,* who had to prove that respect was deserved. This is consistent with Decker's (1978) observation that rural citizens are more likely to see their police as citizens first and as officials second. "What is important is their role as citizen qua citizen, not their occupational identity" (p. 27). A state trooper in rural Missouri told us that if he were off-duty in St. Louis or other cities in Missouri he would be considered just another state employee. However, in the rural area in which he currently worked, ". . . if you are in Bermuda shorts, you are still the state trooper. There is no comparison [between the urban and rural settings]. [In a rural area] you are a pillar of the community and everybody expects certain things out of you. It is like being the local minister."

The bonds between rural police and the community are also strengthened by the practice of hiring local citizens in police agencies. Thus, the officers not only know the community and share many of its values, they are also members of the community and are often involved in community activities. As Decker (1979) noted:

> All members of the sheriff's department had biographies not uncommon to those of the community. The sheriff and his three deputies were all born and educated in the county. Prior to joining the force, every member was involved in an agricultural form of employment, the dominant form of employment for the county. There is evidence of integration into the community in other ways. Each member participates in an important community function; i.e., the softball team, Jaycees, Rotary, Elk's Club, etc. (p. 105)

A former police officer, with experience in communities of varying sizes, reiterated the importance of participation in community organizations:

> The small-town officers are more in tune with the fact that if I'm a member of the Kiwanis or Lions Club, or Jaycees, these people can help me further on. If you're in New York and a member of the Kiwanis and you get into a bind, they aren't going to help you much. If you get into a bind in a small town, the president of the Kiwanis works hand-in-hand with the city manager and he can put in a good word for you. I think most small-town officers realize that, myself included. We're very active in the Jaycees, the Lions, the Kiwanis, and all that stuff.

Given the nature of rural culture and of social interactions in rural areas, it can also be speculated that police-community relations will be very different in rural and urban departments. In rural areas officers are likely to know the offenders and their families, just as the officer and his family will be known by the community. Rural officers are also more likely to know and appreciate the history and culture of an area, and to use that information in their work. In his study of marijuana growers, Weisheit quotes one rural officer who describes his arrest procedure in one of his cases.

> You can't act overly high and mighty with them, you won't get any cooperation. In the big cities, that's what you do, you come on strong, "I'm the boss." That's often a very effective method there, but not out here in the rural areas. . . . This summer I went down and there was a guy with maybe 200 plants spread out over a small farm. I was fairly confident it was there and I pull up in his driveway. He was unloading wood. I'm in the pickup truck, and obviously he knows who I am. I walked up and told him what I was doing there. I said, "I've come to get your marijuana and we're going to be doing an open field search. We're not going to be going through your barns or anything right now. You've got some marijuana out there and I've just come up here to tell you what I'm doing." I helped him unload his wood and then I said, "I'm going down by the pond and look at this marijuana. I'll be back in a minute." I went down, looked at it and came back up. I said, "Well, your marijuana is down there," and then I went ahead and helped him unload some more wood and talked about it. He went to jail with no problem. I think this was the kind of guy who would have liked to have fought you. But because of the way I handled it, he wasn't going to fight anybody. Because, I didn't go in there and say, "You're a marijuana grower and you're worthless." A lot of times if you're dealing with people in these rural areas, they don't have a problem with you coming in and arresting them. They just want to be treated like human beings. (as quoted in Weisheit, 1993, p. 225)

Given the closer social ties between police and their community, it should be expected that rural officers will use policing styles which are more responsive to citizens in their area and that, in turn, local residents would be more supportive of the police. In fact, a 1991 Gallup survey found substantial rural-urban differences in the support that citizens show for the local police. In urban areas, 54 percent of the citizens reported having a great deal of respect for the local police, whereas 61 percent of rural citizens reported this. The differences were much more pronounced when asked about police brutality, where 59 percent of urban residents thought there was police brutality in their area, but only 20 percent of rural residents believed this (*Gallup Poll Monthly*, 1991).

The same features of rural policing that compel officers to be more responsive to the public also mean that rural police have relatively less discretion:

> A major explanation for the high degree of police discretion found in urban areas is the *low visibility* of police actions. In smaller communities the actions of police officers are known to most of the population thanks to the effectiveness and extensiveness of informal communication networks; there they are more highly visible. As a result, small town police enjoy less latitude in deviating from dominant community values. (Eisenstein, 1982, p. 117)

Crank (1990) found that organizational and community factors had a different impact on the adoption of a legalistic police style in rural and urban areas. In urban areas characteristics of the police organization, such as the number of ranks or the ratio of administrators to sworn officers, were better predictors of police style than were characteristics of the community, such as percent of blacks or level of economic distress. In rural areas the relationships were reversed, with community factors being more important than organizational factors. As might be expected, Crank's data suggest that rural departments are more responsive to the local community, whereas urban departments may be more sensitive to the dynamics of the police organization. Or, as a publication of the International Association of Chiefs of Police (IACP, 1990) put it, "The urban officer answers to the police department. The rural or small town officer is held accountable for his actions by the community" (p. 9).

There also may be differences in the way rural and urban police departments evaluate police performance. We were frequently told by rural police administrators, particularly rural sheriffs, that their officers were not judged by the number of arrests they made or the number of tickets they wrote. In fact, making too many arrests was sometimes seen as a reflection of the officer's inability to handle problems informally. As Cain (1971) observed, rural and urban police differed in that for rural departments, "an absence of official reports rather than many of them was considered the hallmark of good policing" (p. 66).

The less formal nature of rural life, along with the small size of many rural departments, makes complex bureaucratic procedures less necessary for day-to-day operations. Thus, rural departments are less likely to have detailed written policies in a variety of areas, a situation which can place them in a legal limbo when problems arise. For example, in their study of police vehicle pursuits, Falcone, Wells, and Charles (1992) observed substantial rural-urban differences in both the number of pursuits and in whether departments had written policies regarding pursuits:

> The paucity of pursuit policy in small departments is of tremendous importance because nearly one third of all Illinois police departments have fewer than one full-time officer. It is the officers working for these small departments who are unaided by policy and who have the highest per officer pursuit ratios . . . officers in departments comprised of 1–10 officers (small agencies) had an average pursuit ratio of over twice that of large agencies and nearly three times that of the next agency category (11–50 officers). (p. 168)

While rural departments, particularly small ones, may be less likely to have detailed written policies than urban departments, our conversations with rural police suggest that written policies are increasingly seen as necessary and worthwhile. It is in the area of developing written policies that state-level agencies and training programs seem particularly helpful for rural departments.

It might be expected that differences in style between rural and urban police would also have implications for police training. When we asked general questions about the adequacy of training in their state, most rural and small-town officers were satisfied with the training they received. One issue that did arise had to do with style and the treatment of citizens. As one officer put it:

> I feel most state training academies are geared for large, urban departments. But it is a different world. I used to send somebody to the academy and when they came back I would have to ride herd on them for two months to get the academy out of them. At the academy, everything is treated as very, very serious. This is the law and this is how it must be done. All traffic stops are felony stops until proven otherwise, stuff like that. I'm sorry, but you really don't get to drag some 60-year-old lady out of the window vent of her car for running a stop sign. In a small town they are people first and suspects second. In a large town they are suspects first and people second. The people management skills, which are so essential in a small town, and probably secondary in a larger community, are not addressed [in the academy].

While we have touched upon a number of issues, there may be a large number of other issues of pressing concern to rural police which have not been systematically studied and therefore do not show up in the literature. There is a clear need to identify these areas and initiate a systematic examination of how they might best be addressed. We will begin to explore these other issues in chapter 5. For now, the focus shifts to the issue of community policing in rural areas and small towns.

Community Policing

The preceding description of policing in rural areas raises a number of obvious questions about parallels with what has been called community policing. The issue has been explored in more detail elsewhere (Weisheit, Wells, & Falcone, 1994; Hawkins & Weisheit, 1997), but it is worth some discussion here.

Community policing is a broad concept that has been interpreted in a variety of ways. Although the term is relatively new, it has already generated a sizeable body of literature (e.g., Moore, 1992; Trojanowicz & Bucqueroux, 1990; Brown, 1989; Wilson & Kelling, 1989; Greene & Mastrofski, 1988; Goldstein, 1987; Thurman & McGarrell, 1997).

Aside from the obvious emphasis on community, it is possible to extract three broad themes from the literature on community policing. The first has to do with the police being *accountable* to the community as well as to the formal police hierarchy. The second is that police will become more *connected* with and integrated into their communities, which means that police will interact with citizens on a personal level, will be familiar with community sentiments and concerns, and will work *with* the community to address those concerns. A third and final theme requires that police will be oriented to *solving general problems*, rather than only responding to specific crime incidents. From the preceding discussion it should be obvious that each of these broad themes is consistent with what rural police have been doing for some time.

Regarding *accountability*, we have already suggested that as elected officials sheriffs must be responsive to the citizenry, particularly in rural areas where most of the voters are likely to know the sheriff personally. In rural areas and small towns, municipal chiefs must also be very sensitive to the wishes of local citizens. As an example of accountability, we have observed that rural sheriffs and small-town chiefs often have their home phone numbers publicly listed. Citizens expect to be able to call them at home at any time, and for the smallest of problems. As one sheriff told us:

> I'm willing to be shown that I'm wrong but it's a lot harder being a sheriff of a small rural county than it is to be the sheriff of [a city] with a population of 250,000 because everybody in that [rural] county—they want to be able to pick up that phone, whether it be Saturday night at 2:00 in the morning and they have a problem. They want to be able to pick up that phone and call that sheriff. They don't want to talk to a deputy, or the dispatcher. They want the sheriff, "I have a problem." It may be dogs barking.

In a 1971 comparison of rural and urban police Cain also noted the responsiveness of rural police to the local community:

> Country policemen differed from city policemen in two main ways: they were *capable* of learning the norms of the communities they policed and *interested* in conforming to them. Neither of these essential ingredients of peace-keeping by consensus was present in the city. Conversely, the members of the rural community also had power to influence the way their policeman undertook his job. [italics in original] (p. 77)

Rural sheriffs and small-town police also seem to be more *connected* to their communities than are urban police. Rural police are more likely to live in the community they serve and to be active members of the community. Because the communities are small, the police know many of the citizens and interact with them in a variety of social situations, such as buying groceries or having their personal car serviced. As one rural officer noted:

> Their [police and citizens'] kids go to the same school. You see them on the street. You see them in the grocery store. It isn't like a city. In fact, I've worked with several cities and their officers are cold. They treat the good people the same way they treat the bad people. They are callous.

Another chief observed:

> I come from a bigger agency. In the bigger agencies, you lose that personal day-to-day touch with the actual citizenry, unless you're there for a specific reason. Here, we're very close to these people. There's not too many of us, so they all get to know you. They come in all the time with their problems, and not just law enforcement-related problems. Yes, we're extremely sensitive. It's a very close knit operation.

This bond between the police and community in rural areas has been observed by others. For example, the International Association of Chiefs of Police (1990) has noted:

> Rural and small town police are closer to their community than are urban police. Rural and small town police are a part of the local culture and community, whereas urban police tend to form a subculture and move apart from the community. . . . Urban police tend to be efficient; rural police tend to be effective. (p. 8)

Similarly, the 1971 work of Cain found that urban police were a more cohesive and unified work group than were rural police. The unity of urban police was important for preventing officers from reporting the misbehavior of other officers. In contrast, rural police showed much less mutual dependence, "either in carrying out the work or socially.

Men lived and worked in isolation from each other. Any misdemeanors were secret, not just from senior officers, but from colleagues too" (p. 89). While rural America may not be as large as when Cain's work was done, there are still many rural areas where her observations about police accountability (discussed above) and cohesion continue to be true.

Another characteristic of community policing is a focus on *general problem solving*, rather than a narrow focus on reactive law enforcement. That is, officers not only respond to specific criminal incidents, but they recognize and respond to more general problems that set the stage for specific criminal acts. The problems need not be limited to "crimes," and the solutions need not involve arrests. When asked about the kinds of problems to which his department was expected to respond, one small-town chief responded:

> Everything, including the kitchen sink. I've had people in here to counsel families on their sex life because they think I'm the Almighty and can do that. I've had people come in who are having problems making ends meet, and we intercede for them in getting assistance, helping them file for welfare. We do a lot of service-oriented work. I consider it non-law enforcement. Somebody needs a ride, like an elderly lady needs a ride to the doctor. We'll take her to the doctor or go get her groceries for her.

Because they are closer to the public they serve, and because they are often one of the only 24-hour service providers in rural areas, rural police receive calls for a wide range of services. If they respond to a wider variety of "nonpolice" problems than urban police, it is not because they are required to do so by statute or because written departmental policies demand it. Rather, it is because they seem to define police work differently, perhaps because the people they serve are not nameless, faceless citizens but neighbors and fellow community members.

Given these observations, we have been surprised to periodically hear observers from outside rural areas comment that little community policing goes on in rural America. Such observations seem to be based on the belief that community policing requires the development of a specific program that has been codified and prescribed in writing. If one accepts this definition of community policing, then it can be argued that community policing is *not* simply and invariably identical to rural policing. Rather, community policing is a formalized and rationalized version of small-town policing—where the purpose is to introduce accountability and provide a measure of legal rationality to what, in rural areas, is a much more spontaneous and informal process. Thus, formal community policing and rural policing are not identical—community policing is small-town policing set in a rational framework, which attempts to formalize the spontaneous acts of good sense and good citizenship found in many rural officers into a systematic "program" which can be taught and which can be monitored and evaluated. This points out one paradox of community policing—in many ways it is the formalization of informal custom and the routinization of spontaneous events.

It is also true that rural policing is not homogenous across the country. One implication of this is that to be effective there can be no "one" program of community policing. Effective community policing must be tailored to the needs and wishes of each individual community, just as rural police tailor their activities to their local communities.

The higher clearance rates for rural police and the more positive perceptions of rural police by their citizens may reflect the benefits of the "community policing" as practiced by rural police. On the other side, the lack of privacy experienced by rural officers is just one illustration of the problems that accompany community policing. The rural setting may also be a good place to examine the concern that community policing will lead to greater problems with corruption. Our study was not designed specifically to address this issue, but it clearly merits further examination. A more general discussion of corruption and excessive force is presented later in this chapter. In that discussion the reader should note the key role of the community in shaping police misconduct.

In summary, rural departments are positioned to be the very embodiment of community policing. Sheriffs and chiefs with whom we spoke frequently saw what they had been doing in rural areas as community policing and believed they were well ahead of urban areas in this regard. One sheriff's comments are typical:

> Yes, there's far more community policing taking place in rural agencies than urban. We have been doing community policing since time began, I believe. We have always stopped and talked with the ranchers, the businessmen, walked the streets, rattled doors, and checked on sick folks. We know the various workers in the community and what they do. We see the kid delivering papers at 6:00 A.M. and talk with him. We have always done that. We are much closer to the people. Consequently, your whole mode of operation changes. Our method of gathering information derives from our personal contact on a day-to-day or minute-to-minute basis. In an urban setting, you're out "developing informants." We do that too, but the vast majority of our information comes from regular folks on a regular basis. I'm a believer in scanners. That would cause cardiac arrest in a lot of agencies. We have gotten more help from folks that have heard

us out on a chase and we have lost the guy. They call up and say, "He's two blocks away going down this street." Plus, it tells them we are on the job, what we're doing.

But is this community policing? Examining rural police practices raises questions about what is meant by the term community policing. Is community policing a formalized, explicitly planned program, or is it what police actually do in maintaining community order and safety? Using the first definition means that little community policing takes place in rural areas because the procedures there are not part of an explicit program derived specifically from this philosophy. Using the second definition means that community policing is a common feature of rural police work because the procedures routinely used there correspond closely to the basic tenets of community policing. Using the first definition means that rural police have much to learn from their urban counterparts. Using the second definition means that urban departments might well look to rural areas for models of community policing.

Violence and Rural Police

It has been argued both that violent crime occurs less often in rural areas and that guns are less often used when committing crimes, although they are much more available in rural areas. Further, rural police more often know the citizenry personally and interact with them in a variety of settings. These factors combined should create an environment in which rural police are less likely to be victims of assault or of felonious killing. As Table 11 shows, however, the available evidence presents a mixed picture. On the one hand, rural officers are least likely to be victims of assault: four times less likely than officers in large urban areas serving 250,000 people or more, and nine times less likely than officers serving urban areas of 100,000 to 249,999 people. In contrast, officers serving very small towns (under 10,000 people) and rural areas are killed at comparatively high rates—rates that are 50 percent higher than for officers serving communities of 250,000 or more. It appears that assaults on rural officers are less frequent but are more often deadly when they do occur. It should also be noted that the highest rates for both assaults and felonious killings of officers are not in the largest cities, but in mid-sized cities of 100,000 to 249,999 citizens (see Figure 11).

Table 11   Average Number of Assaults and Killings of Sworn Law Enforcement
Officers by Population Area for 1988–1995

Area	Avg. No. of Sworn Officers	Avg. No. Assaulted	Avg. Assaults/ 1,000 Officers	Avg. No. Killed*	Avg. Deaths/ 100,000 Officers
Group I Cities 250,000+	255,675	23,168	**90.6**	16.5	**6.5**
Group II Cities 100,000–249,999	35,120	7,987	**227.4**	5.8	**16.5**
Group III Cities 50,000–99,999	39,183	7,292	**186.1**	3.5	**8.9**
Group IV Cities 25,000–49,999	40,159	5,404	**134.6**	2.8	**7.0**
Group V Cities under 10,000–24,999	46,717	4,758	**101.8**	3.1	**6.6**
Group VI Cities under 10,000	60,827	5,104	**83.9**	6.8	**9.9**
Suburban Counties	110,405	9,923	**89.9**	8.1	**7.3**
Rural Counties	75,276	2,040	**27.1**	9.0	**12.0**

*Refers to *felonious* killings only
Sources: The number of sworn officers was drawn from the FBI's *Uniform Crime Reports: Crime in the United States for 1988–1995*, and the number of assaults and killings of officers was drawn from the FBI's *Uniform Crime Reports: Law Enforcement Officers Killed and Assaulted for 1988–1995*.

It is not possible, with the available data, to explain both low assault rates and high rates of felonious killings of rural officers. It is possible to speculate on fruitful avenues to follow in studying the problem. Perhaps assaults on rural officers are seriously underrepresented. If the officer personally knows a belligerent drunk at a wedding, for example, the officer may be less likely to officially record an assault if the drunk takes a swing at him or her. Or, perhaps the high death rate is the product of officers patrolling alone in rural areas, where help will not be called as quickly and where medical assistance is less immediate. Further, even if rural and urban assaults were equally likely to involve guns, rural dwellers might be better marksmen, making their attack more deadly.

Figure 11. Felonious Killings of Police

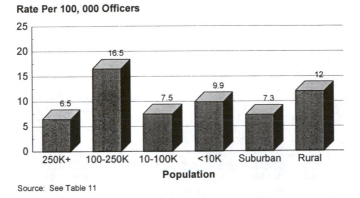

Source: See Table 11

The Use of Deadly Force

Differences by population group in the killing of police suggest a pattern that is contrary to many public stereotypes about the relative dangers of rural and urban policing. Variations in the killing *of police* lead logically to questions about variations in the nature and extent of killing *by police*. Although the *Uniform Crime Reports* provides annual counts of the number of citizens justifiably killed by police, these published figures are not reported by population group. The Criminal Justice Information Services Division of the FBI kindly generated these figures for us for the years 1993 through 1996. The data they supplied included information about the number of justifiable killings by police for each major population group, along with the officially recorded circumstance of the killing in one of seven categories (e.g., "Felon Attacked Police Officer," "Felon Killed in Commission of a Crime," "Felon Resisted Arrest"). As was done with the data for the killing of police, these data were averaged across the available years to smooth out the random fluctuations that are to be expected when working with relatively small numbers.

As Figure 12 shows, the rate of killing per 100,000 arrests for violent crimes declines steadily as one moves from the largest cities to the smallest towns and suburbs but jumps dramatically for rural counties. The rate for rural counties is more than double that for the largest cities and over 14 times the rate for suburban areas. This finding is quite surprising and defies any simple explanation. It might be speculated, for example, that responding as single officers who are often without backup, rural police would be more likely to kill while the felon was

Figure 12 Justifiable Killings by Police

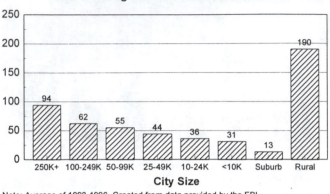

Rate of Killing Per 100K Violent Crime Arrests

Note: Average of 1993-1996, Created from data provided by the FBI

resisting arrest, but this is not the case. In fact, the circumstances under which the shootings occur are relatively consistent across community sizes, with most killings happening because the officer or the officer's partner was attacked by the felon (about 61 percent) and relatively few because the felon resisted arrest (about 6 percent).

There are obvious differences by community size in both the felonious killing of police and the justifiable killing of citizens by police. While the differences may be obvious from the data, it is not clear why these differences exist. The data do reaffirm our general position that the nature of police work may vary considerably by community size and that an urban understanding of both police and citizen conduct may not be adequate for understanding police and citizen behavior in rural areas and small towns. As has happened so often in our study, we again find official numbers intriguing and useful as starting points but insufficient for thoroughly understanding the problem.

Excessive Force and Police Corruption

The problem of violence against rural police has been little studied and is not well understood. Similarly, illegitimate violence by rural police and the corruption of rural police have not been examined systematically. However, beliefs about these issues form part of common stereotypes about rural police, as reflected in popular movies and in "true crime" books. The nature of our study, drawing heavily on the observations and comments of rural and small-town police, made it unlikely that we would gather thorough and accurate information about either excessive force or corruption. In the absence of hard data on this issue, there are many circumstances involved in policing in rural environments that suggest there will be differences in police misconduct between rural and urban areas.

Regarding excessive force, the rural officer is more likely to know the offender personally, as well as his or her friends and family. This may shape the psychology of using force, and it may make the officer more vulnerable to retribution, since these individuals are also likely to know where the officer lives and something about his or her daily routine. It is also possible that when deadly force is used, there may be more sources of emotional support for the officer in the community. Obviously, much will depend on how members of the community viewed both the officer and the offender before the incident occurred. Very different forces are likely to be operating if the offender is a stranger to the area, particularly if destitute and with few connections to people in the community.

Regarding corruption, the high visibility of rural police means that payoffs to police and unusual expenditures by individual officers will be more quickly noticed by residents. At the same time, the very low wages of rural police give them an even greater incentive than urban police to accept payoffs and to engage in profitable illegal activities. Further, if they personally know people they should be arresting, there may be considerable informal pressure to tolerate criminal activity—a tolerance which can eventually lead to their own direct involvement in crime (see Birch, 1983).

Our interviews with rural police (including those who do state- and national-level training and therefore have a larger perspective) suggest a belief that corruption and excessive force are less frequent problems in rural areas than in cities. In some rural communities these problems are particularly serious, but across the nation as a whole they are less pronounced in rural areas. Indirect evidence in support of this can be found in the results of a 1991 Gallup survey in which citizens were asked if they believed that police brutality was a problem in their community (*Gallup Poll Monthly*, 1991). As Figure 13 shows, urban residents were three times more likely than rural residents to believe that police brutality was a problem in their own communities. Although we lack more direct hard data and quantitative measures, such perceptions seem reasonable to us and are consistent with what we have observed about rural police and with what is known about policing in a rural context.

Figure 13. Citizen Belief That Police Brutality is in Their Area

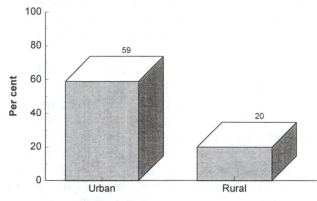

■ Source: Created from data presented in TheGallup Poll Monthly, 1991

The question is whether there is a *pattern* to rural corruption and the use of excessive force that is different from the pattern for urban police. We believe that such a pattern exists and turn now to a description of that pattern. The discussion that follows is highly speculative but consistent with what we have learned about differences between urban and rural policing. The categories we describe merit empirical measurement and assessment to confirm our speculations.

It is common to think of a typology of police misconduct that ranges from participation for the purpose of self-enrichment (e.g., corruption) to participation as an overzealous or exaggerated performance of the police role (e.g., excessive force). Barker and Carter (1994a), for example, draw a strong distinction between "occupational deviance" and "abuse of authority." While this dichotomy might be useful for understanding urban police misconduct, a good understanding of misconduct among rural police requires thinking in another dimension. As with so many other aspects of crime and justice, police misconduct in rural settings can be better understood by also considering the community context in which the misconduct takes place. For the sake of presentation, the discussion begins with two extremes, recognizing that in practice the influence of the community setting may fall anywhere along a continuum between these extremes. Thus, misconduct ranges between: (1) that which violates and offends community values and (2) that which is an expression of community values. The first category of misconduct we will label community-condemned misconduct, and the second will be called community-condoned misconduct. To describe some police misconduct as condoned by the community is not to say that the community openly encourages or approves of the behavior, although that may happen in rare cases. Rather, it implies a tolerance of the misbehavior so that a significant portion of the community would oppose sanctions against the officers involved and would rally around the officers when the misbehavior is discovered by outside investigators.

Community-condemned police misconduct—that which goes against the values of the local community—is the type of misconduct that comes first to most people's minds, and we would suggest it is more prevalent in urban areas. The 1993 case of Michael Dowd is a good example. Dowd was a New York City police officer who dealt in cocaine, snorted it from the dashboard of his patrol car, and was making as much as $8,000 a week in illegal activities (Frankel, 1993). While he had been protected by the silence of other police with whom he worked, there was no public rally in his support and no sense that the community showed anything but contempt and disdain for his illegal acts. Similarly, police departments must often defend themselves from public criticism when incidents of excessive force are made public, as in the 1991 case of Rodney King and the Los Angeles police.

There are no measures to indicate whether community-condemned misconduct is widespread, but it is likely that corruption of this type is far less frequent in rural areas. The rural rate is probably lower because of the greater visibility of rural police, both on and off duty. Police with the amount of illegal income reported by Dowd would be rather quickly spotted, as would an officer who used excessive force in a way that was offensive to the community. A rural officer would need to be far more careful to cover his or her tracks to avoid public suspicion and condemnation.

Corruption for personal gain among urban police is commonly blamed on lax supervision, poor screening of job applicants, and an ineffective bureau of internal affairs within the police department (see Barker & Carter, 1994b). Brutality among urban police is blamed on lax supervision of officers, and the fact that many police have lost touch with the communities they serve (see Dudley, 1991). Interestingly, a common prescription for preventing further misconduct is to increase citizen involvement and oversight of the police. We would argue that such oversight, though informal, is already at a relatively high level in rural areas, which would further support the argument that community-condemned misconduct is less prevalent in rural areas.

In contrast to community-condemned misconduct, it is likely that *community-condoned* official misconduct is *more* prevalent in rural than in urban areas. Unlike community-condemned misconduct, community-condoned misconduct is supported or at least tolerated by local

community values. There are numerous examples of community-condoned misconduct, which has been a popular ingredient in true crime
books involving rural justice. In *Deliberate Indifference,* Howard
Swindle (1993) describes a 1987 case in the rural East Texas town of
Hemphill in which a black motorist passing through an all-white community was taken into custody on Christmas Day by local police without
being told the charges against him and without being allowed to make a
telephone call. When he demanded to make a phone call, the officers
took him from his jail cell and beat him until he was unconscious. He
died several days later. Not only were the local police unrepentant for
their actions, but local citizens rallied around the police:

> . . . after the officers were indicted in Garner's death, residents of
> Hemphill and the rest of Sabine County rallied in defense of the offic-
> ers. One of the town's best-educated and most prominent citizens
> posted bond for two of the officers. A volunteer fire department spon-
> sored a cookout to raise funds for their defense. The town's mayor
> compared the beating death of Garner to an "industrial accident."
> Another noted that Garner should have been at home with his family
> on Christmas Day. "Far as I'm concerned," he said, "the nigger got
> what was coming to him." (p. xiii)

> The few who spoke out publicly in favor of prosecuting the lawmen
> became "outsiders" and "troublemakers" who did not have the best
> interests of their town and county at heart. (p. 179)

Community-condoned misconduct not only includes excessive
force but may also be applied to cases of corruption in which the officer
is engaged in illegal activities that are at least tolerated by the local community. An example can be found in eastern Kentucky, where four sheriffs were convicted by a federal jury on charges of taking bribes to protect drug deals (*Narcotics Control Digest,* 1991). In this section of
Kentucky, known for marijuana cultivation, it has long been known that
in cases of marijuana or drug arrests by local police, action by a local
prosecutor and conviction by a local jury are nearly impossible because
public sentiments protecting the growers are so strong (Weisheit, 1992).
When convictions do occur they are typically at the federal level where
authorities are more willing to arrest, the prosecutor is more willing to
press charges, and juries are less likely to be composed of locals who
are either sympathetic to the defendants or who have been threatened
or otherwise intimidated.

These examples also illustrate how community-condoned misconduct may involve not only the police but other local officials as well,
since they are all influenced by the community in which they work.

Other examples of community-condoned misconduct were discovered in the course of our interviews. One interview was with an attorney for legal services in a northeastern state who provided legal counsel to migrant farmworkers in rural areas. The attorney witnessed a number of instances in which police, prosecutors, and judges in rural areas operated in ways that may have reflected local sentiments but were clearly not in the interests of justice and fairness. This federal attorney gave an example of a case in which a migrant worker who spoke no English borrowed a friend's car that turned out to be stolen. He was taken to jail where:

> He was told by the [local] attorney who saw him a couple of weeks later, "You plead to a misdemeanor and you'll get 90 days." He decided that was a good deal and took the plea . . . So he pled to the 90 days. He was sentenced to 365 days. He's sitting in jail, waiting for his appeal. His appeal will take over 400 days.

As another example, one judge had to be reminded three times that an interpreter was needed for the defendant, who spoke no English. The judge denied the attorney's request, saying, "They've always brought family and friends before and I don't see why they should stop now. Why are you starting trouble? These people are lucky to be here and have jobs." The judge then persuaded the confused defendant to plead guilty to three misdemeanors, although the attorney was convinced that the defendant had no idea what he was pleading to.

None of this discussion is to suggest that community-condoned misconduct is common in rural communities. However, there are rural communities in which it is a problem, and it probably occurs more frequently than in urban areas. More importantly, it is a form of misconduct which has been largely ignored in the research on police. This is unfortunate, because community-condoned misconduct is perhaps more insidious and more difficult to correct than community-condemned misconduct. Community-condoned misconduct also raises interesting ethical issues and questions for proponents of community policing. What if the community to be policed has values that tolerate or even encourage activities considered illegal in the larger society? At what point should local police ignore local sentiments? Are minorities and the poor more likely than others to suffer injustice under this type of misconduct? Community-condoned misconduct may therefore not only represent one illustration of the dark side of rural policing but of community policing as well.

Special Problems

While rural and urban policing may share a variety of concerns, there are also problems which are either unique to the rural setting or are made more complicated by the rural environment. For example, many small municipalities are strapped for funds, which not only makes staffing difficult but may make it impractical for departments to tap into statewide systems for records checks or vehicle registrations. Even a nominal hook-up fee may be more than the department can afford. Further, the self-contained nature of rural communities may make it more difficult to generate support for training, equipment, or services that would increase the routine interactions between the local agency and state or national enforcement groups. In addition, the distances covered by some rural officers may also complicate radio communication.

Rural officers are more likely to find themselves physically isolated but socially under a microscope. This situation is the inverse of that for many inner-city officers. Perhaps the best example of this can be found among conservation officers, whose work is often done alone in remote areas, with backup some distance away:

> Rural officers do not have a police back-up system that will respond to their [request for] assistance within minutes. Game officers usually work alone with their nearest support as much as 50 miles away. They face a population which is generally armed and skilled in the use of weapons. Thus, they must face the threat of danger alone with the knowledge that they have limited, if any, support systems to aid them if they are injured. (Walsh & Donovan, 1984, p. 337)

In our conversations this was an issue commonly raised by police in the most rural areas. When asked "What's the worst thing about being a rural officer?", comments such as this were not unusual:

> That's distance—if you need backup or other emergency services. If you have a bad accident and you're 50 miles outside of town, it's going to take them a while to arrive. Or, if you have a hostage situation where you need backup, they won't be there for an hour.

In small departments, as well as among conservation officers, this isolation is compounded by the fact that there are fewer colleagues with whom they can socialize when off duty. At the same time that officers in small rural departments are physically isolated, they also have less privacy and more difficulty in separating their professional and personal roles. Conservation officers again provide a good illustration of the lack of privacy afforded rural officers.

. . . conservation officers are highly visible members of the community they serve and are in fact never off duty. The officers' homes are their offices, with the game commission logo prominently displayed outside their houses as well as on their vehicles. Their telephone numbers are published statewide. The officers and their families are under constant observation because they are members of the communities where they enforce the law. Thus, they can never develop personal identities other than their official roles. They cannot, like their urban counterparts, disengage from this role, seek comfort in their occupational peer group, and find relief from anxiety privately. Because they lack peer companionship, their families play a very important and sensitive role. However, even then, the officers must be guarded lest confidential case information becomes a source of rural gossip. (Walsh & Donovan, 1984, pp. 337–338)

Similarly, the IACP (1990) has noted that:

The rural or small-town police officer cannot escape his [her] role, and is often viewed by the community as a 24-hour police officer. This generates stress because the officer cannot participate in the social activities of the community as a person but is forced to be constantly identified as a police officer. (p. 9)

Thus, the same familiarity with citizens that facilitates investigations by rural police also takes away from the rural officer's privacy. We have observed there are very few rural chiefs or rural sheriffs whose home telephone numbers are unlisted—and many reported that citizens were more than willing to call them at home at any hour with even minor problems. One rural chief provided a particularly telling example that is unlikely to be duplicated by any urban chief:

In a small town you lose your private life, too. It has taken a toll on my wife and our kids. Two years ago on Thanksgiving we had the family over and then we had a domestic that ended up on my front porch. The husband came over to tell me the problem and then she came over . . . It was pretty embarrassing. I have since put a sign up on my porch that says this is not the police department, it is our home. Dial 911 if you have an emergency. It hasn't worked. The amount of calls that you get at your house, and . . . if you get an unlisted number, they will come by your house. I would rather have them call me.

This chief and a number of others observed that when off duty they could not have a beer at the local bar without starting rumors about them in the community. In such cases it is not unusual for chiefs, sheriffs, and their officers to go to nearby towns if they wish to have a quiet evening or if they wish to have a drink.

In summary, it is true that "police work is police work" and that rural and urban police share many problems and concerns. It is also likely that the more serious the offense, the more similar are rural and urban police practices. In matters of lesser offenses and day-to-day routines, however, there are a number of important rural-urban differences in how work is done, police-citizen interactions, and what citizens expect of the police. These differences raise questions about blindly applying urban models to rural police and may even raise questions about the urban models themselves. Consider the importance urban departments have placed on professionalism and the way in which that term is defined:

> Critics point to the personalized and informal methods of rural and small town police as unprofessional. Perhaps "professionalizing" them would erode their effectiveness. Maybe metropolitan policing could learn something about police effectiveness from rural and small town police. It is possible that "professionalizing" rural and small town police would destroy the close and effective personal relationships they have long enjoyed with their community and its citizens. (IACP, 1990, p. 9)

Although the IACP raises this point without presenting evidence to document it, the idea is a useful starting point for thinking through the role of professionalism in modern policing. Thus, understanding what rural police do and how they do it can provide valuable insights to improve policing in all communities.

Survey of Rural Police Needs

As shown throughout the discussion above, many issues were raised during the course of the study, both in the literature and from interviews and focus groups. The question arose as to whether some issues were of more pressing and widespread concern than others. In matters of setting policy and determining which types of programs should receive priority in funding, it is not enough to know that something is a topic of concern, but it is also important to know which areas are of greater or more immediate concern.

Using interviews, focus groups, and an analysis of existing data, we were able to identify several crime issues seen as important by rural police. Although our methods made it possible to identify a variety of issues and concerns, they were not designed to examine the *distribution* of problems among rural police. This issue was considered using a survey of rural sheriffs and small-town police. A survey made it possible to study a much larger number of departments and to ask standard questions for each department.

This study is based on survey responses from sheriffs and municipal police chiefs in counties for which the 1990 population was 50,000 people or fewer, that is, nonmetropolitan counties. Counties were identified using data from the 1990 Census of the United States, excluding Alaska and Hawaii because they do not have traditional counties and thus no traditional county sheriffs. In 1990, 2,248 of the 3,111 counties in the contiguous United States were nonmetropolitan (72 percent). One-half of these nonmetropolitan counties were systematically selected. A 12-page survey was sent to the sheriff in each selected county. In addition, the largest municipality in each selected county was identified and the chief was sent a survey. Of the selected counties, a total of 218 (19 percent) had *no* municipal police department. The *1994-95 National Directory of Law Enforcement Administrators, Correctional Institutions and Related Agencies* was used to identify the name and mailing address of the sheriff and municipal chief in each sampled county. This information was used to generate a database for mailing surveys and follow-up materials.

In early January of 1996, 2,022 surveys were mailed (1,120 sheriffs and 902 chiefs). Approximately six weeks later a second survey was sent to departments that had not responded. The results presented here are based on the 1,152 surveys (57 percent) received as of June 1, 1996. Chiefs were substantially more likely to respond to the survey than were sheriffs (64 percent vs. 51 percent), although the reason for this difference is unclear. Most of the discussion that follows combines the responses from sheriffs and chiefs, with differences noted in a separate section.

The responding departments were generally small and served small populations. The median number of officers in the surveyed departments was 10, with 80 percent of the sample having 20 or fewer officers. The survey probably underrepresented departments with no full-time officers—only three such departments were in the final sample. These departments are very difficult to locate and may fade into and out of existence, as when staff turns over and vacancies are not immediately filled.

Departments in the survey tended to serve small populations. The median population served by these departments was 9,000 people, with 85 percent of the departments representing jurisdictions of 25,000 or fewer people. Only six of the 1,152 departments reported serving a population of 50,000 or more people at the time of the survey.

Crime Problems

Based on our previous research a list of 14 crime problems was developed. For each problem the sheriff or chief was asked to indicate whether the level of the problem in their jurisdiction was "serious," "minor," or "none." Among the 14 crime problems listed in the survey, the problems most frequently listed as serious were, in descending order: drug use, drunk driving, juvenile crime, drug trafficking, spouse abuse, and handling juvenile offenders. Among the crime areas *least* often listed as serious were: gambling and related crime, gangs, crime in schools, and the dumping of waste and trash. Table 12 shows the percent of departments which described each of the 14 problems as "serious."

Table 12   Percent Saying the Problem is "Serious"

Drug use	79%
Drinking and driving	71%
Juvenile crime	61%
Drug trafficking and production	57%
Spouse abuse	56%
Handling juvenile offenders	54%
Burglary	43%
Child abuse	41%
Vandalism	35%
Dumping waste and trash	13%
Crime in schools	8%
Gangs	7%
Crimes from interstate highways	6%
Gambling and related crime*	3%

N=1,152
*Note: Only 19 percent had a casino in or near their jurisdiction.

Respondents were also given the opportunity to list other problems which our list may have missed. Only 12 percent of the respondents listed another problem, and no single issue seemed to dominate this self-generated list. Among the additional topics raised were: alcohol-related problems, theft, assault, and sexual assault. Other issues tended to be specific to a department or to a region of the country, such as "oil field theft," "breaking into summer homes," and "game violations." Three departments mentioned concerns about right-wing extremist groups.

Next, chiefs and sheriffs were asked to list the one crime problem they considered the most serious in their jurisdiction. For this task, the issue was not whether a problem existed, but whether it was greater or lesser than other problems. Taken together, drug use, drug trafficking, and DUI account for over 62 percent of the top concerns voiced by these chiefs and sheriffs. Thus, substance abuse was by far the single greatest problem reported by chiefs and sheriffs in rural areas and small towns. It might also be argued that the above listing *understates* problems related to substance abuse, since substance abuse, including alcohol, is frequently involved in a number of the other crime problems listed above. Domestic violence, for example, frequently involves alcohol consumption by the abuser, the victim, or both.

The Context of Rural Crime and Policing

Several indicators of community resources were included in the survey. Twenty-one percent of the departments said there was no hospital in their county. Of those counties without a hospital the average distance to a hospital was 12 miles, but 10 percent of the departments without a local hospital reported having to travel 50 or more miles to the nearest hospital. Only a few jurisdictions reported having a juvenile detention facility (14 percent). For the 86 percent without a detention facility the nearest was an average of 60 miles away, and 16 percent of these respondents indicated the nearest juvenile detention facility was 100 or more miles away.

The typical department in this study responded to 25 domestic violence calls per month, with only 9 percent of the departments reporting they received 50 or more calls per month, and only 2 percent of the departments reporting more than 100 calls per month. On average nearly 60 percent of the police calls regarding domestic violence were responded to by one officer. Most jurisdictions had no shelter for battered women (68 percent), with the nearest shelter an average of 36 miles away. Only 1 percent of the departments reported that a shelter for battered women was 100 or more miles away.

Most of the sheriffs and chiefs in this survey reported that a major highway or interstate ran through or near their jurisdiction (83 percent), and most who reported a major highway felt that the impact of the highway was to increase local crime (71 percent). Only 19 percent had a casino in or near their jurisdiction. Those with a casino were evenly split between believing the casino had no impact on local crime (50 percent) and believing the casino increased local crime (49 percent). Only 1 percent thought the casino reduced local crime.

Training Needs

The survey asked about several aspects of training, including training in specific crime problem areas and training in police operations. Finally, several questions focused on access to training for rural police.

Regarding training needs for specific crime problems, respondents were asked if more police training was needed for each of the 14 crime problems described in the previous section. Table 13 shows the percentage of respondents who said more training was needed for each of the specific crime problem areas. The crime problems for which the greatest number of respondents said they needed more training were, in descending order: drug trafficking, drug use, child abuse, handling juveniles, juvenile crime, and spouse abuse. Among the areas in which they were *least* likely to request more training were: dumping waste and trash, vandalism, and drinking and driving.

Table 13   Percent Saying More Training Is Needed

Drug trafficking and production	86%
Drug use	82%
Child abuse	76%
Handling juvenile offenders	74%
Juvenile crime	73%
Spouse abuse	66%
Gangs	62%
Burglary	55%
Crime in schools	50%
Drinking and driving	42%
Vandalism	39%
Gambling*	30%
Crimes from interstate highways	27%
Dumping waste and trash	19%

N=1,152
*Note: Only 19 percent had a casino in or near their jurisdiction.

Two things about Table 13 are worth noting. *First*, for 9 of the 14 items more than 50 percent of the officers said they needed more training. In other words, there was a high interest in training in a variety of crime areas. *Second*, perceived crime problems and training needs did not always match. For example:

- Only 42 percent said they needed more training regarding drinking and driving, even though 71 percent thought DUI was a serious problem. These chiefs and sheriffs may have seen the problem as one for which additional training was unnecessary, or this may be an area in which extensive training was already available.

- Only 7 percent thought gangs were a serious problem in their jurisdiction, but 62 percent wanted more gang-related training.

- While 56 percent thought drug trafficking and production were serious problems, 86 percent wanted more training in this area.

- Regarding the handling of juvenile offenders, 54 percent thought it was a serious problem, but 74 percent wanted more training on the issue.

- Only 8 percent thought crime in schools was a serious problem, but 50 percent wanted more training related to crime in schools.

It is likely that some of these inconsistencies—such as those for gangs, handling juveniles, school crimes, and gambling-related crime—reflect a belief that the problem is currently emerging in their area or is likely to emerge in the near future.

These findings suggest a relatively high interest in training across a variety of areas. The highest interest is in training related to drug trafficking and production, and in drug use. This is closely followed by an interest in issues related to children, including child abuse, handling juvenile offenders, and juvenile crime.

Respondents were also asked about training for nine areas relating to police operations. Table 14 shows the percentage of respondents who thought more training was needed in each area. Table 14 shows a strong interest in training related to computer applications for rural departments, in finding and sharing resources, and in using new communications technology. Each of these areas can help a department compensate for a lack of personnel and a shortage of resources.

There were also eight questions about problems of access to training for rural and small-town police. The percent of responses listing these problems as serious is given in Figure 14. The reported interest among officers in training was high, as was the perceived quality of training. The greatest concerns had to do with freeing up officers' time

Table 14 Percent Saying More Training Is Needed

Computers in rural and small-town departments	86%
Finding and sharing resources	80%
Using new communications technology	79%
Evidence handling and storage	72%
Managing informants	71%
Evasive and high-speed driving skills	66%
Recruiting and using volunteers/reserves	52%
Forming and maintaining task forces	48%
Search and rescue operations	43%
N=1,152	

and the costs of training, once again issues related to personnel and resources. Following these as issues of concern were "relevance of training content for small-town and rural areas" (48 percent) and "distance to training" (47 percent).

Figure 14. Obstacles to Training

(Percent saying "Yes" it is an Obstacle)

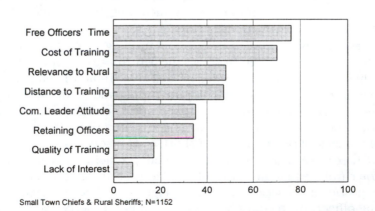

Small Town Chiefs & Rural Sheriffs; N=1152

Very few cited lack of interest by officers as a major obstacle to training (8 percent) and relatively few saw the quality of training as a problem (17 percent). Not surprisingly, when asked to identify the single greatest obstacle to training from the list above, the single most frequently cited issue was "cost of training," ranked first by 41 percent of the respondents, followed by "freeing up officers' time," which was ranked first by 23 percent of the respondents. No other issue was ranked first by more than 10 percent of the respondents. Thus, cost of training and the time involved account for most of the difficulties that rural departments face in getting training to their officers.

As will be noted below, the issue of training costs is a high priority with this group. It was an issue that surfaced at several places in the survey. One question asked for the department's annual training budget. While the majority of responses were reasonable, this question was clearly a sensitive one for respondents. A few gave outrageous figures, such as $5,000,000. Such extreme or improbable responses were not found for other open-ended items, suggesting this was not simply a matter of the entire survey being taken lightly. More likely, this was an issue that bothered them a great deal and stirred strong emotions. To remove these extremes, all responses indicating an annual training budget of $100,000 or more were treated as missing data and excluded from the analysis. This process excluded 73 (6 percent) cases from the analysis. Only a few departments reported training budgets that even came close to this figure. The median annual training budget for the remaining departments was $4,000, with 30 percent of the departments reporting an annual training budget of $2,000 or less.

Our earlier interviews and focus groups suggested that for many rural administrators there is a concern that their agency will finance training for officers who then are able to transfer to larger departments. While this was a concern among the respondents, it was not the majority view. Most thought that additional training made it easier to keep good officers (62 percent). Less than half thought that providing training beyond the minimum required by the state made it easier to recruit new officers (43 percent). Officer time, costs, and concerns about the distance to training all point to the possibility of distance learning, mobile training operations, or an increase in the number of regional training centers. Distance learning is often done through community colleges, which in many states are linked by electronic networks. Unfortunately, 63 percent of the respondents said there was no community college or university in their county. This does not preclude distance learning but may require setting up regional sites within states, using alternatives to the community college system in siting training programs, or developing alternative delivery systems, such as the Internet or even videos provided by mail.

Chiefs versus Sheriffs

As noted earlier, municipal chiefs and county sheriffs may operate under the same broad set of state laws, but there are differences in their responsibilities and in the nature of their work. In this study, there were several differences between municipal chiefs and county sheriffs. The most obvious difference is in the size of their jurisdiction. Municipal chiefs were responsible for jurisdictions that averaged 25 square miles, whereas county sheriffs were responsible for jurisdictions that averaged almost 920 square miles. Sheriffs and chiefs were similar in the number of full-time sworn officers in their departments, but sheriffs were more likely to use part-time officers and full-time civilians. Staffing differences were particularly strong regarding the use of volunteers. Municipal departments used an average of three volunteers per department, while sheriffs used an average of seven volunteers per department. In both types of agency, only about one-fourth of the agencies (24 percent) reported their officers were unionized.

As elected officials, it was not surprising that sheriffs belonged to a larger number of community organizations than did municipal chiefs; they must stay involved in the community to be reelected. This community orientation may also explain why sheriffs were more likely than chiefs to report that a job applicant in their department would find it was an advantage to have grown up in the county (52 percent of sheriffs vs. 39 percent of chiefs).

Sheriffs' offices and municipal police departments hired new officers at approximately the same salary, about $20,000 per year. Other measures suggested that sheriffs generally had fewer resources at their disposal. For example, sheriffs were less likely than chiefs to report that their departments paid all of the monthly health insurance premium for full-time officers—71 percent of chiefs said the department paid the full amount, compared with only 58 percent of sheriffs. In 6 percent of the sheriff's offices, but in only 1 percent of municipal departments, officers paid *all* of their own health insurance premiums.

Despite their many differences, regarding crime problems sheriffs and chiefs were in general agreement. "Drug use," "drug trafficking," and "DUI" were equally likely to be seen as serious by both groups. Differences tended to be among lower ranked concerns. Sheriffs were more likely than chiefs to rate "child abuse," "burglary," and the "dumping of waste and trash" as serious problems. Chiefs were more likely to rate "crime in schools" as a serious problem.

Regarding training on specific crime topics there was general agreement between chiefs and sheriffs on the issues they considered the most serious. Regarding training in police operations there was only one area in which sheriffs and chiefs differed. Sheriffs were much more interested in training on search and rescue operations. Fifty-five percent of sheriffs wanted more training in this area, compared with only 31 percent of municipal chiefs. Much of this difference was probably due to the differences between policing incorporated and unincorporated areas. Overall, sheriffs and chiefs were more similar than different in the crime issues about which they were concerned, and in their interest in training related to these crime issues.

Although they have a much broader mandate and they cover a larger geographic area with about the same number officers, sheriffs had about $1,500 per year less than chiefs in their departments' training budgets. While 88 percent of chiefs said the department provided training beyond the minimum required by the state, only 80 percent of sheriffs' departments provided this additional training. Sheriffs were also more likely than chiefs to report that "freeing up officers' time" was a serious problem in getting training to their officers (80 percent vs. 73 percent). Sheriffs were also more likely to report that community leaders not seeing training as important was a serious problem (42 percent for sheriffs vs. 29 percent for chiefs).

While sheriffs and municipal chiefs may have had many differences in their legal mandates and organizational structure, these data suggested they were more similar than different in the crime problems they were concerned about and in the training they desired.

Summary

A variety of federal, state, and local agencies have jurisdiction in rural areas. However, two types of agencies—sheriffs' departments and municipal police—are the primary providers of rural police services. While municipal police dominate the urban landscape, in rural areas the sheriff's department is more often the central police organization. Sheriffs have not only countywide jurisdiction but a host of duties not assigned to municipal police. These additional duties may include court services, running the local jail, serving civil papers, transporting prisoners, issuing licenses and permits, and collecting county fees and taxes.

Most importantly, sheriffs are usually elected, which makes them directly accountable to the public.

Most police departments, whether they are in rural or urban areas, are small. Almost half have fewer than 10 sworn officers, and 91 percent of all local police agencies have fewer than 50 sworn officers. Not all rural agencies are small, and small agencies are not always in rural areas. Still, small agencies are the most common feature of the rural police environment. Rural departments are not only small, but they are generally funded at about half the level of urban departments, per officer.

The small sizes and small budgets of many rural departments does not mean they are ineffective. To the contrary, rural police typically have higher clearance rates than urban departments. In addition, rural citizens have a more positive image of their police than do urban citizens.

Rural and urban police tend to operate differently. Rural police generally provide a wider range of services and are more closely tied to their communities. Rural police are more likely to come from, and reside in, the community they serve, and they are often active members of community organizations. Closer ties to the community are an advantage for responding to crime, but this closeness costs the rural officer personal privacy. Many aspects of rural police work are consistent with the principle of community policing, although rural departments are not likely to have formal written programs of community policing.

Given the more positive relationship between the police and the community in rural areas, it would be expected that rural police would engage in less violence against citizens and that rural citizens would be less violent against the police. Little is known about violence by rural police against citizens. Although FBI data suggest that rural police are more likely to engage in a justifiable killing of a citizen than are urban police, the available evidence about violence against rural police is contradictory. On the one hand, rural officers less often officially report being assaulted on the job. On the other hand, rural officers are much more likely to be feloniously killed in the line of duty.

While there is much to be learned about rural policing, the evidence suggests important differences between rural and urban police work. More needs to be learned about rural policing, particularly how it varies across rural areas, how rapidly growing rural areas can retain the positive features of rural policing, and what urban departments can learn from rural examples.

There are many areas of concern regarding rural police, but rural police themselves expressed the greatest concern about the problems of drugs and of domestic violence. Next in importance are the handling of juvenile offenders, attracting and retaining rural officers, and getting training to rural police.

Rural police do not operate in a vacuum. In addition to rural citizens, rural police routinely interact with other actors in the criminal justice process, and this interaction seems to be shaped by the rural environment. The focus now shifts to those other components of the rural justice system and their functioning in the rural environment.

Chapter 4

Other Parts of the System

ON BEING A SMALL-TOWN LAWYER

The adversarial nature of law practice is perhaps the biggest problem of the rural practitioner, especially when you have lived here all your life. My family has lived here for four generations. Everybody in town knows us, and I know them. They can't imagine my taking action against them. I have had difficulty [with that] myself. I found it hard to file a suit. I had to get calloused up before I could accept a lot of work. I had reservations about whether I could be zealous against people I went to church with or had been school chums with. One of my first cases was taking the other side of a matter against a fellow I went to school with and whose mother was a school chum of my mother. They both belong to the same garden club. We all belong to the same church. The family doesn't speak to us anymore and that's hard. Some folks don't care what other people think about them but I do. I don't know how thick the callouses have to get before you can do this work without cringing.

Source: Quoted in Landon, 1990, p. 138.

The informal nature of interactions in rural areas has implications for the willingness of citizens to invoke the formal legal process and for the ways in which defense attorneys, prosecutors, and judges conduct themselves. Long-term members of rural communities rely more heavily on informal processes for resolving problems, particularly for lesser offenses. One example of this is Ellickson's (1986) study of northern California ranchers who sustain damage to crops, fences, or livestock herds from the stray cattle of other ranchers. Although the dollar value of damage might be considerable, formal channels are considered inappropriate:

Rural residents deal with one another on a large number of fronts, and most residents expect those interactions to continue far into the future. . . . [italics added] They interact on water supply, controlled burns, fence repairs, social events, staffing the volunteer fire department, and so on. Where population densities are low, each neighbor looms larger. Thus, any trespass dispute with a neighbor is almost certain to be but one thread in the rich fabric of a continuing relationship. (Ellickson, 1986, p. 675)

> The landowners, particularly the ranchers, express a strong aversion to hiring an attorney to fight one's battles. To hire an attorney is to escalate a conflict. A good neighbor does not do such a thing because the "natural working order" calls for two neighbors to work out their problems between themselves. (Ellickson, 1986, p. 683)

In his study of variations in the rate of civil litigation among Illinois counties, Daniels (1982) found that rurality was the single best predictor of civil litigation rates. He concluded that "higher civil litigation rates tend to be characteristic of more urbanized, somewhat more culturally modern and slightly more industrialized counties, and that lower rates tend to be characteristic of more rural, agricultural, and somewhat more culturally traditional counties" (p. 209). That is, rural citizens were less likely to resolve disputes by turning to the formal court process.

Similarly, Engel's (1984) study of personal injury lawsuits in a rural Illinois county found that such formal legal actions were rarely brought. When injury claims were taken to court, awards were very low and the plaintiff was often viewed by the community with hostility and suspicion. Because of the stigma of handling these cases, the majority were handled by attorneys from outside the area. This was in contrast to noncivil actions, which were usually handled by local attorneys. The same pattern was observed by Fahnestock and Geiger (1990) in their study of rural courts in four states.

Interestingly, both Ellickson and Engel found that among cases that were taken to court, most were by plaintiffs who were outsiders, people who were either relatively new to the community or who had weak attachments to the area. As Ellickson (1986) noted, community members in his study considered a 10-year resident among those viewed as "new" to the community.

Landon (1990) has argued that the tendency of rural citizens to avoid formal legal procedures may be fading in some areas but is still a relatively common feature of the rural setting. He also suggests that whether formal actions are sought and the types of issues over which suits are brought varies depending on local custom and culture. Rural citizens may be particularly hesitant to go forward with formal charges if the defendant is another local resident, rather than an insurance company or an individual who is an outsider. As one rural attorney told Landon:

> I just settled an accident case in which the plaintiff did not want to sue the other driver because he knew him. It didn't make any difference that the insurance company would pay. He simply didn't want to hurt the friendship. He collected just enough to cover his medical expenses. He was entitled to a lot more. (as quoted in Landon, 1990, p. 135)

The Practice of Law

It should not be surprising that the distinctive character of rural culture is reflected in criminal justice institutions. For example, the self-imposed isolationism of rural areas is illustrated in Kessler's (1990) description of the problems in establishing a legal services program in a rural community:

> The norms of cooperation, trust and courtesy shared by members of the local bar apply exclusively to attorneys with strong local roots. In general, the legal community is unreceptive to lawyers from outside the county using their local court. Further, members of the local legal community are suspicious of, if not openly hostile to, lawyers born and raised outside the county opening a practice within the county. The attitudes of the legal community to outsiders are illustrated in the comments of one veteran local attorney: "If you're part of the community, practicing law here can be great. But it's not particularly pleasant for out-of-county people. There's a very tight knit organization over here that doesn't particularly care for the outsider." (pp. 274–275)

Perhaps the most thorough examination of legal practice in rural settings was conducted by Landon (1990; 1985), who collected data from attorneys in a small city of about 100,000 and from attorneys in small towns. None of these small towns was larger than 20,000 and over half of the attorneys were from towns with fewer than 5,000 people. In addition, Landon was able to compare his data with that from an earlier study of lawyers from downtown Chicago.

Landon's findings for rural lawyers were consistent with many of the observations made earlier concerning rural police. Compared with urban lawyers, small-town attorneys were generalists who had to handle cases in a wide range of areas. While lawyers as a group tend to be active in community organizations and to see such participation as important for their careers, this was particularly true for lawyers practicing in small towns. Landon also observed that urban lawyers oriented themselves to the interests of their clients and secondarily to their profession. Rural lawyers had to be sensitive to a greater range of influences. They found it necessary to balance the interests of their clients, other local attorneys, and the community. Rural lawyers were accountable to all three groups, and their accountability was further heightened by their high visibility as both citizens and as professionals:

> One of the defining characteristics of country life is the complexity of social connections. Most persons are involved in multiple-interest

relationships. The client who comes to the small town attorney may also serve with the attorney on the local Chamber of Commerce Board, or attend the same church, or also have a son on the high school basketball team, or have a cousin who is married to the attorney's wife's niece. . . . Continual encounters with others are virtually assured, and therefore the motivations that apply to each interactional situation tend to narrow down to those that will make the next encounter comfortable. (Landon, 1985, p. 86)

In many cases the lines between their professional and personal lives were blurred. One exasperated lawyer told Landon:

I'm tired of people coming in as "friends" taking my time and asking for help but assuming that there will be no charge. I refuse to do legal work on the sidewalk any more. For years I couldn't go to the Post Office without being stopped by somebody. I tell them now to come to my office. The meter goes on and things go forward in a business-like manner. Some don't like it, but I've got to earn my living as a lawyer. (as quoted in Landon, 1990, p. 130)

In small towns where everyone knows everyone, there is also the problem of lawyer-client confidentiality:

Potential clients, knowing the speed with which information gets around town, may well be anxious about how tight-lipped the office staff is. If they think that their affairs will leak out into the community through the secretary they are very likely to take matters to an attorney in a neighboring county. Sometimes just being seen walking into a lawyer's office in a small town sets the rumor mill in operation. (Landon, 1990, p. 130)

Finally, Landon argued that informality was a common feature of legal practice, perhaps even the defining feature. Communications between attorneys were more likely to occur through the telephone than through formal motions. "This informality and courtesy characteristic of country practice is essentially professional interaction based on the norm of reciprocity. It expects attorneys to be cooperative, rather than contentious; trustworthy, not tricky; reasonable, not radical" (Landon, 1990, p. 144). Small-town lawyers who violated this trust or who too aggressively pursued the interests of their clients were subject to a range of informal "sanctions" by their fellow attorneys. "When an attorney here violates those understandings, the word is quickly passed around. We begin dragging out the interrogatories and imposing the technical rules until the guy gets the message that that's not the way we do things around here" (Landon, 1990, p. 142). Thus, even though rural and urban lawyers work within the same formal set of laws and procedural rules, the rural setting has an impact on how those rules are carried out.

Successful rural attorneys are first and foremost businesspeople whose economic survival depends on good relationships with clients, other attorneys, and the larger community.

Prosecutors

The rural environment also shapes the work of prosecutors. The rural prosecutor is more likely to be familiar with the judge, defense attorney, offender, and the victim. In addition, the relationship between the rural prosecutor and the police is likely to be much closer than in urban jurisdictions. As Thorne (1976) has noted:

> A prosecutor is the chief law enforcement official in his jurisdiction. . . . For the small-office prosecutor, the opportunity will usually exist to know each law enforcement official personally. This facilitates the opportunity to meet with the enforcement units to explain prosecutorial policy, answer questions, and receive suggestions. . . . Awareness of such policies are as important to the police function as staying abreast of case law affecting their actions. (p. 311)

Hoffman's (1996) account of prosecutors in the state of New York, which has 10 part-time district attorneys, illustrates some of the problems these attorneys face. One prosecutor "has such perks as a cinderblock office that seats three—if he keeps the door propped open." Aside from scarce resources, prosecutors must deal with the conflicts that arise from the close personal ties among citizens and from the fact that the part-time prosecutor also serves as a private attorney for many local citizens.

> Conflicts also arise in the district attorney's staff, whose members all have outside law practices. A lawyer must abide by attorney-client confidentiality rules and cannot, in a later case, even appear to use that knowledge against a former client. . . . Once, Richard Brown, an assistant prosecutor who has two other law jobs to make ends meet, was asked by a client whether he could get more money from an insurance company because his car had burned. Shortly thereafter, the district attorney's office charged the man with arson and insurance fraud in connection with the car. A judge had to appoint a special prosecutor from the criminal defense bar. (Hoffman, 1996, p. A16)

A similar picture is painted by Maroules (1998) in a preliminary report of his study of 26 rural prosecutors in Illinois, each of whom practiced in a county of fewer than 21,000 people and none of whom had an assistant or an investigator. Maroules observed that:

> Prosecutors noted the tendency of residents to view the state's attorney as their private lawyer. They spoke of being stopped or called at all hours of the day—at work, on the street, or at home—by people wanting to discuss their speeding tickets, DUIs, probate matters, rumors about drugs, and other issues. They described some of the complex relationships involved in being state's attorney, an elected politician, and a lawyer in private practice (and for some, a small business owner as well) simultaneously. Their descriptions of conversations they have had with people charged with crimes makes it clear that they are as concerned for the person as much as they are the case. In sharp juxtaposition to what one would find in more populous counties, these prosecutors indicate that they rarely recuse themselves from cases when they have a personal relationship with an individual (an acquaintance, friend, or even family member) charged with a crime. (p. 15)

The prosecutors included in the Maroules study also indicated concerns about the impact of some sentencing laws, including mandatory minimums and mandatory community service. There were concerns that such laws required resources the county did not have and closed the door to alternative sentences that would mete out justice while also operating within the limited budget of the county.

Our own data gathering did not focus on prosecutors in particular. However, during the course of our study we had occasion to view a trial of a man with antigovernment sentiments who was stopped for having no license plates on his car and then was found to have no driver's license and to be carrying a concealed weapon. The man was a lifelong resident of the area, as was the prosecutor. Jury selection was a problem because so many people knew both the prosecutor and the defendant. For example, one juror told the judge that he knew the State's Attorney on a personal level, another had spoken to a relative of the defendant about the case, another knew the State's Attorney because they were both members of the local hospital board, one juror knew the State's Attorney as a neighbor, another personally knew both the defendant and his parents, another juror knew both the state trooper and her family, and another juror knew one of the witnesses as a fellow employee. One woman revealed that she knew the State's Attorney, the defendant, the defendant's parents, and the three witnesses. Further, she revealed that her husband was a retired state trooper. She was called before the bench with the prosecutor to be questioned about her ability to be a neutral juror. When asked how she would assess any information given her by the prosecutor, she put her hand on the prosecutor's shoulder and said, "Now Kevin, I've known you all of your life and I know that you would *never* lie to me." Eventually, four potential jurors were excused and the remaining twelve formed the jury panel.

Beyond the issues raised by the social setting, rural prosecutors often must work with limited resources. This can influence their ability to pay for laboratory analyses, the use of experts, and the labor of investigators. The problem is illustrated in a 1998 case in Jasper, Texas, a rural community in which three white men bound a black man and then dragged him to death behind their pickup truck. The prosecutor was interested in pursuing the death penalty in this murder and another that happened at about the same time. The problem, however, was that the expense of pursuing these cases had the potential to cost more than 15 times the annual budget for his office, and possibly more than the entire county had taken in from taxes in the previous year (Fields & Parker, 1998).

As is true of police, the rural setting shapes the environment in which prosecutors work, and that setting has the potential to make his or her job more personal and satisfying. At the same time, it can make the job immensely complicated.

Rural Courts

The rural setting also shapes the operation of courts. Going as far back as Wiers's 1939 study of juvenile court cases, a number of researchers have compared the operation of rural and urban courts. Wiers found the crime rate was lower in rural areas and that courts more often handled cases informally. More recently, Austin (1981) found that social background factors were more important in rural criminal courts, whereas urban courts were more legalistic and formal. In his analysis of juvenile justice in Minnesota, Feld (1991) observed:

> Urban courts operate in communities with more disrupted families, more racially heterogeneous populations and less residential stability, all of which provide fewer mechanisms for informal social control. . . . Accordingly, urban counties place greater emphasis on formal, rather than informal, mechanisms of social control. (pp. 206–207)

In another study, Feld (1993) identified some of the differences between rural and urban juvenile courts, and suggested how those differences influenced the handling of juvenile offenders:

> Urban courts appear to cast a broader, more inclusive net of control that encompasses proportionally more and younger youths than do

suburban or rural courts. There also appears to be a relationship between social structure, procedural formality, and severity of sanctions. The more formal, urban courts hold larger proportions of youths in pretrial detention and sentence similarly charged offenders more severely than do the suburban or rural courts. (pp. 158–159)

Others have not only considered the structure of rural courts but have compared the sentencing practices of rural and urban courts. Hagan (1977) found that urban courts were more bureaucratized, had heavier caseloads, and had larger, better-trained staff. Hagan also found that the less formal nature of rural courts accounted for the harsher treatment of minorities in rural courts. Myers and Talarico (1986) concluded that simple rural-urban distinctions in sentencing were too simplistic. For example, urban courts were more likely to sentence rapists to prison, though when rural judges used prison they gave longer sentences. They also suggest that using an official label for a crime (such as homicide) may mask important rural-urban differences in the nature of the offense.

In her study of rural courts, Golden (1981) also emphasized how activities which appear similar on the surface may have very different meanings in rural and urban courts. She gives the example of plea bargaining, which is common in both urban and rural courts but is used very differently in each. In busy urban courts, plea bargaining is used to expedite case processing, whereas in rural courts plea bargaining may more often be the result of "informal personal interaction between the functionaries in the system, as well as their proximity and familiarity" (p. 41).

In rural areas, this close professional network extends beyond lawyers and judges to include most actors in the justice system. The number of actors in rural justice systems is small, and their interactions are frequent and expected to be long-term. As Fahnestock (1991) notes:

> Over half of the rural counties in the United States rely on part-time prosecutors. The active bar often consists of a dozen or fewer members, including the prosecutor and the attorney(s) who represent local government. Often, there are five or fewer sheriff's deputies and a single probation officer, and each is known to the judge. The clerk of the court's staff frequently numbers two or three. In short, fewer than 30 people routinely work together, a group about the size of a small family reunion. (p. 14)

The extent to which these close working relationships can shape the operation of the justice system in rural areas is well illustrated by a judge who commented that he was hesitant to find defendants not guilty because that "would be like saying the sheriff lied" (Fahnestock, 1991, p. 19).

In addition to these professional networks, rural justice professionals may be strongly connected to their rural communities through long-standing social and family networks, some of which span generations:

> The small scale of rural communities results in a web of inter-relationships among justice system workers and the community at large. The defendant may be the judge's mother's hired hand. The plaintiff may attend the judge's church or be his or her daughter's Little League coach. The prosecutor may be the judge's former law partner. Rural judges cannot recuse themselves every time they know someone involved in a case. Indeed, many rural judges recuse themselves only when they have witnessed the alleged offense or they have a direct interest in the matter before them. (Fahnestock, 1991, p. 14)

Under these conditions it becomes nearly impossible for criminal justice officials to separate their social and professional lives. Thus, it has been observed that judges in rural areas have no truly private lives, similar to the condition we noted earlier regarding rural police:

> Unlike the urban judge, the rural judge has no anonymity. Whether eating out, grocery shopping, seeing a movie with the family, playing golf, or walking down the street, the rural judge is often scrutinized. Whatever the rural judge does outside the court reflects on the judicial office. (Dilweg, 1991, p. 28)

> Rural judges are always accessible, so they always must be "on." They cannot run out for milk or gas up the car without an awareness of their judicial role. . . . Nearly every rural judge has stories about encountering the mother of someone they have just sent to prison. (Fahnestock, 1991, p. 65)

Because they are highly visible as both citizens and officials, the professional, community, and family roles of rural justice officials sometimes collide. As one judge recounted:

> You know, I had to sentence my own son to prison. When he got arrested, I thought about recusing myself. But then I thought about how it would look to the community. Folks would say, "He can sentence other people's sons to jail, but he won't send his own." So I stayed on the case. I took his plea and gave him a stiff sentence. It was the hardest thing I've ever done, but it was the right thing to do for the court. (as quoted in Fahnestock, 1991, p. 13)

Fahnestock and Geiger (1993) argue that rural and urban courts function differently and that assessing them may require different criteria. While urban courts may emphasize speed and procedural correctness, rural courts are more focused on using the court as a forum to solve problems. As they have observed:

> To rural judges, parties are not just docket numbers and fact patterns. They are known individuals, with families and problems, whose actions are viewed in the context of community values. At their best, rural judges can fashion responsive, tailored solutions that address the actual needs of defendants, victims, and litigants. (p. 258)

> Therefore, rural courts regard movement of the entire caseload as less important than their ability to deal with any one case in a way that satisfies the interested parties and the community. (p. 262)

The picture of law that emerges suggests important points of difference between urban and rural areas. Like rural police, rural courts are compelled to be more responsive to the local community. Urban courts are more likely to focus on following proper procedures and on the processing of cases. In contrast, rural courts are more likely to focus on outcomes—i.e., given what is known about the offender, the victim, and the community, what is the most just disposition of a case? For officials in urban courts, determining whether "justice" has been served requires focusing on the process, whereas in rural courts "justice" is more likely to be measured by looking at outcomes.

Probation

Although technically part of court services, probation is sufficiently different from trial and other court proceedings that it merits a separate discussion. Probation also merits discussion because of the number of offenders it includes. There are two and a half times as many people on probation as in prison, making probation the most popular disposition among sentencing judges. In 1993 alone, more than 1.4 million adult felons entered probation (Snell, 1995).

Considering its frequent use as a disposition, probation has been understudied. At its inception in 1841, probation was based on the idea of both monitoring offenders released into the community and linking offenders with community resources, such as education, job training, and substance abuse counseling. In recent years, probation work increasingly has come to emphasize offender monitoring and rule enforcement rather than providing treatment or services for the offender (see Crank, 1996).

While probation in general has been understudied, research on rural probation is almost nonexistent. For rural probation officers emphasizing enforcement, one might expect the issues they face to be similar to those facing rural police. For rural probation officers emphasizing treatment one might expect a variety of community issues to be important, including the availability of services, the distance to clients, and the close social connections between rural clients and other citizens in the community. It is also possible that rural probation officers express a greater commitment to treatment and service to clients than do urban officers. All of these are reasonable speculations, but each lacks supportive empirical research.

Ellsworth and Weisheit (1997) compared metropolitan and non-metropolitan probation admissions on a variety of factors. They found that admission rates were 50 percent higher in nonmetropolitan counties than in metropolitan counties (see Figure 15) and that nonmetropolitan admissions were more likely to be for misdemeanors than were metropolitan admissions. In addition, nonmetropolitan admissions were generally younger, with fewer prior arrests but more prior probations than was true for metropolitan admissions. Unfortunately, using only probation admissions data, it was not possible to determine if these observed differences were the result of differences in probation practices, differences at earlier stages of the process that filtered the cases going to probation, or some combination of the two. Their research provides an empirical starting point for comparing rural and urban probation practices.

Kuhn (1995), a federal probation officer who grew up in Appalachia, surveyed federal probation officers in the region for their perceptions of the unique problems and concerns of officers and clients in Appalachia. His observations, and the comments of responding probation officers, were consistent with many of the ideas of rural culture discussed in chapter 1 about the wariness toward outsiders, mistrust of government, and the informal nature of rural life. As he noted:

> Having grown up in Appalachia, this writer recalls the most scathing insult that could be levied upon someone was to be called "nosey." With a three-century tradition of having few close neighbors and keeping everything "in the family," Appalachians often see periodic home visits by well-dressed probation officers who ask prying questions as unjust additional punishment. . . . Like the Whiskey Rebellion and the Battle of Blair Mountain, Federal supervision is viewed as another example of exploitative intrusion from Washington. (pp. 4–5)

Figure 15. Monthly Probation Admissions

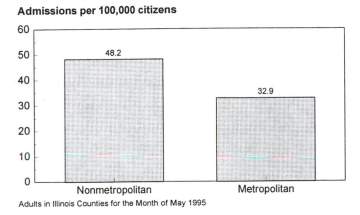

Admissions per 100,000 citizens

Adults in Illinois Counties for the Month of May 1995

Appalachian culture also prescribes subservient roles for women. This can present problems when the probation officer is a woman supervising a male offender. As one female officer noted:

> Some simply cannot adjust to a female probation officer being an authority figure and may attempt intimidation. Some may be unable to develop adequate communication with female officers because living a socially isolated life has made them extremely shy. . . . Due to his shyness, a male offender may let his wife "do all the talking" to the probation officer. (as cited in Kuhn, 1995, p. 5)

Kuhn also noted that officers who were too formal and business-like in their demeanor were seen as arrogant and cold by the residents. One officer listed his first two rules for probation work in Appalachia as: "Never wear a tie" and "Get to know the postmasters. They know where everyone lives." Once an officer has been accepted by the offender and the offender's family, new problems arise from this familiarity (1995, p. 5):

> The greatest challenge in supervising some offenders is finding a diplomatic method of leaving without a mess of pole beans, a piece of fruitcake, some four o'clock seeds, and a puppy. Anyone who refuses to sit down (regardless of furniture cleanliness) and have a cup of coffee risks that scathing Appalachian indictment: They think "they're too good" to sit down in my home (p. 4). . . . One officer relates that he politely declined a bag of fresh vegetables from an offender's garden only to find the bag tucked away on the back floorboard of his vehicle after he left. (p. 7)

Kuhn also commented on the importance of firearms to Appalachian residents and the perceived severity of laws that prohibit gun ownership by misdemeanants while on probation and permanently prohibit guns for those convicted of felonies. One of his responding officers noted: "A lot of my people would rather spend a couple of years more in jail than give up hunting, if they had that option" (p. 7).

Taken together, the work of Ellsworth and Weisheit (1997) and Kuhn (1995) only scratch the surface of what is to be learned about rural probation. Ellsworth and Weisheit's work is based on official records and is thus ill suited to an understanding of social processes. Kuhn's work is focused on a very particular rural population, one might even say a population with the most exaggerated of rural characteristics. Both studies suggest that probation work in rural areas may be very different from that in urban areas, and these differences are worth further examination.

Rural Jails

In addition to the judicial branch, some discussion has focused on rural jails, which are generally the responsibility of local sheriffs. As was true of police departments, research tends to focus on urban jails, but by far the greatest number of facilities are in rural areas. According to the 1988 National Jail Census, two-thirds of the jails in the United States have a daily population of less than 50 inmates (Innes, 1990).

Most observers agree that while urban jails tend to be seriously overcrowded, rural jails are more likely to operate *under* their rated capacity (Klofas, 1990). Mays and Thompson (1988) found that rural jails not only are underutilized but are often older than urban jails and more poorly staffed. Because the fixed costs of running a jail exist apart from whether the cells are full or empty, the per-inmate cost of running jails in rural areas is about double that in urban areas. Further, the lack of staff and programming mean that rural inmates are less often separated by age and are less often supervised, which may partly account for their substantially higher rates of homicide, suicide, and death from illness and natural causes (Mays & Thompson, 1988). In rural areas, the fiscal conservatism which leads to small budgets for jail structures and jail services may create problems for the local sheriff, who can still be held "individually liable for the safety and welfare of inmates" (p. 432).

Mays and Thompson (1988) also argue that sheriffs in rural areas have fewer support services available to process inmates more quickly

and move them out of the jail. For example, limited probation services may leave fewer alternatives to jail for misdemeanants. Also, the rural practice of relying on part-time judges may have a direct impact on the jail. "The result may be less-than-timely dispositions in bail hearings, preliminary hearings, trials, and other functions that require a judge's presence" (p. 431).

The economic plight of some rural areas leads local sheriffs to raise money by housing jail inmates from urban areas or from rural areas that have no jails. Federal authorities also contract with local jails to hold prisoners or to house illegal aliens for the Immigration and Naturalization Service (e.g., *New York Times*, 1993). Housing inmates for other jurisdictions may be a good fiscal move by the sheriff whose jail receives the inmates and a practical necessity for the official who must reduce overcrowding. Little is known, however, about the full implications of this practice. For example, what is the impact of separating the inmate from local connections, both legal and illegal? These connections would include family, friends, employers, and legal counsel. Another issue is the type of inmate sent to these rural jails. Do urban facilities send the most troublesome inmates to rural jails, and does this facilitate the spread of gang influence and other criminal networks, particularly when inmates are shipped across state lines? Other questions arise about the treatment of these inmates. It has been argued earlier in this report that the behavior of rural police is relatively visible, and they are accountable to local citizens. It is possible that these immediate controls over police behavior are substantially reduced when the "client" is not a local citizen—perhaps not even a citizen of the United States. Further, while little is known about rural jails, even less is known about short-term lockups and holding facilities in rural areas.

Prisons

The United States has been in a prison-building boom for over a decade, and most state and federal prisons are built in rural areas. In rural areas with high unemployment and no strong economic base, citizens often lobby hard for new prisons (Patrico, 1992). However, the idea that a rural community would actively seek out a prison is relatively new. As Lamb (1996) has noted:

> A generation ago, rural America found the notion of accepting a prison so repellent that many communities sued their state governments to keep them out. . . . [today] small towns from California to Florida are battling to get a penitentiary in their backyard. In many cases they are offering free land, utilities and cash incentives for the chance to get a slice of what is turning out to be the public works mega-project of the 1990s.

> In jobs and job security, prisons are doing for Main Street U.S.A. what military bases did during the cold war. (p. A1)

The percentage of prison inmates housed in nonmetropolitan counties has steadily increased over time. While only 82 nonmetro prisons were opened in the 1960s and 1970s combined, between 1980 and July of 1991 213 nonmetro prisons were opened. By 1991, 44 percent of all state and federal prisoners were housed in nonmetropolitan counties, even though only 23 percent of the total U.S. population was in those counties (Beale, 1993). In sparsely populated rural counties the impact of the prison can be substantial. As Beale (1993) found:

> The population of new prisons accounted for 5 percent of the national increase in nonmetro population from 1980–90. In nonmetro counties acquiring a prison, the new inmate population amounted to nearly half of all 1980–90 population growth. This growth was supplemented by in-movement of new employees and their families and by retention of local people who would have moved away in the absence of the new jobs and their stimulus to local business. (p.17)

In general, prisons are attractive to the same economically depressed areas that are willing to house other undesirable industries, including power plants, new landfills, hazardous waste facilities, and recovery plants for garbage (Shichor, 1992). These areas have the added advantage of high unemployment and concomitant low labor costs, with little or no union representation. This is particularly appealing for privately run prisons, which operate under fewer employment restrictions than public facilities.

Prison construction and the accompanying employment have had a substantial impact on rural America. The long-term impact of prison construction on economic development and on crime is less clear. A prison may provide stable employment, but the stigma of having prisons may make it more difficult to attract other types of business. ". . . prisons are a weak tool for economic development. They are less likely to foster long-term economic growth or higher incomes than public investments in education, research or basic infrastructure, for example" (Moberg, 1996, p. 17). There is little evidence that siting a prison in an economically depressed rural area is an economic bonanza for the area. At best, prisons appear to halt or slow economic decay. For some communities the prison becomes an economic lifesaver, something that keeps the community from economic ruin but also keeps it from dramatic growth. As one mayor whose community was pursuing a prison observed, "When you're looking at a 22 percent unemployment rate, there are some things you do that you wouldn't do otherwise" (Moberg, 1996, p. 16).

One consequence of building prisons in rural areas is the cultural and racial difference between the predominantly white rural staff and urban minority inmates (Jacobs & Kraft, 1978). Our informal interviews with prison guards suggest that although they frequently come from racially and culturally homogeneous rural communities, they receive little or no training designed to help them understand cultural differences in language, demeanor, and styles of communication between themselves and urban minority inmates.

There is no clear evidence that the threat to citizens from escapes is a serious problem (Shichor, 1992). Nor is there conclusive evidence that a prison brings an increase in local crime, although not all studies are in agreement (Shichor, 1992). Prison visitors do not generally move to the area, nor do inmates generally settle in the area upon their release. Both of these situations may change. It is possible, for example, that gang leaders who run drug operations from their prison cells will have confederates move to the community to facilitate communication with outside operatives. Research in the state of Oregon found that inmates, after release from prison, often remained in the local community for after-care programs, which were required as a condition of parole (Caillier & Versteeg, 1988). In the course of our interviews we have also heard of isolated incidents in which male inmates developed relationships with female staff and remained in the community after their release. The extent to which this is a problem, and whether it is becoming more frequent, is unclear. As the drive to build more prisons continues, and as new prisons are increasingly sited in rural areas, it will become crucial to understand why crime appears to accompany prisons in some communities and not in others.

The lengths to which some rural communities will go to attract a prison is perhaps a testament both to the current economic condition of these areas and to the perceived prospects for other forms of economic development in the future. It is not difficult to see how residents of these communities might come to view illegal gambling, marijuana cultivation, smuggling, or a variety of other consensual crimes as necessary for survival.

Aside from providing jobs, prisons have an impact on the local criminal justice system. In most states felonies that occur within prisons can be prosecuted in the local county. Although little is known about this issue, Eichenthal and Jacobs (1991) have done preliminary work and raise some interesting questions. For example, they found large variations in the willingness of prison officials to pursue prosecutions through the local courts, as well as variations in the willingness of local prosecutors to bring charges. Among the problems associated with investigating prison crimes, they note:

> The police investigators, *especially when they are from rural counties* [italics added], are likely to have special problems in establishing rapport with potential inmate witnesses and in understanding the complex norms and dynamics of the inmate social system, which provide the context for the crime and the key to the investigations. (p. 292)

Eichenthal and Jacobs found that in some areas prison cases accounted for as many as 25 percent of the cases handled by local prosecutors. Thus, the burden on local courts will be raised correspondingly. The cost of handling prison cases can be substantial for these rural communities, even when they are partially reimbursed by the state. These costs include legal defense services for indigent defendants, increased courtroom security, and secure detention facilities during the trial. In addition, "Inmate defendants also may be more litigious and less willing to settle the cases against them quickly. Indeed, for some inmates the opportunity to travel back and forth to court and the county jail may be viewed as a desirable break from the deadening prison routine" (Eichenthal & Jacobs, 1991, p. 294–295). In fact, Eichenthal and Jacobs found that some local prosecutors routinely declined to prosecute prison crimes because of the costs involved. In addition, a locally elected prosecutor has little to gain by spending time on crimes within the local prison if that means less time on local criminal concerns. An exception to this might be cases in which inmates assault guards who are local citizens.

With the hundreds of studies that have been done about prisons it is ironic that so little has been done with respect to exploring the relationship between prisons and the rural communities in which most prisons are located. With no immediate end to widespread prison construction, it is important to have a better understanding of the impact of prisons on the rural communities in which they are built.

Summary

It appears that criminal justice institutions operate differently in rural and urban areas. In particular, rural officials are likely to have much closer working relationships with others in the system and to be less able to separate their professional and private lives. Rural courts are less formal than urban courts, though not always less harsh. Further, the flexibility which accompanies the less formal approach to case processing may also lead to greater racial disparity in sentencing. In general, rural and urban courts may operate under different definitions of "justice," with urban courts more focused on justice as a process and rural courts more focused on justice as an outcome.

Nationally, most jails are small and in rural areas. Unlike urban jails that tend to be overcrowded, rural jails are more likely to operate under their rated capacity. It is not unusual for rural jails to house inmates from other jurisdictions as a way to offset operating costs.

Prisons are usually built in rural areas. Many rural communities, particularly those with high unemployment and a small tax base, actively lobby to attract new prisons. Locating prisons in rural areas sets the stage for conflicts between rural white staff and urban minority inmates. While a prison may not generate a substantial amount of crime in the surrounding community, it may increase the workload of the local justice system in states where felonies committed in the prison are prosecuted locally. The boom in prison construction in rural areas suggests the importance of further studying this area.

There are few aspects of the rural justice system that are thoroughly understood, and there are some, such as probation, about which almost nothing is known. It is clear that rural justice, like rural crime, is shaped by the culture and geography of small towns and rural areas.

Chapter 5

Where Do We Go from Here?

RESEARCHERS INCREASINGLY HAVE COME TO APPRECIATE THE value of comparative studies of crime and justice. Comparing crime and justice in America with that in other countries not only provides a better understanding of our own system but demonstrates a variety of alternatives. It is ironic that such comparative work has exclusively focused on cross-national studies, ignoring the substantial variations in crime and justice within the United States.

This book is the product of more than eight years of study of rural crime and rural policing. Unfortunately, most research on rural crime and justice has lacked a broad conceptual framework within which knowledge can be organized and interpreted. It is often assumed—we believe erroneously—that rural issues are simply small versions of urban issues, that things operate in fundamentally the same way in both settings. Throughout the book we have demonstrated a variety of ways in which urban and rural areas differ regarding both crime and justice. We also argue that the differences follow general patterns. At the same time, we recognize there are respects in which urban and rural areas do share common problems and that there is considerable variation among rural areas. It is difficult to make sense of the patterns of these similarities and differences without adopting a broader framework for their interpretation.

The conceptual framework for this study has organized information around two interconnected themes: geographic isolation and the nature of rural culture. Compared with life in a central city, rural life is characterized by greater levels of *physical distance* among citizens but lower levels of *social distance.* For example, in a rural area it may take longer for the local (volunteer) fire department to respond to a fire, but the firefighters are more likely to know the person whose house or field is burning. Similarly, the urban resident who moves to a rural area may be struck by the juxtaposition of feelings both of being in open countryside and that one is living "under a microscope." These two features, geography and culture, shape the nature of crime and the responses to it. Understanding geography and culture helps explain urban-rural differences in crime and justice, as well as variations across rural areas.

Taken as a whole, our study suggests that research and policies aimed at rural crime problems cannot ignore the unique features of rural culture that shape crime, citizen responses, police activities, and the operation of the courts. At the same time, we would argue that the contrast between rural and urban areas is a fruitful starting point for gaining a better understanding of each.

Broad Issues

Any further pursuit of specific issues related to rural and small-town crime and justice requires that several general issues be considered. First, defining such terms as "rural" and "urban" is no simple task, as we demonstrate in Appendix A. Throughout much of our discussion we have tried to simplify things by making comparisons between the most rural areas and the most urbanized central cities. Comparing the extremes is a useful tool for making our major points. Our approach, however, has also left out some very interesting areas that are neither urban nor rural. Sheriff Buchanan of Yavapai County, Arizona, has referred to these areas as "ruburban." In the early 1900s, Galpin, one of the founding scholars in rural sociology, coined the label "rurban" to designate areas that did not fit neatly into either rural or urban categories (Galpin, 1918). Recent sociologists and demographers seem to prefer the label "exurban" for such areas (Bell, 1992). We intentionally neglected these suburban areas in our current discussion, but they are extremely important. They remind us that communities do not exist only in the simple categories of rural or urban but along a continuum between those two extremes.

A second general issue is to explore differences *among* rural areas. It is *not* true that "sticks is sticks." For example, the culture and crimes of rural Appalachia are quite different from those of southwestern migrant workers or of reservations in the plains states. Thus, research on rural crime problems in one area may have limited applicability in another rural area. One of the challenges for future research will be to distinguish more clearly those features that are common across rural areas from those unique to particular rural locations.

The third and final general issue concerns the development and application of research methods that overcome some of the problems of doing research in rural areas. Both the geography and the culture in rural areas present problems in gaining access to rural subjects. A better understanding of rural culture is clearly essential both to conducting research and to interpreting what is observed. For example, street-corner interviews with urban drug addicts have no counterpart in rural areas, and it is not clear how rural drug users who have not been identified by authorities might be conveniently located by researchers in rural areas. This is a particular problem if the researcher is not from the local community. These general issues form the backdrop or setting for examining more specific problems in rural areas. The challenges facing researchers and policymakers in rural areas and small towns are formidable, but the needs of these areas are real and deserve attention.

The further pursuit of these broad issues, and of the specific topics listed below, is based on the assumption that "rural" is an important aspect of American society and that it will continue to be so for some time. In the 1970s it was thought that rural America was disappearing, being replaced by a mass society. In the 1990s there are still people who speak of rural America in the past tense—as a concern in developing countries but no longer in America. However, to paraphrase Mark Twain, rumors of the death of rural America are greatly exaggerated. Rural America has not disappeared, but it has changed. Agriculture no longer dominates. Rural citizens are primarily employed in service industries and manufacturing, much like urban citizens. Many rural areas have also seen economic growth from tourism and from an influx of retirees. Note, however, that this rural growth does not signal a "return to the way things used to be." The resurgence seems to be more of a renaissance than a revival in many rural areas, reflecting broad contemporary global developments (see Herbers, 1986; Browne et al., 1992).

Rural areas have also been affected by technology that makes it possible for growing numbers of professionals to work at home. It has been argued, for example, that Montana has become the first state in which rural professionals are so numerous that they have a substantial influence on state lawmakers. Accelerating this trend are corporate and government agency policies that encourage telecommuting. This allows employees to live farther from their company offices, sending in their work by mail or electronically. For a growing number of professionals, living and working in a rural area has become a realistic option, an option they may be inclined to choose if they grow tired of the crime, congestion, and pace of urban life.

Finally, recent political shifts have magnified the importance of rural populations and communities. Notably, there has been an increasing emphasis on defining and solving social problems at the local level. This means a shifting of attention away from large metropolitan centers, of which there are relatively few, to smaller municipalities and counties, of which there are many. Rather than being absorbed, rural communities and governments are becoming more autonomous and empowered as political units.

In short, political trends, technology, improved highways, the movement of some industries into rural areas, and a dissatisfaction with urban life all combine to make rural areas increasingly important, albeit in new ways. As rural areas change politically and economically, we can expect corresponding changes in rural crime. Much needs to be done to anticipate the needs and crime-related problems that will face rural America in the next few decades. Anticipating future problems, however, first requires a good understanding of the current state of affairs. Such an understanding is sorely lacking. This book has addressed a variety of issues, but more needs to be done. Many of the issues we included have been given only a superficial treatment—which is as much as the available evidence allowed. Our attention now shifts to some of the issues about which more should be learned.

Special Topics

This study has covered a wide range of issues relating to rural crime and rural justice. As a summary and overview work, however, it simply was not possible to cover any single issue in great depth. Further, most of the issues touched upon in this book have not been adequately studied, leaving much to conjecture. What follows is a list of specific topic areas that merit further study. Some of them were touched on in earlier chapters. Others were not mentioned because there was too little information even for informed speculation. Our listing begins with issues related to crime and then turns to topics more directly related to the operation of criminal justice agencies.

Domestic Violence

We have suggested that while stranger-on-stranger violence is much less frequent in rural areas, violence among intimates is as frequent in rural areas as in cities. However, there is too little research to say much more with any confidence. There are many unanswered questions about rural domestic violence, including both spouse abuse and child abuse. For example: How do the detection of and response to domestic violence differ in rural and urban areas? Do the interpersonal connections among police and citizens in rural areas have an influence on the way in which rural police respond to domestic violence? What are the options for disposing of domestic violence cases in rural areas? How do the resources for victims in rural areas compare with those in urban areas, and what are the problems in service delivery to battered women in rural areas? Are there cultural factors in rural communities that shape the use of violence, the willingness to report, and the manner in which local agencies respond? What about child abuse and neglect in rural communities?

Drugs

When considering the large volume of research on urban drug problems, the paucity of information about rural drugs is striking. Very little is known about drugs in rural areas. It appears that drugs are readily available to rural citizens, but little else is known. For example: How do rural and small-town drug networks differ from urban drug networks? What role do rural areas play in the production and transshipment of drugs that are eventually consumed in urban areas? What is the nature of the drug use problem in rural areas, and what features of the rural environment have an effect on drug treatment? Do police play a greater role in drug prevention programs in rural areas?

Arson

Surprisingly little is known about rural arson. In particular, much more needs to be learned about how the profiles of rural arsonists compared with those of urban arsonists. There is also a paucity of knowledge about variations in the problem of arson across rural areas. In 1996, the country was outraged by the burning of black churches in the South. Upon closer investigation, it was proposed that although race was a factor in some of the burnings, an equally important factor was the physical location of the church. In particular, it appeared that burned churches were frequently in relatively remote rural areas, and the buildings themselves were often left unattended during the week (Fields & Price, 1996). It was also concluded that although the problem was given unprecedented attention, the number of church burnings in 1996 was not very different than in previous years. Having revealed this, the story generally disappeared from public discourse, although the issue of rural arson still has not been addressed.

Timber Theft

Almost nothing is known about timber theft in the United States, although one group cites the former head of the U.S. Forest Service as testifying before Congress that in the national forests timber theft may amount to "as much as $100 million per year and may account for one in ten trees cut within the National Forest System" (Action Alert: Timber Theft Letter, 1997). Considering that only a small percentage of the trees in America grow in the national forests, the overall scope of tree theft may be enormous. As a resource that is being harvested faster than it can be replaced, the value of wood is likely to continue climbing and the incentives for theft will grow accordingly. Unfortunately, most of the information about tree theft appears to be speculation, with little research having been done to measure the nature and extent of the problem.

Gangs and Gang Influences

There appears to be a public concern that urban gangs are moving into rural areas, and we have suggested some of the avenues by which this might happen. However, our observations are highly speculative. As with most other issues, the study of gangs in rural areas is very inadequate. Given that crime and policing are different in rural and urban areas, we might expect differences between urban and rural gang activity. Further, we should expect that effective strategies for responding to gangs in urban areas may need to be modified to fit the rural environment. Unlike the issues of domestic violence or drugs, there are questions about the very existence of gangs in rural areas. Examples of such questions include: Is there a gang problem in rural areas and small towns? What is the nature of the problem? How can it be documented? If there is a problem, what is the appropriate response? How are the problems and solutions different in rural and urban areas? An important first step in exploring the issue of gangs in rural areas is making a distinction between urban-based gang activities that have an impact on rural areas and gang activity that is centered in and directed from rural areas. The first category, which would include such things as drug trafficking, is probably more frequent than the second. At this point, however, neither type is well understood. Our re-analysis of gang survey data suggests that whether a rural area is adjacent to a larger city is an important correlate of gang activity in the rural community. This, however, needs to be verified and further explored.

Crime and Violence in Rural Schools

Following an era of school consolidation, deciding what constitutes a rural school may be more complicated than in the past. However, just as there are differences in the cultures of urban and rural communities, we would expect differences in the environments of rural and urban schools. Examples of questions concerning rural schools would include: Are violence, drugs, and guns a problem in rural schools? What features of the rural environment shape the response to crime and violence in these schools? What impact does school consolidation have on the problem? Are the links between schools and communities different in rural areas, and what are the implications of this for crime prevention?

Crimes Connected to Highways

Highways play a key role in moving people through rural areas and in connecting rural and urban communities. We have already suggested that highways allow rural areas to serve as transshipment points for drugs and may make it easier for gang members to extend their activities into small communities well outside of urban areas. More needs to be known, however. For example: How has the construction of interstate highways influenced crime in rural areas and small towns? Are rest-stop crimes a problem and, if so, what is the role of rural police in dealing with the problem?

Impact of Casinos and Legal Gambling

State-sanctioned gambling has become a fact in most states. It is common to put casinos and riverboats outside of large cities, often in rural areas. The issue becomes particularly complex when the casinos are operated on reservations, where jurisdictional issues can be a problem. Despite the enormous growth of legalized gambling and the extent to which rural areas may be affected, more needs to be known. For example: What is the impact of casinos and riverboats on rural and small-town crime? Gambling establishments generally have good security systems, but what about burglary and theft in surrounding communities? What impact does this crime have on local resources?

Impact of Technology on Crime and the Victimization of Rural Citizens

While we would argue that modern telecommunications have not meant the end of rural culture, such technology has made it easier for criminals to reach out beyond their immediate community. For example: Have such things as satellite communications, improved telephone systems, faxes, and modems made rural citizens more susceptible to fraud and high-tech deceptive practices? How has technology helped in rural crime prevention and calls for assistance?

Environmental Crimes

Rural areas may provide an important setting for crimes against the environment and crimes by environmentalists. There is every reason to believe that issues related to the environment will become more important over time, and this will be particularly true in rural areas where it is more difficult to monitor the dumping of waste and where a variety of groups have an interest in preserving areas in their natural state.

Crime in Areas of Transition

It was noted that where rural communities undergo rapid growth, the crime rate often grows even more quickly. The trend toward building factories in remote rural areas is just one example of how such change can occur almost overnight. Another development has been the increased use of telecommuting, where work can be done at home and sent to the office through fax or modem. In this situation the worker can live almost anywhere, including remote rural areas. Examples of questions to consider would include: What happens to crime when rural areas undergo sudden change, such as building a factory or rapid urban sprawl?

Crime by and the Victimization of Special Populations

These special populations have been generally ignored in discussions of crime in rural areas. Questions about special populations would include: What special services or considerations are required of the criminal justice system when senior citizens begin moving into a rural community in large numbers? What are the issues that arise when populations undergo dramatic seasonal shifts because of tourism? What about the victimization of tourists, for whom returning to testify may prove difficult and expensive? What about migrant workers, who have neither ties to the community nor extensive resources?

Crime by and against Minorities in Rural Areas

Compared with cities, there are relatively few minorities in rural areas. The tendency to equate crime with minority status, particularly in the media, is a distortion of what happens in urban areas, but it may be completely inaccurate in rural areas. Unfortunately, the link between minority status and crime in rural areas has not been carefully explored. The issue does raise a number of questions. For example: Does the low representation of minorities in rural areas change the way they are treated by other citizens and by the criminal justice system? What about crime and justice in those rural areas with relatively large minority populations?

Rednecks, White Trash, and Trailer Trash

Although such groups are an integral part of everyday discourse, they have been little studied and almost nothing is known about their involvement in crime. Documenting these groups and studying their criminality is a conceptual and methodological challenge that needs to be addressed.

Native Americans

Native Americans are among the only minorities more highly represented in rural areas than in large cities. The rise of casinos and the issue of using reservation lands for smuggling goods across the United States-Canadian border are only two of the issues recently gaining national attention. In the course of this study the literature on Native American crime was examined, and a number of people knowledgeable about the issue were interviewed. Despite this effort, we do not feel we have a thorough understanding of the complexities of Indian crime, justice, and culture. For this reason we did not include an extended discussion of Native American issues as they relate to rural crime and justice. Such a discussion is needed, however. Understanding Native American crime issues requires considering not only the rural setting itself, but also complex jurisdictional and sovereignty issues, as well as substantial variation in culture among Indian tribes.

Victim Services

We have seen one brief article describing the problems of resources and distances that influence the provision of victim services in rural areas (Sifferd, 1998). There are also several brief mentions of victim service issues in Websdale's (1998) study of domestic violence in rural Kentucky. Aside from this, little has been done to understand how the rural setting shapes the crime problems for which victim services are needed, and the problems of providing those services in rural areas.

Impact of Prisons on Crime and Justice in Rural Areas

The United States is currently undergoing a prison construction boom. Most of this construction occurs in rural areas. More needs to be known about the impact of this construction on the local community. For example: What is the impact of a prison on the local community's crime rate? What is the impact on the local justice system—particularly the prosecutor and the courts? Are there problems when minority staff are transferred into communities with few minorities?

Getting Training to Rural Police

In the course of the study we repeatedly heard about the problem of getting training to rural police. The cost of training for financially strapped departments is only part of the problem. Where the number of officers in a department is small, sending an officer away for a week or two of training puts a hardship on the officers who remain. In some cases it may mean periods with no local police service for the community. Problems with access to training are compounded in areas where the travelling distance required to get training is long. Are there strategies for dealing with these problems? How can training be modified to incorporate the reality of rural policing, such as single-officer patrols, no immediate backup, and limited resources for storing and maintaining evidence?

Attracting and Retaining Rural Police Officers

While it appears that many officers enjoy working in rural areas, the low salaries and more limited opportunities for training and professional advancement may play a role in the high turnover of rural police. More needs to be known about this issue. For example: What steps can rural and small-town departments take to improve the retention of police officers? Why do some rural departments seem to be training grounds for police who wish to move to larger departments, while other rural departments have a relatively stable work force?

Reserve, Volunteer, and Part-Time Police

It is not unusual for police departments to supplement their full-time sworn officers with part-time, reserve, or even volunteer officers. In rural areas that are short of resources, these individuals may play a more important role than in cities or in wealthier rural areas. There are rural departments in which part-time and reserve officers substantially outnumber full-time sworn officers. Also, some states are increasing the restrictions on who can be hired in this less-than-full-time capacity, and on the training they will be required to receive. Although they may be vital to the delivery of police services in rural communities, these rural officers have not been extensively studied.

Part-Time Departments

In addition to studying part-time officers, research should be directed at departments with no full-time officers. The number of these departments is substantial, and they play an important role in providing police services to sparsely populated areas and small towns.

Handling Juvenile Offenders in Rural Areas

Discussions of juvenile delinquency seldom consider rural delinquency and generally ignore juvenile justice in rural areas. We observed that in many states there are a limited number of juvenile detention centers. For rural police this may mean transporting arrested juveniles to facilities in other counties, often at a considerable distance and at considerable expense to the local community. How does the distance from detention facilities influence the decisions of police? What are the options for handling delinquent juveniles in rural areas? Do rural and small-town police handle juveniles differently than do urban police?

Urban Police Officers Who Begin Working in Rural Areas

It is our observation that some of the rural-urban differences in policing we have reported are most evident to officers who leave urban settings to work in the rural environment. It is also our impression that such a move is relatively common for retiring urban police who view the move as a second career. The adjustment is often difficult for both the officer and the local community. Our observations, however, merit further study. How frequently do urban police begin working in rural environments? How common are the adjustment problems? What characteristics of the officer and of the community help smooth the transition? What can the study of these officers tell us about fundamental differences in rural and urban policing, and how can an understanding of these differences be used to improve policing in both settings?

A Job Task Analysis of Rural Police Work

We have argued that rural and urban policing are fundamentally different, particularly in the day-to-day details. The two settings differ both in the way in which things are done and in what is expected of the officer. That is, "good" police work in rural areas may not be identical to good police work in urban areas. Our study was designed to outline the broad landscape of rural policing but was not designed to provide more empirical measures for comparing rural and urban police activity. Conducting a job task analysis would be a useful next step in better understanding the differences and similarities between rural and urban policing. Precisely how do rural and urban police work differ? What are the implications of these differences for the content of training and the evaluation of police performance?

Evaluating Rural Criminal Justice Agencies

In addition to a job task analysis, there is a pressing need for studies to determine whether the measures we traditionally use to assess the performance of criminal justice officials and agencies are appropriate for rural officials and rural departments. We have argued throughout the book that crime and justice in rural and urban areas are different. This implies, although it is not necessarily true, that it might be necessary to use different criteria for determining a well-run police department and proper police behavior, as examples.

Women and Minorities in Rural Police Work

Nearly all studies of women and minorities in police work have been done in urban areas. Cities have sizeable minority populations and police forces large enough for there to be several women and minority officers working in the same department. Thus, women in an urban department will generally have other women in the department with whom they can discuss problems and decide upon solutions. However, in small rural departments a woman or a minority might well have no other women or minorities in the department with whom they can socialize. If policing is considered a traditionally male occupation, and rural areas are more conservative generally than are cities, then the adjustment of women in rural police work may be particularly difficult. A logical starting point is to study whether women and minority police in rural areas are doubly isolated—both from citizens and from other women/minorities in the department with whom they can socialize.

Explaining the High Rate of Felonious Killings of Rural Police

One of the more disturbing findings of this study was the relatively high rate of felonious killings of rural police. The finding was also unexpected, given what is known about the more positive relationships between rural police and the citizens they serve. Thus, a series of questions are raised: Why is the felonious killing of police so much higher in rural and suburban areas than in central cities? Is it because of police practices or because of the kinds of people with whom the police must

deal—or a combination of the two? What can be done to lower the felonious killing rates in rural and suburban areas?

Killings by Rural Police

A companion question to that about the killing *of* rural police is the
issue of killing *by* rural police. Our analysis of FBI data in chapter 3 suggests this is a serious problem that has not been addressed in the
research. As with other rural issues, variations across rural areas is an
important place to begin such research.

Role of Rural Police in Crime Prevention

It is our impression that rural police are more oriented to crime prevention than are urban police. This is an issue that merits further empirical
study. It would be useful, for example, to compare the role of DARE programs in rural police departments with those same programs in urban
departments. Given their greater ties to their communities, do rural and
small-town police play a greater role in crime prevention? Does their
informal knowledge of much of the citizenry help them identify problems in their earliest stages?

Innovative Uses of Technology by Rural Police

There have been recent efforts to make greater use of technology across
all aspects of the criminal justice system. It is also possible that some of
the problems faced by rural police can be addressed with developing
technologies. For example, in many parts of the rural West it is difficult
for individual officers to maintain radio contact with the local department in all parts of their patrol area. Satellite communication systems
may reduce such problems and may soon be affordable for small
departments. The availability of less expensive computers, the expansion of communication capabilities, and similar advances in technology
may have a considerable impact on rural police. Information sharing,
remote site training, and improved communications across large jurisdictions are examples of how technology may benefit small departments. Further, the falling prices of this technology make it within the
reach of rural departments more than ever. What are some of the most
innovative uses of new technology by rural departments, and what can
be done to make them more widely available?

Rural Resource Sharing

In rural areas with low tax bases and scarce resources, departments often must do more with less. One way to do this is to share resources. For example, local pilots or the local civil air patrol may donate time for aerial searches or surveillance. Given their closer ties to the community, resource sharing may be more easily accomplished in rural areas than in cities, but more needs to be learned about rural resource sharing. It has also been our observation that in rural areas there is often a greater interdependence between municipal departments and sheriffs' offices. For example, the sheriff's office will provide coverage when a municipal department cannot provide twenty-four-hour coverage. We have also observed a tendency in some areas for small towns to eliminate their municipal department and contract with the county sheriff for routine patrol. Finally, in many rural counties small municipal departments may rely on the sheriff for investigations, criminalistics, and even dispatch. Questions about resource sharing include: What are some innovative examples of resource sharing that seem to work particularly well for rural police? What is the best way to make other rural departments aware of these innovative ideas? Can the state or federal government play a role in linking rural departments with resource providers?

Community Policing in Rural Areas

We have argued that much of what is already done in rural areas is consistent with what has been called community policing. Rural areas raise interesting questions in this regard. For example: Sheriffs provide some of the best examples of community policing, but how does the concept of community fit across a countywide jurisdiction? How can a further study of rural policing help outline the benefits and limits of community policing? What aspects of the rural police style are transferrable to urban areas, and which are unique to the rural setting? Conversely, might there be aspects of community policing in urban areas that make little sense in rural communities? For example, there are roads in rural Wyoming that are so remote that even the FM radio band is empty. In such settings the idea of foot patrol or patrol on bicycles is absurd.

Working Relationships among Rural Justice Agencies

From our interviews it appears that rural police, courts, and other agencies work together more closely than in urban areas. Research is needed to document the extent to which this is true and to explain variations from one rural area to the next. For example, it may be that adopting a unified court system reduces some of the personal familiarity between judges and others in the system. How does this influence the handling of cases and the quality of justice meted out?

Local, State, and Federal Cooperation

While the relationship between local and state or federal authorities is strained in some rural areas, there are jurisdictions in which local authorities speak highly of state and federal agents. Why are working relationships among local, state, and federal authorities more positive in some rural areas than in others? How does the trend toward defining an increasing number of crimes as federal offenses affect crime and justice in rural areas? From a local perspective, are there offenses for which federal penalties are helpful, and are there offenses for which this trend is counterproductive?

This listing of issues that merit further study was not intended to be exhaustive but to demonstrate the range of topics about which more needs to be learned and to encourage further research. These issues range from applied policy questions to more academic concerns. All, however, can fill in important gaps in our understanding of rural crime.

Summary

This text has outlined a broad framework for understanding rural crime and rural justice. Within this framework a variety of issues merit further consideration. Rural areas are undergoing changes, and as they change it is likely that rural crime will change too. The study of rural crime illustrates a point to which many researchers pay lip service but promptly forget in practice: *The nature and extent of crime is shaped by its context.* Responding to rural crime and understanding rural justice requires an understanding of the physical and social features of the rural environment, as well as an appreciation of how these features vary *among* rural areas. Rural crime and justice are not esoteric subjects of interest to a limited audience. To the contrary, what can be learned about the relationship among crime, geography, and culture in the rural setting has implications for crime and justice elsewhere.

Appendix A

What Is Rural?

UNDERSTANDING WHAT IS MEANT BY THE TERM "RURAL" IS essential to the study of rural and small-town crime and justice. Like such concepts as "truth," "beauty," or "justice," everyone knows the term rural, but no one can define the term very precisely. As one sheriff told us, "Rural is like pornography, I can't precisely define it but I know it when I see it." As with the term pornography, our difficulty in precisely defining the term rural may complicate our efforts at applying it or measuring it in specific cases, but it does not render the term useless. While precise definition may be difficult, there is something to the idea of "rural" that distinguishes it in intuitively and sociologically important ways from what is called "urban." Further, this distinction has important implications for understanding the social dynamics of crime and for developing informed criminal justice policies that apply to a variety of settings.

How the term rural is defined is important for three reasons. First, in *conceptual* terms, our definition specifies exactly what we are studying and indicates the terms by which we are thinking about it. Thus, definition serves to clarify the content and scope of our ideas. Second, in *operational* terms our definition of rural determines how rural events and characteristics are measured and empirically counted. Thus, it determines the kind of data we collect on rural crime and directly shapes the findings we can reach with these data. Finally, the way rural is defined has a *practical* impact on the way in which communities, locations, and people are targeted by policies addressing rural crime issues, as well as what kinds of interventions are relevant for them. Thus, it can shape the crime control policies developed from our research.

Despite its apparent simplicity in commonsense terms, there is nothing mechanical or straightforward about developing a systematic working definition of rural. Indeed, rural sociologists have struggled for decades (without much resolution) with how to define rural adequately in social scientific terms. The following discussion initially outlines some of the basic conceptual questions involved in specifying what rural means. Next, it moves to a discussion of how rural can be measured empirically. Finally, we consider some of the key analytical issues regarding how the rural variable might be used to expand our knowledge of crime and policing in different areas.

Conceptual Issues

While "rural" is commonly treated as a single unitary idea—both in research and in everyday conversations—careful reviews have pointed out its multidimensional nature (Bealer, Willits, & Kuvlesky, 1965; Deavers, 1992; Miller & Luloff, 1981; Sjoberg, 1964). Most uses of the term rural reflect a mixture of different ways in which a place (or a group of people) can be described as distinctively rural. Drawing on the discussion of Bealer, Willits, and Kuvlesky (1965), we can identify at least four basic dimensions of meaning: (1) demographic, (2) economic (or occupational), (3) social structural, and (4) cultural.

Demographic

The most obvious sense of what rural means is the demographic dimension, referring simply to how many people are concentrated in an area, along with where they are located (Wilkinson, 1991). Rural means areas of sparse populations, either in the small total number of people who live there or in their low concentration (i.e., ratio of people to available space). A related but distinct idea reflects concerns about distance as well as density—i.e., rural places are also geographically isolated, physically removed from other population areas and from major urban centers. For example, outlying less densely populated areas of counties that contain a large city often are not counted as really rural (even though they have many of the social attributes) because they are near urban populations. Instead, they are variously labeled as "metropolitan fringe," "rurban" (Galpin, 1918; Ball, 1977), or "exurban" (Bell, 1992) areas.

A further element in the demographic meaning of rural is location outside the political boundaries of an urban area. People and places located inside the city limits (or other formally designated municipal boundaries) are counted as urban, while everyone and everything located outside the city limits is labeled rural. The issue here is not population size or density, but geopolitical location relative to official urban boundary designations. A community may have few people (e.g., a small town of 2,600 persons) yet not be considered rural, because it is within an officially incorporated or census-designated area. Defining rural in demographic terms depicts it as a numerical, physical attribute of a place or a population, referring only to where people live and how many of them live there—not to who they are or what they do. While this has the virtue of being objective, concrete, and quantitative, strictly demographic definitions are often criticized for missing the true meanings of rural and urban (e.g., Beale, 1984; Herbers, 1986; Jacob & Luloff, 1995).

Economic

Beyond mere demographics, the idea of rural also has an economic meaning. It traditionally implies something about how the people in the area make a living. We stereotypically think of rural as a place where people tend to "live off the land"—i.e., are close to nature and depend directly on the exploitation of natural resources. In its traditional meaning, rural has been treated as a synonym for agricultural—i.e., an area where farming is done, in which people are mostly farmers. Note that this defines rural in occupational terms, applying it to less technologically developed communities where the economy is simple, nonindustrial, and labor intensive. While this obviously refers to farming, it might also include mining, fishing, logging, or hunting as primary subsistence activities.

While the identification with farming remains a central part of the common meaning of rural, technological and economic developments during this century have radically changed the role of agriculture in the U.S. economy (Browne, et al., 1992; Castle, 1995). Today farming ranks well behind manufacturing and service-provision as a source of employment and income in the rural areas. Less than 10 percent of the rural labor force is significantly involved in farming, and less than 10 percent of the rural population actually lives on farms. Thus, the common definition of rural (which simply equates it with farming) needs to be modified to remain relevant to contemporary conditions.

Rural as an economic classification also may be defined by the functional simplicity of an area—i.e., a single common industry within the community (in which most residents are engaged), resulting in a simple division of labor and a low degree of economic specialization. Here rural—as synonymous with economic simplicity—implies a lack of variety in the ways by which people make a living and a low degree of functional differentiation in the community's social structure.

Social Structure

Another common meaning of rural includes social structural consider-ations that reflect the distinctive character of social life and social order in rural communities. In social interactional terms, the defining attributes of rural life are intimacy, informality, and homogeneity. In social structural terms, the rural life is defined by smaller but denser networks of social bonds. By virtue of the smaller numbers of people in rural settings, social connections are more immediate (face-to-face), more intense or primary (often based on kinship ties), and more com-plete (based on knowledge of personal biographies rather than formal role positions). Because of the greater familiarity, rural social order is maintained through informal mechanisms of social control (based on kinship and personal acquaintance) rather than through formal mech-anisms and legal institutions. In addition, rural areas are characterized by a lack of social resources commonly associated with large population centers—e.g., mass transportation, central markets or exchanges, spe-cialized medical facilities, newspapers, airports, television stations, museums, zoos, social services.

Cultural

The fourth component of the common meaning of rural is cultural, referring to distinctive sets of attitudes, beliefs, values, knowledge sys-tems, and behavioral habits that characterize the people living in rural areas. Rural culture "has been pictured as traditional, slow to change, provincial, and fatalistic" (Bealer, Willits & Kuvlesky, 1965, p. 264). Rural culture has also been characterized as stable but relatively intol-erant of diversity and as relatively unaccepting of outsiders. In short, rural is interpreted in terms of a distinctive worldview, a way of thinking that is different from what is common among urban dwellers. Viewing rural as a cultural phenomenon that goes beyond geographic or demo-graphic conditions has much intuitive appeal. This is expressed in the commonsense wisdom, "You can take the boy out of the country but you can't take the country out of the boy." However, defining rural in cultural terms complicates the attempt to do systematic research on rural events. First, it makes the idea of rural rather subjective and difficult to study objectively, since the idea of culture is notoriously difficult to quantify. Moreover, it limits by definition issues that might otherwise be regarded as matters for empirical investigation—e.g., variations in values, outlooks, attitudes, or lifestyles across rural and urban areas. That is, while considerable disagreement exists about whether distinctive rural-urban cultural differences still exist in modern societies as a result of the pervasive influences of mass communication and transportation, this should remain an empirical question rather than a definitional mandate.

Conceptualization of "Rural"

Given the many dimensions of rural and the confusion this can produce, what is the correct definition of the term? Unfortunately, there is no one correct definition of rural. Our aim is not to prescribe a correct meaning but to outline the forms of meaning already in use and to suggest how these may be compared. Some researchers (e.g., Deavers, 1992; Wilkinson, 1991) favor restricting the meaning of rural to a single dimension, almost always demographic and based on Census Bureau categories. This approach seems desirable because it is more objective, quantitative, analytically straightforward, and readily measured through available census data. It also seems most conceptually basic and straightforward. The difficulty with a simple demographic notion is that for most people, rural means much more than statistical population sizes or densities. The alternative is to define rural as a broad, multifaceted umbrella term referring to an array of different attributes, variables, and dimensions that, while historically correlated, cannot be meaningfully reduced to a single category or number. In a broad summary review such as this, we are utilizing the latter approach to be as inclusive as possible. We suggest that whatever approach is selected, an important requirement is that researchers spell out clearly how rural is defined in their particular study, along with indicating how this relates to the data being collected and analyzed.

Besides the problem of multiple content dimensions, several additional analytical issues greatly affect how rural is defined and studied. One issue is whether rural is to be defined in *positive* versus *negative* terms. A positive definition of rural defines it by the *presence* of certain characteristics or conditions that are viewed as distinctively rural, such as farming as a major economic activity or low population density. Positive definitions require that we specify the essential features of what counts as rural, providing for some specific variations within the category. A negative definition of rural defines it implicitly by the *absence* of certain conditions or community attributes that are viewed as distinctively urban. In these terms, rural is defined by default as not-urban—

i.e., whatever remains after urban areas have been designated. Negative definitions, because they define rural implicitly and diffusely (as merely the miscellaneous remainder of urban classification), inherently provide for little differentiation among the diversity of rural places. Criminological research in recent decades has relied heavily on such negative definitions of rural areas reflecting: (a) a singular preoccupation with urban problems of crime and policing, and (b) a strong reliance on census-based data. Strictly speaking, such definitions of rural by subtraction have little meaningful content of their own, constituting an amorphous "leftovers" category that is difficult to interpret and for which effective policy development will be impossible.

Moreover, the meaning of rural in a negative definition varies implicitly but invisibly according to how "urban" categories are defined and measured. For example, the Census Bureau makes a distinction between *urban* places (referring to incorporated or Census-designated settlements of at least 2,500 population) and *metropolitan* areas (referring to counties or clusters of counties that contain at least 100,000 population and an urban center with at least 50,000 population). Note that while urban and metropolitan seem like synonyms, they have different referents. Urban may refer to small towns, while metropolitan refers to large counties. Rural sometimes is negatively defined as not-urban while in other instances as not-metropolitan, even though these are not all equivalent. Which negative definition is used depends on what kind of data (municipal or county-level) are available for an analysis. Thus, what are seemingly equivalent definitions may lead to the same community being classified and counted as rural in one data set but as nonrural in another.

Another issue is whether rural should be conceptualized in *relative* terms or in *absolute* terms. Defining rural in terms of farming activity tends to ascribe to it a fixed, objective character. Alternatively, many descriptions of rural define its content as relative to specific social and historical contexts. This especially applies when rural is defined by contrast to urban areas, where whether an area is counted as rural depends on what is considered urban in that time and place. For example, in 1790 there were only eight cities in the United States with more than 5,000 people, and the largest city (Philadelphia) had only 42,000 people. What was considered a large city in 1790 would hardly be termed that today. Indeed, many recent studies (which count "small towns and cities" as part of the rural landscape) define rural to include communities of 5,000 to 50,000 people. The relativity may be based on social structural or cultural considerations, as may be seen when comparing the meaning of rural in different regions of the country. Many "rural" areas of Delaware and New Jersey would be considered urban by residents of Wyoming or Montana. We note that even in the last few decades, the Census Bureau has considerably modified its own definitions of what is an urban place and what counts as a metropolitan county. As a result many previously rural locations have been officially transformed into urban or metropolitan areas, even though their population sizes or social resources did not change appreciably, because Census Bureau definitions were changed.

Yet another issue in determining what rural means is the level of description or reference. To what kinds of things does the term rural meaningfully apply? In simplest terms, rural may be used to characterize single residences or persons, as in much survey research that is administered by individual interviews or household questionnaires. Usually, however, rural has a locational rather than personal meaning; it refers to a place rather than an individual. The most basic level is a focus on rural simply as all *unincorporated areas*, i.e., areas outside of city limits. At a second level, rural can refer to *communities*, including not only incorporated municipalities but also villages and towns that are not viewed as fully urbanized. Third, for some purposes it is useful to focus on rural *counties*. Where rural is defined demographically as nonmetropolitan, this automatically applies to the county level, since the census category of metropolitan applies to county units. Usually, analysis at this level involves distinguishing rural (nonmetro) counties from urban (metro-central) and suburban (metro-fringe) counties. An unacknowledged complicating factor is that sizes of counties as geographic units of analysis vary tremendously between eastern and western states—e.g., some western counties are larger than some entire eastern states. Fourth, it is possible to aggregate even further and focus on rural states, in which the entire state is classified as either rural or nonrural, based on population characteristics (population density or percentage in urban places) or economic factors (importance of farming, mining, and fishing within the state's economy). Finally, some research is focused on rural *countries*, where the category rural applies to the entire society or nation. This societal level is not a concern in most studies, particularly those we considered for this review which have a distinctly local focus, but it does apply to cross-cultural or international research aimed at assessing the social effects of large-scale economic and political development.

Each of these levels has been used when referring to the idea of rural. The meaning of rural, along with its implications for understanding rural crime and criminal justice, are very different across these levels. As Farmer, Luloff, Ilvento, and Dixon (1992) note, data collected at different levels of aggregation (e.g., local municipalities vs. counties vs. states) do not necessarily yield the same findings regarding the social characteristics of rural areas, especially as analyses become complex and multivariate.

Another conceptual issue in specifying what rural means is how to depict the distinction between rural and urban—as qualitative or quantitative. Is rural-urban a dichotomy describing two discrete categories of social settings with distinctly different social dynamics? This corresponds to most discussions of the rural ideas in recent policy-focused research, since policy decisions tend to be structured in terms of either-or alternatives. Even the Census Bureau, which generally favors quantitative numerical descriptions, defines rural in dichotomous terms by either an urban/not-urban or a metro/nonmetro categorization. Most discussions of the rural-urban distinction (particularly those relying on intuitive, commonsense ideas about what is rural) invariably are phrased in such discrete, dichotomous terms. In contrast, can rural-urban more reasonably be viewed as a continuum that varies between rural and urban as polar extremes with lots of intermediate gradations representing varying degrees of rurality? This latter possibility corresponds to social science descriptions where rurality and urbanism are treated as more complex dimensions of community organization. In the latter research, questions about the rural-urban distinction are replaced by analyses of the rural-urban continuum.

Any description of rural that involves translating numbers into categories raises additional questions: How many categories are needed to capture the real distinction between rural and urban—two (rural and urban); three (rural, urban, suburban); four (rural-farm, rural-nonfarm, urban, suburban); or more (rural-open country, rural-village, nonmetropolitan small city, metropolitan fringe, metropolitan center)? The number chosen seems arbitrary and debatable, reflecting a compromise between convenience (i.e., what kinds of data are available) and validity (what kinds of research or policy questions are being asked) rather than naturally occurring divisions.

The discussion above has focused on the variety of complications that enter into any effort to clarify what we mean by rural. Given these complications and the absence of any single standard, it is not surprising that researchers have adopted a wide range of strategies for measuring the concept. Our focus now shifts to a discussion of these strategies to illustrate some of the options available for measuring the concept.

Measurement Issues

Beyond the problem of spelling out what rural means conceptually is the task of measuring it. While most people have a strong and conceptually rich sense of what "rural" means, when it comes to measuring the idea and collecting data, practical constraints often require that the content of "rural" be greatly narrowed. As the preceding discussion suggests, the idea of rural can be defined in a variety of ways with widely varying results.

Operational definitions of rural in research on crime and criminal justice have taken several basic approaches. These include measurements: (a) by intuition; (b) by demographic conditions; (c) by occupational characteristics; (d) by composite measures; and (e) by subjective self-ratings. We note initially that the most common operational approach is not to explicitly define rural at all, but to rely on implicit, common intuitive understandings of the term. This presumes that the meaning of rural is so clear cut, familiar, and widely shared that it requires no specification or elaboration. In this approach, cases are chosen for analysis based on prima facie judgments by researchers about their rural character. In our review of 90 studies on rural crime, most (62 percent) gave no explicit (i.e., measurable) definition of the term rural. Moreover, the most widely cited collection of research studies and policy analyses of rural crime (Carter, Phillips, Donnermeyer, & Warschmidt, 1982) includes no operational definition of rural, even though a number of chapters analyze statistical data on "rural" crime and report empirical rural-urban comparisons. The lack of a precise definition for rural in this collection reflects the clear (but doubtful) presumption that its meaning is well understood in everyday language.

The intuitive approach to measuring rural draws heavily but implicitly on occupational, social structural, and cultural factors for deciding when an area (or population) is really rural. Such factors seem obvious and commonsensible, but they are very difficult to quantify. Often the reliance on intuitive or implicit definitions works well only for average cases that fit neatly into unambiguous ideal-type categories of rural-urban. It does not address the variations that may occur across rural settings about which there is less consensus. Such an implicit approach also hides the underlying principles or criteria by which rural conditions are recognized and understood. As a result, it limits the ability to generalize beyond the specific cases being studied, and in the process limits both the knowledge and the policy applications that the research should generate.

Beyond intuitive judgment, the second approach to measuring rural makes use of demographic information, utilizing categories and criteria of rural-urban prescribed by the federal census. This has the advantages of yielding data that are objective, official, standardized, quantitative, and readily available. However, because the Census Bureau's primary focus is on measuring degrees of urbanism, rural places are defined and measured in negative terms, with the attendant difficulties noted earlier. In census data, the category of rural simply includes those areas or populations left over after urban categories have been classified and counted. The rural-urban distinction from census data is primarily based on population size, which seems numerical and unambiguous. However, technically it leads to two different definitions of rural. One refers to rural as nonmetropolitan areas, while the other refers to nonurban areas. In census terms, metropolitan refers to geographic areas containing an urbanized center of at least 50,000 persons plus contiguous areas having strong economic and social ties to that urban center. In contrast, urban refers to *incorporated places* containing at least 2,500 population. The metropolitan category applies to counties as units-of-data while the urban category applies to municipalities (or census-designated equivalents). Thus, while both Census Bureau definitions of rural are based on a combination of geographical area and population size, the two are not identical. Some urban areas are located within nonmetropolitan counties, and metropolitan counties often contain nonurban areas. This means that the size of the rural population, as well as its location across geographic areas, will depend on which negative definition is used.

Overall, approximately 25 percent of the U.S. population was nonurban in 1990, while less than 23 percent was nonmetropolitan. However, the disagreement is larger than the difference between these two percentages because the two groups have only partial overlap. At least 20 million persons categorized as rural residents by one definition were not counted as rural by the other. In geographic terms, the overlap is even smaller. Herbers (1986) notes that less than 10 percent of the total land area within counties designated as metropolitan areas in the United States is classified as urban under federal definitions (p. 191). Importantly, neither of the Census Bureau's definitions of rural include information about the social, economic, occupational, or cultural characteristics of areas. As Beale's (1984) insightful analysis shows, many areas demographically classified as metropolitan by current census definitions lack the basic social structural features by which the concept of metropolitan generally is defined.

Use of demographic statistics to measure rural places and populations necessarily involves two additional issues. One is the numerical criterion used to distinguish rural from urban. What number best captures the change from rural to urban? Even among agencies of the federal government, a variety of different official definitions of rural appear. As already noted, the Census Bureau uses two different numbers to define urban and metropolitan, and these numerical criteria have been changed several times as a result of political/administrative decisions.

For example, the criteria for designating a county as a metropolitan area have been changed three times since being created for the 1950 census (Beale, 1984), reflecting the fact that these are political (rather than sociological) categories. As official governmental designations, the urban and metropolitan labels serve as eligibility criteria for many federal programs providing funding for urban development and renewal. This provides considerable economic incentives for many rural communities to be reclassified and generates political pressures on the Census Bureau to make the criteria more inclusive. Consequently, within the past two decades a number of communities or counties have changed from rural to urban/metropolitan without any real increase in population size or social services. Other agencies besides the Census Bureau also designate rural categories. The Farmer's Home Administration rural housing loan program includes cities up to 20,000 population in its rural category. In contrast, the Rural Electrification Act excludes places with more than 1,500 population from its rural category, while the community development block grants program counts cities as rural (nonurban) with populations up to 50,000 (Gilford, Nelson, & Ingram, 1981).

The other issue is the number of categories needed to reasonably distinguish rural and urban settings. The most extensive and systematic elaboration, developed by the Economic Research Service of the U.S. Department of Agriculture (Butler, 1990; Cook & Mizer, 1994) uses a combination of demographic and geographic information to yield a ten-category rural-urban continuum. It classifies counties by their urban population size as well as by their proximity to major urban centers, which allows for a much more detailed classification of places from completely rural to highly urban. For nonmetropolitan areas, this approach considers whether they are *adjacent* to a metropolitan county, including both physical proximity and whether it provides significant employment to that adjacent area. Thus, the USDA-ERS system takes into account suburbs, "bedroom communities," outlying small towns, nonurbanized fringe areas, and remote, "completely rural" areas. However, like most elaborations of rural-urban, this system remains mostly urban focused, providing more and finer gradations among urban places. It distinguishes only two categories of rural (adjacent and nonadjacent to metropolitan areas) versus eight categories of urban. This system does not include economic, occupation, social, or cultural considerations, however, being based only on census-provided demographic data.

A third approach to measuring rural places is based on occupational or economic information. Where rural is conceptualized in terms of farm country, the ruralness of areas is often measured by the prevalence of farming as a major economic activity or by other agricultural events as indicators of farming. This approach might also include data on indicators of other primary extractive industries, such as mining, fishing, or logging. However, these are much less frequently used, given the common identification between rural areas and farming. As noted earlier, this rural-farming equation is based on an historical correlation that is increasingly incorrect and inappropriate, limiting its usefulness as a general measurement strategy. Note, however, that occupational data may sometimes be combined with demographic data to provide useful subdivisions of rural areas—e.g., rural-farm versus rural-non-farm.

A fourth approach seeks to incorporate cultural, social, and life-style factors into the measurement of rural (Miller & Luloff, 1981). While no researchers define or measure rural solely by such factors (which are notoriously hard to measure objectively), some researchers have developed *composite* measurements of rurality (Lowe & Peek, 1974; Willits & Bealer, 1967). These combine demographic data with additional sociological information on the attitudes, values, and social practices of populations in areas. While appealing for theoretical reasons, this form of measurement is much more difficult to carry out, since the necessary data are not readily available or systematically collected. Moreover, research results have been inconclusive as to whether it actually works better than simple demographic indicators in differentiating among rural areas or between rural and urban populations.

A final method for measuring rurality makes use of subjective self-identifications. In contrast to census-data definitions, questionnaire surveys generally ask respondents to categorize their community, based on their perceptions of its demographic and social characteristics, into a rural-urban classification. For example, a common survey question asks respondents to indicate whether they live in an urban, suburban, small-town, or rural area; or they may be asked to make a more detailed and quantitative description (e.g., reporting the estimated population of their community). Many national surveys use this format (e.g., surveys of delinquent behavior among high school students, household surveys of drug use or of domestic violence among the general adult population). In practice, the criteria applied here probably lead to classifications that are not far from the Census Bureau's definition. However, they are by nature more subjective and unverifiable.

Mostly, the study of rural has focused on counties, communities, or more localized places as the unit of analysis. Although not as commonly used, another strategy is to identify rural *states*. At this level, the GAO, for example, defines rural states as those with fewer than 50 people per square mile and identifies 18 states that meet this criterion (General Accounting Office, 1990). Rather than defining states dichotomously as either rural or urban, another strategy is to rank order states from the most rural to the most urban, based on their population density (e.g., Photiadis & Simoni, 1983). The two-category system used by the GAO is the simpler of the two approaches and is undoubtedly easier to apply when considering national policies and programs for rural areas. For example, if the federal government were to fund anti-crime programs for rural areas it would be useful to have a single (and simple) cutoff that would separate rural areas from others. However, simplicity and ease of application come at a price. It is a system based on a state's *overall* population density, without regard for how that population is spread out across the state. In reality many states have *both* rural and urban regions. For example, under the GAO's definition Utah is a rural state because in 1990 its population density was 21 people per square mile. However, 87 percent of Utah's population lives in *urban* areas. In contrast, Vermont is classified as nonrural, even though only 32 percent of its citizens live in urban areas.

Perhaps the best illustration of the inherent difficulties in declaring states as rural or nonrural based on population density is California. With an average of 191 people per square mile in 1990, California is clearly a nonrural state under the GAO definition. Yet, as the following description shows, California has both rural and urban elements:

> California is an urban state that defines its own scale. Some 95 percent of the state's 30 million persons live in metropolitan areas, yet it is the leading agricultural producer in the United States. . . . However, behind the urban front is a significant, although frequently overlooked, rural backwater that has 2.2 million persons. Were a rural California to be a state by itself, its population would be larger than 18 other states, and it would have four congressional representatives. (Bradshaw, 1992, as quoted in *Sage Urban Studies Abstracts*, p. 140)

Although making a simple urban-rural distinction may be useful for policy purposes, using gradations of rural may make more sense for analytical (i.e., research) purposes. In this case, the focus may be not only on whether an area is rural, but also on the extent of rurality.

Analytical Issues

Deciding what is meant by rural requires thinking through the many meanings of the term and settling on a system for measuring it. In addition, those who would study rural issues must sort through a series of issues related to how the idea will be used in the analysis. These analytical issues include:

Rural as a Quantitative Variable versus a Typological Category

In quantitative terms, rural refers to a continuum of social contexts that ranges from most rural to most urban. The rurality of communities can be measured by their location along this scale. In typological terms, rural refers to a discrete category of social places that is distinctly and qualitatively different from urban places. Rural represents a dichotomous either-or classification of places rather than a scalable quantity of some attribute.

Rural as a Scope Condition versus a Causal Variable

Of these two views, the former means that analysis of social processes (e.g., of crime and criminal justice) must be done separately for rural and urban settings. The causal models that apply to people in rural settings only hold in that context; they do not work in urban places and vice versa. This means that separate models or explanations must be developed and tested in rural and urban settings. The latter view means the inclusion of rurality as one more variable in a multivariate model, which can be estimated and tested along with the other causal variables. The effects of rurality are additive with the other social variables in a single common model that applies across both rural and urban settings.

General versus Localized Analysis

The social meaning of rural is not universal and constant. It varies greatly across locations (expressing regional variations in geography and culture) and over time (with changes in economic modes and technological developments). Emphasis on the substantial heterogeneity of rural settings can mean that different communities (or types of communities) must be studied and explained separately, adopting a more idiographic, case-study approach that preserves the individual uniqueness of different rural settings or regions. Alternatively, much research, especially that aimed at formulation of national policies and programs, deals with rural as a more-or-less unitary phenomenon, having relatively homogenous categories of settings. The emphasis on the basic commonalities of rural settings means that rural events can be analyzed to find general and uniform processes. Data from different locations and regions can be pooled together to develop more reliable and broadly applicable explanations of rural trends, which are used in turn to develop broad general policies for rural crime control and criminal justice.

Rural as a Single Variable versus Many Different Variables

The first of these two views implies that the rurality of a place can be sensibly summarized in a single number or classification. The second view argues that each place must be indexed by a number of different variables, each one reflecting a different facet of the concept of rural (e.g., population density, social isolation, economic modes of production, networks of social ties, cultural values, identities and memberships, divisions of labor, role structures, cultural values, and technology). While it might appear that the solution is to combine these dimensions into a single indicator of rural, it is unclear how this could be done. Even if the substantial problems of measuring each dimension were overcome, it is unclear how much weight should be attached to each. For example, it has already been suggested that the occupational dimension is probably less important than the cultural, but *how much* less?

Rural as a Dependent versus an Independent Variable

Demographic measures (such as population density) are generally treated only as independent variables. That is, we assume that density may shape behavior (such as crime) and not that behavior shapes density. In contrast, cultural definitions of rural are equally well suited to be handled as either dependent or independent variables. For example, rural culture may shape the occurrence of violent crime. In this example, rural culture is treated as an independent variable. At the same time, there are dozens of popular books exploring how a particularly heinous crime rattles the value system and beliefs of small-town residents. In this case rural culture is treated as a dependent variable, as having been influenced by something else.

Finally, the dimension of rural that is selected both shapes and is shaped by the research methods used. For example, understanding rural culture and patterns of interaction may require either case studies or observational research. In contrast, survey research and official records may be the best way to study the occupational and demographic dimensions, and a focus on multiple dimensions may require multiple methods.

These analytical issues must be taken into account in any research on rural crime and rural justice. While they may be of lesser immediate concern to policy makers and program implementers, considering them can provide both groups with valuable insights. Appreciating these analytical issues makes it easier to evaluate research used in policy and program decisions, and to determine what research is most needed in the future.

Problematic Assumptions

Research on rural crime has uniformly reflected several misguided assumptions about rural life and social control that seem especially problematic. These have limited our efforts to understand what rural crime actually involves and how it differs from the more familiar processes of urban crime. These assumptions are:

The Magnitude Assumption

This is the presumption that the differences between rural and urban processes are essentially a matter of sizes, numbers, or amounts. They reflect a belief that social control varies in *quantity* but not in *quality* across urban and rural areas. Urban areas are composed of more people, more interactions, more strangers, fewer kinship connections, more problems, and less informal controls—but the same basic variables apply to each area. In these terms, the rural-urban distinction reflects differences of degree rather than differences of kind. While this assumption is conveniently consistent with the linear statistical models and data analytic procedures that are currently popular in criminological research, it seems highly presumptuous, if not simply wrong. We cannot simply assume that rural areas are "urban processes written small," at least not without more empirical evidence and systematic analysis to indicate it is reasonable to do this.

The Homogeneity Assumption

This is the common presumption that rural areas are very similar in their social conditions and dynamics and can thus be treated as the undifferentiated hinterland—i.e., what is true of one rural area will be generally true of them all. This represents a kind of "urban myopia" that seems to characterize much criminological research, expressing an urban stereotype of rural areas captured in the phrase, "Once you leave the city, sticks is sticks." While it appears that enormous variations exist across rural areas, there has been little to document these variations and their implications for crime and criminal justice policy.

The Implicit Definition Assumption

This is the assumption that "rural" and "urban" are simple and familiar categories that need little explication, elaboration, or definition. It assumes that everyone knows what "rural" means and that everyone defines it in pretty much the same terms. It also assumes that the operational definitions used in collecting and reporting crime statistics correspond closely with the common conceptual definitions of rural and urban. In reality, what constitutes rural and how it is to be measured has never been resolved in a consistent manner.

Summary

In conducting interviews for this study, the question we are most commonly asked is our definition of rural. It is a question to which we have no simple answer. In fact, rural police officials with whom we spoke were themselves usually vague about the term. The purpose of this discussion is not to develop a single correct definition of rural which can become a standard for all circumstances. To the contrary, it is hoped that the discussion illustrates that a single definition is not only impossible, but undesirable. The "correct" definition of rural will vary from one situation to the next, depending on why it is used, what data are available for measuring the idea, to whom it is applied, and the way in which the idea of rural will be used in the analysis. For example, policy makers may prefer the two-category distinction of rural versus nonrural in establishing programs to fund rural crime initiatives. In contrast, two categories may be too few for the researcher who is determining crime patterns across varying degrees of rurality.

Rather than a concrete measurable idea, the concept of rural might best be described as a "sensitizing concept." Some years ago, Herbert Blumer (1953) made the distinction between definitive or precisely measurable concepts and sensitizing concepts:

> A definitive concept [has] . . . a clear definition in terms of attributes or fixed benchmarks. . . . A sensitizing concept lacks

such specification of attributes or benchmarks. . . . Instead, it gives the user a general sense of reference and guidance in approaching empirical instances. Whereas definitive concepts provide prescriptions of what to see, sensitizing concepts merely suggest directions along which to look. Hundreds of our concepts—like culture, institutions, social structure, mores, and personality—are not definitive concepts but are sensitizing in nature. They lack precise reference and have no benchmarks which allow a clean-cut identification of a specific instance and of its content. Instead, they rest on a general sense of what is relevant. (p. 7)

Understanding rural as a sensitizing concept is also a good reminder that the study of rural crime should not become so focused on defining rural that it becomes bogged down. The most reasonable strategy is for studies to select a definition that (1) makes intuitive sense, (2) is relatively easy to use, and (3) allows for comparisons with other research. In addition, the researchers should, whenever possible, make their definition explicit. Our own study requires that the issue be approached from a number of directions, including a review of the relevant literature, interviews with rural police, and the re-analysis of existing data that include information about rural areas. Consequently, we have approached the issue with considerable flexibility, allowing for a wide range of definitions when using the work of others. Similarly, when selecting rural sheriffs and police chiefs to interview, we have consciously included areas that cover a wide range of definitions of rural. This is done both to reflect a sensitivity to the range of definitions used and to help us better understand the consequences of using various definitions.

Appendix B

The Study

THE INFORMATION PRESENTED IN THIS BOOK WAS FIRST developed as part of a large two-year study of rural and small-town crime and policing funded by the National Institute of Justice. That study, which began in 1992, involved collecting and reviewing relevant literature, conducting focus groups with rural sheriffs and municipal police, locating and cataloging data sets relevant to rural crime, and interviewing officials familiar with rural crime and rural policing. This book is based primarily on the literature review, supplemented with information from interviews, with information provided by eight focus groups, and from a survey of small-town police chiefs and rural sheriffs regarding their concerns. To monitor emerging issues we have also kept track of related news stories and public opinion surveys. The purpose of our work is to develop a broad conceptual framework for looking at rural crime and rural justice, a framework that facilitates adding new issues as they arise and modifying our descriptions to incorporate changes to our existing arguments. An important objective of our work is to stimulate thinking and suggest patterns that merit further study.

Literature Review

Rural and small-town crime issues can be found in the literature from a variety of fields and from sources that vary greatly in their concern with detail and accuracy. In addition, rural is often only one of many variables embedded within a larger discussion and is not mentioned in either the title or the abstract. Thus, using key word searches to go through indexes quickly will identify many sources but will miss many others.

Regarding the academic literature, we focused our search efforts on materials published since 1980. Indexes prior to 1980 were much less comprehensive. Further, much of the literature prior to 1980 had already been assembled by Hubbard and Horton (1980) in *Rural Crime and Criminal Justice: A Selected Bibliography.* The search included a computerized search through the DIALOG Information Retrieval Service in an examination of the following indexes/abstracts:

- Criminal justice abstracts
- Criminology and penology abstracts
- Criminal justice periodical index
- Current contents
- Sociological abstracts
- Social work abstracts
- Human resources abstracts
- PAIS Bulletin: Public Affairs Information Service

In addition, we also kept abreast of developing literature by routinely examining the annual programs for the American Society of Criminology and the Academy of Criminal Justice Sciences and requesting copies of appropriate presentations. Finally, we used what those involved in meta-analysis refer to as the "ancestry method," by which the references in identified publications are searched to identify other publications on the same topic.

This study was highly exploratory and was intended to go beyond the existing academic literature to include emerging issues and patterns, as well as those issues which had been neglected in the academic literature. This aspect of the study included searches of newspapers and magazines and directly contacting organizations that might have produced documents relevant to rural crime. A sampling of these organizations includes: The National Crime Prevention Association, the Committee for Arson Control, the U.S. Fish & Wildlife Service, the U.S. Forest Service, the Centers for Disease Control, the American Bar Association, Klanwatch, the U.S. Commission on Civil Rights, and a number of organizations concerned with Native American law.

Interviews

At the conclusion of our original study we had interviewed over 180 people from a variety of perspectives relevant to rural and small-town crime, including sheriffs, municipal chiefs, state police, conservation officers, judges, attorneys, coroners, and other authorities in specific areas. In the years since our study began we have continued to visit rural settings and conduct interviews. Most of the focus has been on sheriffs and municipal chiefs from a variety of rural areas throughout the country. In our original study most of our interviews were with sheriffs in rural counties or in counties with substantial rural areas (N=67), and with police chiefs in small towns in rural areas (N=64). Of these original 131 interviews, 17 (13 percent) were face-to-face and the remainder were by telephone. While we wanted to include jurisdictions of varying sizes, the focus was on the most rural jurisdictions. Among interviewed municipal chiefs the size of their community ranged from 287 to 50,000 people with an average of 7,500 people. Departments ranged in size from 1 to 66 uniformed officers, with an average of 17 officers. Among interviewed county sheriffs, departments ranged in size from 1 to 182 uniformed officers, with an average of 23 officers. This figure is a very rough approximation, since department size is difficult to compute for sheriffs' departments (which sometimes have high numbers of part-time employees, where jail staff are sometimes also sworn officers, and where there are sometimes a large number of reserves). The population of the counties served by these sheriffs ranged from 2,100 to 712,000 people, with only 8 of the 67 sheriffs working in a county of more than 50,000. Since the original study concluded, we have interviewed and visited several dozen more criminal justice officials—some through formal interviews and some more casually.

As an exploratory study, locating subjects for interviews focused on identifying individuals from the widest possible range of social and physical environments, rather than on "average" rural settings. Indeed, the differences across rural areas are so substantial that speaking of averages is probably misleading and is certainly of limited utility for policy. Rural Montana and rural Delaware, for example, probably have as many differences as similarities. To capture as much of this range as possible we selected police officers from across the country, attempting to include every state and giving a particular focus to the 18 states identified as rural by the U.S. Government's General Accounting Office (1990).

As an exploratory study we felt it important to use unstructured interviews. Appreciating rural variation, and always keeping it in mind, we were still interested in identifying common themes. Thus, we used the available literature, and information gathered from a series of preliminary interviews, to develop a list of question areas to be covered in the course of the interviews. However, we also encouraged subjects to explore other areas they thought were important. Question areas included crime concerns, police-citizen interactions, police practices, and the working relationship between police and other criminal justice agencies. The length of interview ranged from 20 minutes to 2 hours but was typically about 40 minutes long.

Focus Groups

In addition to the interviews, eight focus groups were conducted in the original study. One was with rural sheriffs from around the country who were identified with the assistance of the National Sheriffs' Association. The remaining seven focus groups were sheriffs and/or municipal police from different geographic regions of the country. Focus groups were very important early in our study to help us identify key issues. However, at later stages in the research there was little reason to continue with this method of data collection.

Survey of Rural Police

With support from the Federal Law Enforcement Training Center, a survey of rural chiefs and sheriffs was conducted. The survey systematically sampled every other county in the United States with a population under 50,000 as of 1995, using Census Bureau population estimates. In each of the selected counties a survey was sent to the sheriff and to the chief of the police department in the largest municipality in the county. Surveys were sent to 1,120 sheriffs and 902 municipal chiefs—19 percent of the counties had no municipal department. Of the 2,022 mailed surveys, 1,152 (57 percent) were returned. The content of the surveys and the patterns of responses are reported in chapter 4.

References

Abadinsky, Howard (1986). *Organized crime* (2nd ed.). Chicago: Nelson-Hall.

Abadinsky, Howard (1989). *Drug abuse: An introduction.* Chicago: Nelson-Hall.

Action alert: Timber theft letter (1997, October 28) [Timber theft group sign-on letter]. Available: www.accessone.com/gap/www/timberlet.htm

Angle, Paul M. (1980). *Bloody Williamson.* New York: Alfred A. Knopf.

Applebome, Peter (1987, December 12). Some say frontier is still there, and still different. *New York Times,* p. 11.

Arthur, John A. (1991). Socioeconomic predictors of crime in rural Georgia. *Criminal Justice Review, 16*(1), 29–41.

Auletta, Ken (1982). *The underclass.* New York: Random House.

Austin, D. Mark, Woolever, Cynthia, & Baba, Yoko (1994). Crime and safety-related concerns in a small community. *American Journal of Criminal Justice, 19*(1), 79–97.

Austin, Thomas L. (1981). The influence of court location on type of criminal sentence: The rural-urban factor. *Journal of Criminal Justice, 9*(4), 305–316.

Bachman, Ronet (1992a, June). *Crime victimization In city, suburban, and rural areas* (Report for the Bureau of Justice Statistics) [NCJ–135943]. Washington. DC: U.S. Department of Justice.

Bachman, Ronet (1992b). Crime in nonmetropolitan America: A national accounting of trends, incidence rates, and idiosyncratic vulnerabilities. *Rural Sociology, 57*(4), 546–560.

Badger, Lee W. (1989). Reporting of child abuse: Influence of characteristics of physician, practice, and community. *Southern Medical Journal, 82*(3), 281–286.

Bai, Matt (1997, March 31). White storm warning: In Fargo and the prairie states, speed kills. *Newsweek,* p. 66.

Baker, James N., King, Patricia, Murr, Andrew, & Abbott, Nonny (1989, April 3). The newest drug war: In rural America, crack and "crank" are now hot commodities in the backwoods. *Newsweek,* pp. 20–22.

Baker, Russell (1997, January 25). The new out crowd. *New York Times,* p. 23.

Ball, Richard A. (1977). Emergent delinquency in a rurban area. In Theodore Ferdinand (Ed.), *Juvenile delinquency: Little brother grows up* (pp. 101–120). Beverly Hills: Sage.

Bankston, William B., & Allen, H. David (1980). Rural social areas and patterns of homicide: An analysis of lethal violence in Louisiana. *Rural Sociology, 45*(2), 223–237.

Bankston, William B., Jenkins, Quentin A. L., Thayer-Doyle, Cheryl L., & Thompson, Carol Y. (1987). Fear of criminal victimization and residential location: The influence of perceived risk. *Rural Sociology, 52*(1), 98–107.

Barker, Thomas, & Carter, David L. (1994a). A typology of police deviance. In T. Barker & D. L. Carter (Eds.), *Police deviance* (3rd ed., pp. 3–10). Cincinnati: Anderson.

Barker, Thomas, & Carter, David L. (Eds.). (1994b). *Police deviance* (3rd ed.). Cincinnati: Anderson.

Barkun, Michael (1994). *Religion and the racist right: The origins of the Christian Identity Movement.* Chapel Hill: University of North Carolina Press.

Bass, Jay (1995). Rural policing: Patterns and problems of "micro" departments. *The Justice Professional, 9*(1), 59–74.

Bastian, Lisa (1995, May). *Criminal victimization 1993* (Report for the Bureau of Justice Statistics) [NCJ–151658]. Washington, DC: U.S. Department of Justice.

Bastian, Lisa D., & Taylor, Bruce M. (1991). *School crime: A national crime victimization survey report.* Washington, DC: U.S. Department of Justice.

Baumer, T. (1978). Research on fear of crime in the U.S. *Victimology, 3*(3/4), 254–64.

Bayley, David H. (1988). Community policing: A report from a devil's advocate. In J. R. Greene & S. D. Mastrofski (Eds.), *Community policing: Rhetoric or reality* (pp. 225–237). New York: Praeger.

Beale, Calvin L. (1984, January). Poughkeepsie's complaint or defining metropolitan areas. *American Demographics, 6*, 29–31, 46–48.

Beale, Calvin L. (1993). Prisons, population, and jobs in nonmetro America. *Rural Development Perspectives, 8*(3), 16–19.

Bealer, Robert C., Willits, Fern K., & Kuvlesky, William P. (1965). The meaning of "rurality" in American society: Some implications of alternative definitions. *Rural Sociology, 30*(3), 255–266.

Bell, Daniel J. (1986). Domestic violence in small cities and towns: A pilot study. *Journal of Crime & Justice, 9*, 163–181.

Bell, Daniel J. (1989). Family violence in small cities: An exploratory study. *Police Studies, 12*(1), 25–31.

Bell, Michael (1992). The fruit of difference: The rural-urban continuum as a system of identity. *Rural Sociology, 57*(1), 65–82.

Belyea, Michael J., & Zingraff, Matthew T. (1985). Monitoring rural-urban drug trends: An analysis of drug arrest statistics, 1976–1980. *The International Journal of the Addictions , 20*(3), 369–380.

Belyea, Michael J., & Zingraff, Matthew T. (1988). Fear of crime and residential location. *Rural Sociology, 53*(4), 473–486.

Benson, Katy (1995, March). Rural crime: Being a cop in the country requires a unique approach to policing. *Police,* pp. 46–49, 68–69, 76–77.

Birch, James W. (1983). Reflections on police corruption. *Criminal Justice Ethics, 2*(2), 2, 83–85.

Bishop, K. (1990, August 10). Military takes part in drug sweep and reaps criticism and a lawsuit. *New York Times,* p. A11.

Bjorgo, Tore, & Witte, Rob (Eds.). (1993). *Racist violence in Europe.* New York: St. Martin's Press.

Blumer, Herbert (1953). What is wrong with social theory? *American Sociological Review, 19,* 3–10.

Boggs, S. L. (1971, Summer). Formal and informal crime control: An exploratory study of urban, suburban, and rural orientations. *Sociological Quarterly, 12,* 319–327.

Bonnen, James T. (1992). Why is there no coherent U.S. rural policy? *Policy Studies Journal, 20*(2), 190–201.

Bonnen, James, & Wimberley, Ronald (1991). Rural data needs in changing times: A summary. In R. C. Buse & J. L. Driscoll (Eds.), *Rural information systems* (pp. 419–439). Ames: Iowa State University Press.

Bordua, David J., & Lizotte, Alan J. (1979). Patterns of illegal firearms ownership. *Law & Policy Quarterly, 1*(2), 147–175.

Bradshaw, Ted K. (1992). In the shadow of urban growth: Bifurcation in rural California communities (Working Paper No. 569). Berkeley Institute of Urban and Regional Development, University of California at Berkeley. Cited in *Sage Urban Studies Abstracts* (May 1993), *21*(2), 140.

Bradshaw, Ted K., & Blakely, Edward J. (1982). The changing nature of rural America. In William P. Brown & Don F. Hadwiger (Eds.), *Rural policy problems: Changing dimensions* (pp. 3–18). Lexington, MA: Lexington Books.

Brandon, Karen (1996, November 18). Suburbia sprouts in California's valley of plenty. *Chicago Tribune,* pp. 1, 10.

Bridges, George S. (1993). *Racial disproportionality in the juvenile justice system.* Report submitted to the Commission on African American Affairs and Management Services Division/Department of Social and Health Services, State of Washington, Olympia, Washington.

Bristow, A. P. (1982). *Rural law enforcement.* Boston: Allyn & Bacon.

Brodsky, Harold (1990). Emergency medical service rescue time in fatal road accidents. *Transportation Research Record* 1270, pp. 89–96.

Bromley, David G. (1991). The satanic cult scare. *Society, 28*(4), 55–66.

Brown, David L., & Hirschl, Thomas A. (1995). Household poverty in rural and metropolitan-core areas of the United States. *Rural Sociology, 60*(1), 44–66.

Brown, Lee R. (1989). *Community policing: A practical guide for police officials.* Washington, DC: National Institute of Justice.

Browne, William P., Skees, Jerry R., Swanson, Louis E., Thompson, Paul B., & Unnevehr, Laurian J. 1992. *Sacred cows and hot potatoes: Agrarian myths in agricultural policy.* Boulder, CO: Westview Press.

Bryan, Frank M. (1981). *Politics in the rural state: People, parties, and processes.* Boulder, CO: Westview Press.

Bryan, Frank M. (1986). Defining rural: Returning to our roots. In J. Seroka (Ed.), *Rural public administration: Problems and prospects* (pp. 9–20). New York: Greenwood Press.

Bukro, Casey (1991, February 19). Blood feud. *Chicago Tribune,* Section 2, pp. 1, 10.

Bureau of Justice Statistics (1990a, July). *Handgun crime victims* (Special Report for the U.S. Department of Justice) [NCJ–123559]. Washington, DC: U.S. Department of Justice.

Bureau of Justice Statistics (1990b). *Law Enforcement Management and Administrative Statistics (LEMAS), 1990* [computer file]. Washington, DC: U.S. Department of Justice, BJS [producer]. Ann Arbor, MI: Inter-University Consortium for Political and Social Research [distributor].

Bureau of Justice Statistics (1992). *Drug enforcement by police and sheriffs' departments, 1990.* Washington, DC: U.S. Department of Justice.

Burrough, Bryan (1989, October 29). In Clay County, Ky., It takes some doing to avoid a sizemore. *New York Times,* pp. 1, 23.

Butler, Margaret A. (1990). *Rural-urban continuum codes for metro and nonmetro counties.* Washington, DC: United States Department of Agriculture.

Caillier, Mark W. and Versteeg, Karyn D. (1988). *Preliminary conclusions: Correctional impact on the City of Salem police services.* Salem, OR: Salem Police Department. Cited in Shichor (1992), Myths and realities in prison siting, *Crime and Delinquency, 38*(1), 70–87.

Cain, Maureen (1971). On the beat: Interactions and relations in rural and urban police forces. In Stanley Cohen (Ed.), *Images of deviance* (pp. 62–97). Baltimore, MD: Penguin.

California pesticide thefts on the rise. (1992, September 17). Pesticide Action Network North America Update Service. Available: http://rtk.net/E2701T598

Carter, Timothy J. (1982). The extent and nature of rural crime in America. In Timothy J. Carter, G. Howard Phillips, Joseph E. Donnermeyer, & Todd N. Wurschmidt (Eds.), *Rural crime: Integrating research and prevention* (pp. 20–33). Totowa, NJ: Allanheld, Osmun.

Carter, Timothy J., Phillips, G. Howard, Donnermeyer, Joseph F., & Wurschmidt, Todd N. (Eds.). (1982). *Rural crime: Integrating research prevention.* Totowa, NJ: Allanheld, Osmun.

Castellano, Thomas C., & Uchida, Craig D. (1990). Local drug enforcement, prosecutors and case attrition: Theoretical perspectives for the drug war. *American Journal of Police, 9*(1), 133–162.

Castle, Emery N. (Ed.). (1995). *The changing American countryside: Rural people and places.* Lawrence: University of Kansas Press.

Chandler, Kathryn A., Chapman, Christopher D., Rand, Michael P., & Taylor, Bruce M. (1998). Students' reports of school crime: 1989 and 1995. (Report #NCES 98–241/NCJ–169607). Washington, DC: U.S. Department of Education and U.S. Department of Justice.

Chavez, Linda (1996, April 10). Want motive for Unabomber? Media should ask more questions about Kaczynski's ties to radical environmental group. *USA Today,* p. 11A.

Chicago Tribune (1989, August 4). Illegal drug trade spreads to rural areas, p. 5.

Chicago Tribune, (1997, June 2). Vandals free thousands of minks, p. 6.

Chitty, Michael C. (1994). *Conservation police and wildlife poaching: An exploratory study.* Unpublished master's thesis, Illinois State University, Normal, IL.

Clayton, Richard R. (1995). *Marijuana in the "Third World": Appalachia, U.S.A.* Boulder, CO: Lynne Reinner.

Clemente, E., & Kleiman, M. B. (1976). Fear of crime among the aged. *Gerontologist, 16*(3), 207–210.

Clemente, E., & Kleiman, M. B. (1977). Fear of crime in the United States: A multivariate analysis. *Social Forces, 56*(2), 519–531.

Coates, James. (1987). *Armed and dangerous: The rise of the survivalist right.* New York: Hill and Wang.

Coates, James, & Blau, Robert (1989, September 13). Big-city gangs fuel growing crack crisis. *Chicago Tribune,* pp. 1, 8.

Coates, James, & Weingarten, Paul (1990, April 2). U.S. marijuana cartels flower inside and out. *Chicago Tribune,* pp. 1, 6.

Colvin, Rod (1992). *Evil harvest.* New York: Bantam Books.

Conklin, J. E. (1971, Winter). Dimensions of community response to the crime problem. *Social Problems, 18,* 373–385.

Conklin, J. E. (1976). Robbery, the elderly, and fear: An urban problem in search of a solution. In J. Goldsmith & S. S. Goldsmith (Eds.), *Crime and the elderly* (pp. 99–110). Lexington, MA: Lexington Books.

Cook, Peggy J., & Mizer, Karen L. (1994). *The revised ERS county typology: An overview.* (Rural Development Research Report 89). Washington, DC: Economic Research Service, U.S. Department of Agriculture.

Corcoran, James (1990). *Bitter harvest: Gordon Kohl and the Posse Comitatus.* New York: Penguin.

Cordner, Gary W. (1989). Police agency size and investigative effectiveness. *Journal of Criminal Justice, 17*(1), 145–155.

Crank, John P. (1989). Civilianization in small and medium police departments in Illinois, 1973–1983. *Journal of Criminal Justice, 17,* 167–177.

Crank, John P. (1990). The influence of environmental and organizational factors on police style in urban and rural environments. *Journal of Research in Crime and Delinquency, 27*(2), 166–189.

Crank, John P. (1996). The construction of meaning during training for probation and parole. *Justice Quarterly, 13*(2), 265–290.

Crank, John P., & Wells, L. Edward (1991). The effects of size and urbanism on structure among Illinois police departments. *Justice Quarterly, 8*(2), 169–185.

Cronk, Christine, & Sarvela, Paul D. (1997). Alcohol, tobacco, and other drug use among rural/small town and urban youth: A secondary analysis of Monitoring the Future data set. *American Journal of Public Health, 87*(5), 760–764.

Cronk, Shanler D. (Ed.). (1977). A beginning assessment of the justice system in rural areas. Conference Report Sponsored by the National Rural Center, American Bar Association.

Crouch, Ben M., & Damphouse, Kelly (1991). Law enforcement and the satanism-crime connection: A survey of "cult cops." In James T. Richardson,

Joel Best, & David G. Bromley (Eds.), *The satanism scare* (pp. 191–204). New York: Aldine de Gruyter.

Curry, G. David, Ball, Richard A., & Decker, Scott H. (1996). Estimating the national scope of gang crime from law enforcement data. In C. R. Huff (Ed.), *Gangs in America* (2nd ed., pp. 21–36). Thousand Oaks, CA: Sage.

Curry, David G., Ball, Richard A., & Fox, Robert J. (1994). Gang crime and law enforcement recordkeeping. *Research in brief*. Washington, DC: National Institute of Justice. Office of Justice Programs, U.S. Dept. of Justice.

Daniels, Stephen (1982). Civil litigation in Illinois trial courts. *Law & Policy Quarterly, 4*(2), 190–214.

Dasgupta, Satadal (1988). *Rural Canada: Structure and change.* Lewiston/ Queenston: Edwin Mellen Press.

Davidson, Osha Gray (1990). *Broken heartland: The rise of America's rural ghetto.* New York: Free Press.

Deavers, Ken (1992). What is rural? *Policy Studies Journal, 20*(2), 184–189.

DeBoer, Larry, & Mann, Jeffrey P. (n.d.). *City-county consolidation for Indiana: An outline of the issues.* West Lafayette, IN: Purdue University Cooperative Extension Service.

Decker, Scott H. (1978). The working personality of rural policemen. *LAE Journal of the American Criminal Justice Association, 41*(3), 19–27.

Decker, Scott H. (1979). The rural county sheriff: An issue in social control. *Criminal Justice Review, 4*(2), 97–111.

Dees, Morris (1993). *Hate on trial.* New York: Villard Books.

DeFrances, Carol J., & Smith, Steven K. (1994). *Crime and neighborhoods* (Report for the Bureau of Justice Statistics). Washington, DC: U.S. Department of Justice.

deLama, George (1994, October 27). West chomping at the bit over federal control. *Chicago Tribune*, pp. 1, 4.

deLama, George (1994, October 31). For militias, invaders of U.S. are everywhere. *Chicago Tribune*, pp. 1, 10.

DeLeon, David (1978). *The American as anarchist.* Baltimore, MD: John Hopkins University Press.

Dewey, Richard (1960). The rural-urban continuum: Real but relatively unimportant. *American Journal of Sociology, 66*(1), 60–66.

deYoung, Mary (1994). One face of the devil: The satanic ritual abuse moral crusade and the law. *Behavioral Sciences and the Law, 12*, 389–407.

Dilweg, Vivi L. (1991). Balancing right from wrong: What the new ABA Code of Judicial Conduct says. *The Judges' Journal, 30*(2), 26–29, 70–71.

Donnermeyer, Joseph F. (1992). The use of alcohol, marijuana, and hard drugs by rural adolescents: A review of recent research. In Ruth W. Edwards (Ed.), *Drug use in rural American communities* (pp. 31–75). New York: Haworth Press.

Donnermeyer, Joseph F. (1994). *Crime and violence in rural communities.* Paper presented at the 1994 Annual Meeting of the Academy of Criminal Justice Sciences, Chicago, IL.

Donnermeyer, Joseph F., & Mullen, Robert E. (1987). Use of neighbors for crime prevention: Evidence from a state-wide rural victims study. *Journal of the Community Development Society, 18*(1), 15–29.

Donnermeyer, Joseph F., & Phillips, G. Howard. (1982). The nature of vandalism among rural youth. In Timothy J. Carter, G. Howard Phillips, Joseph F. Donnermeyer, & Todd N. Wurschmidt (Eds.), *Rural crime: Integrating research and prevention* (pp. 124–146). Totowa, NJ: Allanheld, Osmun.

DuBow, F. McCabe, E., & Kaplan, G. (1979). *Reactions to crime: A critical review of the literature.* U.S. Department of Justice, Law Enforcement Assistance Administration. Washington, DC: U.S. Government Printing Office.

Dudley, William (Ed.). (1991). *Police brutality.* San Diego: Greenhaven Press.

Dunkelberger, John E., Clayton, J. Mark, Myrick, Rebecca S., & Lyles, Gladys J. (1992). *Crime and Alabama farms: Victimization, subjective assessment and protective action* (Bulletin 616). Auburn: Auburn University, Alabama Agricultural Experimental Station.

Dyer, Joel (1997). *Harvest of rage: Why Oklahoma City is only the beginning.* Boulder, CO: Westview Press.

Economist, The (1996, May 25). Gangs in the heartland, pp. 29–30.

Edwards, Ruth W. (Ed.). (1992). *Drug use in rural American communities.* New York: Haworth Press.

Egan, Timothy (1995, April 25). Federal uniforms become target of wave of threats and violence. *New York Times,* pp. A1, A10.

Eichenthal, David R., & Jacobs, James B. (1991). Enforcing the criminal law in state prisons. *Justice Quarterly, 8*(3), 283–303.

Eisenstein, James (1982). Research on rural criminal justice: A summary. In Shanler Cronk, Joanne Jankovic, & Ronald K. Green (Eds.), *Criminal justice in rural America* (pp. 105–143). Washington, DC: U.S. Department of Justice.

Ellickson, Robert C. (1986). Of Coase and cattle: Dispute resolution among neighbors in Shasta County. *Stanford Law Review, 38,* 623–687.

Ellsworth, Thomas, & Weisheit, Ralph A. (1997). The supervision and treatment of offenders on probation: Understanding rural and urban differences. *The Prison Journal, 77*(2), 209–228.

Engel, David M. (1984). The oven bird's song: Insiders, outsiders, and personal injuries in an American community. *Law and Society Review, 18,* 551–553.

Erskine, H. (1974, Spring). The polls: Fear of crime and violence. *Public Opinion Quarterly, 38,* 131–145.

Esseks, J. Dixon, Schmidt, Harvey E., & Sullivan, Kimberly L.(1998). *Living on the edge: The costs and risks of scattered development.* Washington, DC: American Farmland Trust.

Esselstyn, T. C. (1953). The social role of a county sheriff. *Journal of Criminal Law, Criminology, and Police Science, 44,* 177–184.

Fahnestock, Kathryn (1991). The loneliness of command: One perspective on judicial isolation. *The Judges' Journal, 30*(2), 13–19, 64–66.

Fahnestock, Kathryn, & Geiger, Maurice D. (1990). *Time to justice: Caseflow in rural general jurisdiction courts.* Montpelier, VT: Rural Justice Center.

Fahnestock, Kathryn, & Geiger, Maurice D. (1993). "We all get along here": Case flow in rural courts. *Judicature, 76*(5), 258–263.

Falcone, David N., & Wells, L. Edward (1995). The county sheriff as a distinctive policing modality. *American Journal of Police, 14*(3/4), 123–149.

Falcone, David N., Wells, L. Edward, & Charles, Michael T. (1992). *Police pursuit in pursuit of policy: The empirical study, Volume II.* Washington, DC: AAA Foundation for Traffic Safety.

Farm thieves reaping big profits from agricultural chemicals. (1995, April 30). *Evansville Courier*, p. A16.

Farmer, Frank L., Luloff, Albert E., Ilvento, Thomas W., & Dixon, Bruce L. (1992). Rural community studies and secondary data: Aggregation revisited. *Journal of the Community Development Society, 23*(1), 57–70.

Federal Bureau of Investigation (FBI). (1980 through 1997). *Uniform crime reports: Crime in the United States.* Washington, DC: U.S. Government Printing Office.

Federal Bureau of Investigation (FBI). (1988 through 1995). *Uniform crime reports: Law enforcement officers killed and assaulted.* Washington, DC: U.S. Government Printing Office.

Feld, Barry (1991). Justice by geography: Urban, suburban, and rural variations in juvenile justice administration. *Journal of Criminal Law and Criminology, 82*(1), 156–210.

Feld, Barry C. (1993). *Justice for children: The right to counsel and the juvenile courts.* Boston, MA: Northeastern University Press.

Fields, Gary, & Parker, Laura (1998, June 16). Jasper, Texas, weighs cost of death penalty trials. *USA Today*, p. 4A.

Fields, Gary, & Price, Richard (1996, June 28–30). Why are churches burning? *USA Today*, pp. 1A–3A.

Finn, Leila, & Kerr, Mary Lee (1991). Mobile homes. *Government That Works, 19*(4), 64.

Fischer, Claude S. (1980). The spread of violent crime from city to countryside, 955 to 1975. *Rural Sociology, 45*(3), 416–434.

Fischer, Claude S. (1981, June). The public and private worlds of city life. *American Sociological Review, 46*, 306–316.

Fischer, David H. (1989). *Albion's seed: Four British folkways in America.* New York: Oxford University Press.

Flanagan, Timothy J. (1985). Consumer perspectives on police operational strategy. *Journal of Police Science and Administration, 13*(1), 10–21.

Flynn, Kevin, & Gerhardt, Gary (1989). *The silent brotherhood: Inside America's racist underground.* New York: Free Press.

Forsyth, Craig J., & Marckese, Thomas A. (1993). Thrills and skills: A sociological analysis of poaching. *Deviant Behavior, 14*(2), 157–172.

Frankel, Bruce (1993, September 28). Ex-NYC officer tells stark tale of cops gone bad. *USA Today*, p. 3A.

Freudenburg, William R. (1986). The density of acquaintanceship: An over-looked variable in community research. *American Journal of Sociology,* *92*(1), 27–63.

Freudenburg, William R., & Jones, Robert Emmett (1991). Criminal behavior and rapid community growth: Examining the evidence. *Rural Sociology,* *56*(4), 619–645.

Friend, Tad (1994). The white trashing of America. *New York, 27*(33), 22–31.

Frisch, Suzy (1997, October 30). County's mink farm release linked to others: Activists targeting quality operations across the Midwest. *Chicago Tribune,* pp. 1, 4.

Frisch, Suzy (1997, November 13). Mink farmers brace for vandalism wave. *Chicago Tribune,* pp. 1, 8.

Fritchen, Janet M. (1991). *Engangered spaces, enduring places: Change, identity, and survival in rural America.* Boulder, CO: Westview Press.

Fuguitt, Glenn V., Brown, David L., & Beale, Calvin L. (1989). *Rural and small town America.* New York: Russell Sage Foundation.

Gagne, Patricia L. (1992). Appalachian women: Violence and social control. *Journal of Contemporary Ethnography, 20*(4), 387–415.

Gallup Poll Monthly (1991). Americans say police brutality frequent, 306, pp. 53–56.

Galpin, Charles J. (1918). *Rural life.* New York: Century.

Gardner, LeGrande, & Shoemaker, Donald J. (1989). Social bonding and delinquency: A comparative analysis. *Sociological Quarterly, 30*(3), 481–500.

Garkovich, Lorraine (1989). *Population and community in rural America.* Westport, CT: Greenwood Press.

Garkovich, Lorraine (1991). Governing the countryside: Linking politics and administrative resources. In Kenneth E. Pigg (Ed.), *The future of rural America: Anticipating policies for constructive change* (pp. 173–193). Boulder, CO: Westview Press.

Garmire, Bernard L. (Ed.). (1982). *Local government police management* (2nd ed.) Washington, DC: International City Management Association.

Geisler, Charles C., & Mitsuda, Hisayoshi (1987). Mobile-home growth, regulation, and discrimination in upstate New York. *Rural Sociology, 52*(4), 532–543.

Geller, William (Ed.). (1991). *Local government police management* (3rd ed.) Washington, DC: International City Management Association.

General Accounting Office (GAO). (1990). *Rural drug abuse: Prevalence, relation to crime, and programs.* Washington, DC: U.S. General Accounting Office.

Gibbs, Nancy (1993, May 3). Fire storm in Waco. *Time,* pp. 26–27, 30–36, 39–43.

Gilford, Dorothy M., Nelson, Glenn L., & Ingram, Linda (Eds.). (1981). *Rural America in passage: Statistics for policy.* Washington, DC: National Academy Press.

Goad, Jim (1997). *The redneck manifesto.* New York: Simon & Schuster.

Goldberg, Carey (1996, June 20). Alarm bells sounding as suburbs gobble up California's richest farmland. *New York Times,* p. A10.

Golden, Kathryn (1981). Rural courts: An Illinois study. *Criminal Justice Review*, 6(1), 38–42.

Goldstein, Herman (1987). Toward community-oriented policing: Potential, basic requirements, and threshold questions. *Crime & Delinquency, 33*(1), 6–30.

Gouveia, Lourdes, & Donald D. Stull (1995). Dances with cows: Beefpacking's Impact on Garden City, Kansas, and Lexington, Nebraska. In Donald D. Stull, Michael J. Broadway, & David Griffith (Eds.), *Any way you cut it: Meat processing and small-town America* (pp. 85–107). Lawrence: University of Kansas Press.

Greenberg, Michael R., Carey, George W., & Popper, Frank J. (1987). Violent death, violent states, and American youth. *The Public Interest, 87*, pp. 38–48.

Greenburg, Jan Crawford (1996, December 2). Brady gun bill under attack. *Chicago Tribune*, p. 4.

Greene, Jack R., & Mastrofski, Stephen D. (Eds.). (1988). *Community policing: Rhetoric or reality.* New York: Praeger.

Gyimah-Brempong, Kwabena (1987). Economies of scale in municipal police departments: The case of Florida. *Review of Economics and Statistics, 69*(2), 352–356.

Hackenberg, Robert A. (1995). Joe Hill died for your sins: Empowering minority workers in the new industrial labor force. In Donald D. Stull, Michael J. Broadway, & David Griffith (Eds.), *Any way you cut it: Meat processing and small-town America* (pp. 231–264). Lawrence: University Press of Kansas.

Hafley, Sandra Riggs (1994). *Rural organized crime: Marijuana growers in Kentucky.* Unpublished master's thesis, University of Louisville, Louisville, KY.

Hagan, John (1977). Criminal justice in rural and urban communities: A study of the bureaucratization of justice. *Social Forces, 55*(3), 597–612.

Hall, Bob (1995). The kill line: Facts of life, proposals for change. In Donald D. Stull, Michael J. Broadway, & David Griffith (Eds.), *Any way you cut it: Meat processing and small-town America* (pp. 213–230). Lawrence: University Press of Kansas.

Hamm, Mark S. (1993). *American skinheads: The criminology and control of hate crime.* Westport, CT: Praeger.

Hanaback, M. (1992, October). Poaching: Crime in our wilderness (Part I). *Outdoor Life,* 57–59, 70–75.

Hart, John Fraser, & Morgan, John T. (1995). Mobile homes. *Journal of Cultural Geography, 15*(2), 35–53.

Harvey, David (1996). *Justice, nature and the geography of difference.* Cambridge, MA: Blackwell.

Hastings, Don (1985). Big bucks for poachers. *Illinois Department of Conservation: Outdoor Highlights, 13*(6), 8–11.

Hawkins, Carl W., Jr., & Weisheit, Ralph A. (1997). The state of community policing in small towns and rural America. In Quint C. Thurman &

Edmund F. McGarrell (Eds.), *Community policing in a rural setting* (pp. 19–25). Cincinnati, OH: Anderson.

Heges, Stephen, Hawkins, Dana, and Loeb, Perry (1996, September 23). The new jungle. *U.S. News and World Report*, pp. 34–44.

Herbers, John (1986). *The new heartland*. New York: Time Books/Random House.

Hicks, Robert (1991). *In pursuit of Satan: The police and the occult*. Buffalo, NY: Prometheus Press.

Hoffman, J. (1996, August 27). In rural New York, neighborliness can be a headache. *New York Times*, p. A16.

Howlett, Debbie (1997, September 10). Easy-to-concoct drug often makes users turn violent. *USA Today*, pp. A1, A2.

Hubbard, Robert D., & Horton, David M. (1980). *Rural crime and criminal justice: A selected bibliography*. Washington, DC: National Institute of Justice.

Huff, C. Ronald (Ed.). (1996). *Gangs in America* (2nd ed.). Newbury Park, CA: Sage.

Illinois State Police (1994). *Crime in Illinois*. Springfield: ISP Division of Forensic Services and Bureau of Identification.

Innes, Christopher A. (1990). *Population density in local jails, 1988*. U.S. Department of Justice. Washington, DC: Bureau of Justice Statistics.

Insurance Research Council (1993). *Public attitude monitor, 1993*. Oak Brook, IL: Insurance Research Council.

International Association of Chiefs of Police (IACP). (1990). *Managing the small law enforcement agency*. Dubuque, IA: Kendall/Hunt.

International Association of Fire Chiefs, Inc. (IAFC). (1989). *Rural arson control* (Report No. EMW–86–C–2080). Washington, DC: Federal Emergency Management Agency, United States Fire Administration.

Jackson, Patrick G. (1988). Assessing the validity of official data on arson. *Criminology, 26*(1), 181–195.

Jacob, Steve, & Luloff, A. E. (1995). Exploring the meaning of rural through cognitive maps. *Rural Sociology, 60*(2), 260–273.

Jacobs, James B. (1989). *Drunk driving: An American dilemma*. Chicago: University of Chicago Press.

Jacobs, James B. (1993). The emergence and implications of American hate crime jurisprudence. *Israel Yearbook on Human Rights, 22*, pp. 39–65.

Jacobs, James B., & Kraft, Lawrence J. (1978). Integrating the keepers: A comparison of black and white prison guards in Illinois. *Social Problems, 25*(3), 304–318.

Jenkins, Philip (1995, September). Home-grown terror. *American Heritage*, pp. 38–40, 42, 44–46.

Jensen, Gary E, Stauss, Joseph H., & Harris, William V. (1977). Crime, delinquency, and the American Indian. *Human Organization, 36*(3), 252–257.

Johnson, Charles (1994, February). Call the ag patrol. *Farm Journal*, p. 30–31.

Johnson, Dirk (1998, June 24) Growth of factory-like hog farms divides rural areas of the Midwest. *Christian Science Monitor* [electronic edition]. Available: www.csmonitor.com/yr/mo/day/news/national/hog-factories.html

Johnson, Eric C., & Monkkonen, Eric H. (Eds). (1996). *The civilization of crime: Violence in town and country since the middle ages.* Urbana: University of Illinios Press.

Johnson, Kenneth M. (1993). Demographic change in non-metropolitan America, 1980 to 1990. *Rural Sociology, 58*(3), 347–365.

Kelley, Daryl (1993, September 14). Rancher gets 3-year sentence for exploiting migrants. *Los Angeles Times,* pp. A3, A21.

Kennedy, Leslie W., & Krahn, Harvey (1984). Rural-urban origin and fear of crime: The case for "rural baggage." *Rural Sociology, 49*(2), 247–260.

Kessler, M. (1990). Expanding legal services programs to rural America: A case study of program creation and operations. *Judicature, 73*(5), 273–280.

Kilman, Scott (1995, May 4). Iowans can handle pig smells, but this is something else: Giant hog "factories" strain inherent neighborliness of a rural community. *Wall Street Journal,* pp. A1, A6.

Klanwatch Intelligence Report (June 1995). Over 200 militias and support groups operate nationwide, p 1.

Klein, Malcolm W. (1995). *The American street gang: Its nature, prevalence, and control.* New York: Oxford University Press.

Klockars, Carl B. (1988). The rhetoric of community policing. In J. R. Greene & S. D. Mastrofski (Eds.), *Community policing: Rhetoric or reality* (pp. 239–258). New York: Praeger.

Klofas, John M. (1990). The jail and the community. *Justice Quarterly, 7*(1), 69–102.

Kowalewski, David, Hall, William, Dolan, John, & Anderson, James (1984). Police environments and operational codes: A case study of rural settings. *Journal of Police Science and Administration, 12*(4), 363–372.

Kowalski, Gregory, & Duffield, Don (1990). The impact of the rural population component on homicide rates in the United States: A county-level analysis. *Rural Sociology, 55*(1), 76–90.

Krannich, Richard S., Berry, E. Helen, & Greider, Thomas (1989). Fear of crime in rapidly changing rural communities: A longitudinal analysis. *Rural Sociology, 54*(2), 195–212.

Kuhn, Danny R. (1995). Appalachians on probation: Cultural considerations for the officers who supervise them. *Federal Probation, 59*(3), 3–9.

Lamb, David (1996, October 9). Main street finds gold in urban crime wave: Once-struggling rural America sees economic salvation in one of the nation's fastest-growing, most recession-proof industries—prisons. *Los Angeles Times,* pp. A1, A12.

Landon, Donald D. (1985). Clients, colleagues, and community: The shaping of zealous advocacy in country law practice. *American Bar Foundation Research Journal, 1,* pp. 81–112.

Landon, Donald D. (1990). *Country lawyers: The impact of context on professional practice.* New York: Praeger.

Lane, Roger (1997). *Murder in America: A history.* Columbus: Ohio State University Press.

Lanning, Kenneth V. (1989, October) Satanic, occult, ritualistic crime: A law enforcement perspective. *Police Chief,* pp. 62–83.

Laub, John H. (1981). Ecological considerations in victim reporting to the police. *Journal of Criminal Justice, 9*(6), 419–430.

Laub, John H. (1983a). Patterns of offending in urban and rural areas. *Journal of Criminal Justice, 11*(2), 129–142.

Laub, John H. (1983b). Urbanism, race, and crime. *Journal of Research in Crime and Delinquency, 20*(2), 183–198.

Lebowitz, B. D. (1975). Age and fearfulness: Personal and situational factors. *Sociological Focus, 13*(1), 696–700.

Lee, Gary R. (1982). Residential location and fear of crime among the elderly. *Rural Sociology, 47*(4), 655–669.

Lee, Helene R. (1997, April 2). Watch who you're calling "trailer trash." *Chicago Tribune*, p. 11.

Leukefeld, Carl G., Clayton, Richard R., & Myers, Jo Ann (1992). Rural drug and alcohol treatment. In Ruth W. Edwards (Ed.), *Drug use in rural American communities* (pp. 95–116). New York: Haworth Press.

Linedecker, Clifford L. (1993). *Massacre at Waco, Texas.* New York: St. Martin's Paperbacks.

Littlewood, T. B. (1969). *Homer of Illinois.* Evanston, IL: Northwestern University Press.

Littrell, Donald W., & Littrell, Doris P. (1991). Civic education, rural development, and the land grant institutions. In Kenneth E. Pigg (Ed.), *The future of rural America: Anticipating policies for constructive change* (pp. 195–212). Boulder, CO: Westview Press.

Lowe, George D., & Peek, Charles W. (1974). Location and lifestyle: The comparative explanatory ability of urbanism and rurality. *Rural Sociology, 39*(3), 392–420.

Lundstrom, Marjie, & Sharpe, Rochelle (1991). Getting away with murder. *Public Welfare, 49*(3), 18–29.

Lyerly, Robert R., & Skipper, James K. (1981). Differential rates of rural-urban delinquency. *Criminology, 19*(3), 385–399.

Marenin, Otwin, & Copus, Gary (1991). Policing rural Alaska: The village public safety officer (VPSO) program. *American Journal of Police, 10*(4), 1–26.

Maroules, Nick (1998). Study looks at unique roles of prosecutors in rural areas. *The Compiler, 17*(4), 15–16.

Martin, Douglas E. (1995). Crime along rural interstate highways. *Free Inquiry in Creative Sociology, 23*(2), 105–108.

Mayhew, B. H., & Levinger, R. L. (1977). Conflicting interpretations of human interaction. *American Journal of Sociology, 83*, 455–459.

Mays, G. Larry, & Thompson, Joel A. (1988). Mayberry revisited: The characteristics and operations of America's small jails. *Justice Quarterly 5*(3), 421–440.

McConnell, Malcolm (1989, February). Crack invades the countryside. *Reader's Digest*, pp. 73–78.

McCormick, John, & O'Donnell, Paul (1993, June 21). Drug wizard of Wichita: Did the chemist concoct a killer narcotic? *Newsweek*, p. 32.

McDowell, Edwin (1992, October 28). Threat of crime rises on the main highways. *New York Times*, p. A7.

McIntosh, William Alex, Fitch, Starla D., Staggs, Frank M., Nyberg, Kenneth L., & Wilson, J. Branton (1979). Age and drug use by rural and urban adolescents. *Journal of Drug Education, 9*(2), 129–143.

Meagher, M. Steven (1985). Police patrol styles: How pervasive is community variation? *Journal of Police Science and Administration, 13*(1), 36–45.

Metropolitan Life Insurance Company (1993). *The American teacher 1993: Violence in America's public schools.* New York: Louis Harris and Associates.

Miller, Martin G., Hoiberg, Eric O., & Ganey, Rodney E. (1982). Delinquency patterns of farm youth. In Timothy J. Carter, G. Howard Phillips, Joseph F. Donnermeyer, & Todd N. Wurschmidt (Eds.), *Rural crime: Integrating research and prevention* (pp. 87–103). Totowa, NJ: Allanheld, Osmun.

Miller, Michael K., & Luloff, Albert E. (1981). Who is rural? A typological approach to the examination of rurality. *Rural Sociology, 46*(4), 608–625.

Milofsky, Carl, Butto, Anthony, Gross, Michael, & Baumohl, Jim (1993). Small town in mass society: Substance abuse treatment and urban-rural migration. *Contemporary Drug Problems, 20*(3), 433–471.

Moberg, David (1996). State jobs: Economic boon or bust? *Illinois Issues, 22*(2), 14–23.

Molnar, Joseph J., Nelson, Robert G., & McGranahan, David (1991). Rural social structure and populations. In R. C. Buse & J. L. Driscoll (Eds.), *Rural information systems* (pp. 339–351). Ames: Iowa State University Press.

Moore, Mark Harrison (1992). Problem-solving and community policing. In Michael Tonry & Norval Morris (Eds.), *Modern Policing* (pp. 99–158). Chicago: University of Chicago Press.

Mount, Charles (1992, February 23). Counties planning a united effort to combat gang problems. *Chicago Tribune*, p. 23.

Mullen, Robert E., & Donnermeyer, Joseph F. (1985). Age, trust, and perceived safety from crime in rural areas. *Gerontologist, 25*(3), 237–242.

Murray, Charles (1986). White welfare, white families, "white trash." *National Review, 38*(5), 30–34.

Myers, Martha A., & Talarico, Susette M. (1986). Urban justice, rural injustice? Urbanization and its effect on sentencing. *Criminology, 24*(2), 367–391.

Narcotics Control Digest (1991, August 28). Four sheriffs guilty, p. 2.

National Center on Child Abuse and Neglect (1981). *Study findings: National study of the incidence and severity of child abuse and neglect.* Department of Health and Human Services. Washington, DC: U.S. Government Printing Office.

National Center on Child Abuse and Neglect (1988). *Study findings: National study of the incidence and severity of child abuse and neglect.* Department of Health and Human Services. Washington, DC: U.S. Government Printing Office.

National Fire Prevention Association (NFPA). (1992). *U.S. arson trends and patterns—1991.* Quincy, MA: National Fire Prevention Association.

National Institute of Justice (1993). *Controlling chemicals used to make illegal drugs: The Chemical Action Task Force and the Domestic Chemical Action Group.* Washington, DC: U.S. Department of Justice.

National League of Cities (1994). School violence in America's cities: NLC survey overview. Unpublished report.

National Safety Council (1992). *Accident facts: 1992 edition.* Washington, DC: National Safety Council.

National Sheriffs' Association (1979). *County law enforcement: An assessment of capabilities and needs.* Washington, DC: National Sheriffs' Association.

New York Times (1993, June 28). Haitians suffer from isolation in rural jails, p. A8.

Nisbett, Richard E., & Cohen, Dov (1996). *Culture of honor: The psychology of violence in the South.* Boulder, CO: Westview Press.

O'Brien, Darcy (1996). *Power to hurt.* New York: HarperCollins.

O'Dea, Patrick, Murphy, Barbara, & Balzer, Cecilia (1997). Traffick and illegal production of drugs in rural America. In Elizabeth Robertson, Zili Sloboda, Gayle M. Boyd, Lula Beatty, & Nicholas J. Kozel (Eds.), *Rural substance abuse: State of knowledge and issues* (pp. 79–89). Rockville, MD: National Institute on Drug Abuse.

Office of Juvenile Justice and Delinquency Prevention. (1997). *The 1995 national youth gang survey.* Washington, DC: U.S. Department of Justice.

Ollenburger, J. C. (1981, March). Criminal victimization and fear of crime. *Research on Aging, 3,* 101–118.

Orr, Richard (1997, October 27). Scientists call for study of how farm animals are treated. *Chicago Tribune,* p. 3.

Ostrom, Elinor, & Smith, Dennis C. (1976). On the fate of "Lilliputs" in metropolitan policing. *Public Administration Review, 36*(2), 192–200.

Pash, P. (1986). Poacher wars. *Illinois Department of Conservation: Outdoor Highlights, 14*(1), 3–9.

Patrico, Jim (1992, January). Lock up prison profits. *Farm Journal,* pp. 32–33.

Perkins, Craig, & Klaus, Patsy (1996). *Criminal victimization 1994* (Report for the Bureau of Justice Statistics). Washington. DC: U.S. Department of Justice.

Peters, Victoria J., Oetting, E. R., & Edwards, Ruth W. (1992). Drug use in rural communities: An epidemiology. In Ruth W. Edwards (Ed.), *Drug use in rural American communities* (pp. 9–29). New York: Haworth Press.

Photiadis, John D., & Simoni, Joseph (1983). Characteristics of rural areas. In Alan W. Childs & Gary B. Melton (Eds.), *Rural Psychology* (pp. 15–32). New York: Plenum Press.

Pimentel, David, & Pimentel, Marcia (1997, October 30). U.S. food production threatened by rapid population growth. Unpublished manuscript prepared for the Carrying Capacity Network.

Pope, Victoria (1996, April 22). Crack invades a small town: Sandy Level, Va., is trying to fight back, but cocaine is winning. *U.S. News and World Report* pp. 34, 37–39, 42–44.

Possley, Maurice (1997, April 20). "Code of the West" updated to help city slickers. *Chicago Tribune* pp. 1, 9.

Potter, Gary, & Gaines, Larry (1990). *The organizing of crime in Appalachia.* Paper presented at the Academy of Criminal Justice Sciences. Denver, CO.

Potter, Gary, & Gaines, Larry (1992). Country comfort: Vice and corruption in rural settings. *Journal of Contemporary Criminal Justice, 8*(1), 36–61.

Rachel's Hazardous Waste News #66 (1988, February 29). The new urban garbage solution: Dump it in poorer, rural areas. Available: http://www.rtk.net/E3391T132

Rand, Michael R., Lynch, James P., & Cantor, David (1997). *Criminal victimization, 1973–95* (Report for the Bureau of Justice Statistics). Washington. DC: U.S. Department of Justice.

Rangel, Charles B. (1991, April 4). Stemming the tide of youth gangs. *Chicago Tribune*, p. 11.

Reaves, Brian A. (1992a). State and local police departments, 1990. *Bureau of Justice Statistics Bulletin*, pp. 1–13.

Reaves, Brian A. (1992b). Sheriffs' departments 1990. *Bureau of Justice Statistics Bulletin*, pp. 1–12.

Reaves, Brian A. (1993). *Census of state and local law enforcement agencies, 1992.* Washington, DC: U.S. Department of Justice, Bureau of Justice Statistics Bulletin No. NCJ–142972.

Richardson, James T., Best, Joel, & Bromley, David G. (Eds.). (1991). *The satanism scare.* New York: Aldine de Gruyter.

Ringel, Cheryl (1997). *Criminal victimization 1996; Changes 1995–96 with trends 1993–96.* (Report for the Bureau of Justice Statistics). Washington. DC: U.S. Department of Justice.

Rosenbush, Steve (1998, June 17). Tech leaders warn of "great divide." *USA Today*, pp. 1B, 6B–7B.

Rural Missouri (1992, May). Research looks at rural roads, p. 7.

Salomon, Sonya (1997). Culture. In Gary A. Goreham (Ed.), *Encyclopedia of Rural America: The Land And People, Volume I* (pp. 169–172). Santa Barbara, CA: ABC–CLIO.

Saltiel, John, Gilchrist, Jack, & Harvie, Robert (1992). Concern about crime among Montana farmers and ranchers. *Rural Sociology, 57*(4), 535–545.

Sampson, Robert J. (1986). The effects of urbanization and neighborhood characteristics on criminal victimization. In Robert M. Figlio, Simon Hakim, & George E. Rengert (Eds.), *Metropolitan crime patterns* (pp. 3–25). Monsey, NY: Willow Tree Press.

Schildgen, Bob (1996). Murphy's laws: 1. hogs rule 2. you pay. *Sierra, 81*(3), 29.

Schlegel, Kip, & McGarrell, Edmund F. (1991). An examination of arrest practices in regions served by multijurisdictional drug task forces. *Crime and Delinquency, 37*(3), 408–426.

Security Systems Digest (1985). Rural arson, a growing problem, p. 10.

Seroka, Jim, & Subramaniam, Seshan (1991). Governing the countryside: Linking politics and administrative resources. In Kenneth E. Pigg (Ed.), *The future of rural America: Anticipating policies for constructive change* (pp. 213–231). Boulder, CO: Westview Press.

Setterberg, Fred and Shavelson, Lonny (1993). *Toxic nation: The fight to save our communities from chemical contamination*. New York: John Wiley & Sons.

Shichor, David (1992). Myths and realities in prison siting. *Crime and Delinquency, 38*(1), 70–87.

Short, James F. (1998). The level of explanation problem revisited—The American Society of Criminology 1997 presidential address. *Criminology, 36*(1), 3–36.

Sifferd, Katrina (1998). Victim services stretched far in rural areas. *The Compiler, 17*(4), 11–14.

Sims, Victor H. (1988). *Small town and rural police*. Springfield, IL: Charles C Thomas.

Sjoberg, Gideon. (1964). The rural-urban dimension in preindustrial, transitional, and industrial societies. In Richard E. L. Faris (Ed.), *Handbook of modern sociology* (pp. 127–159). Chicago: Rand-McNally.

Smith, Brent L. (1980). Criminal victimization in rural areas. In Barbara Raffael Price & Phyllis Jo Baunach (Eds.), *Criminal justice research: New models and findings*. Beverly Hills: Sage.

Smith, Brent L., & Huff, C. Ronald (1982). Crime in the country: The vulnerability and victimization of rural citizens. *Journal of Criminal Justice 10*(3), 271–282.

Smith, Georgia, & Lab, Steven (1991). Urban and rural attitudes toward participating in an auxiliary policing crime prevention program. *Criminal Justice and Behavior, 18*(2), 202–216.

Smith, Wes (1995, October 8). Loose talk, not radical sheik, bugs prison town. *Chicago Tribune*, p. 4.

Smith, Wes (1996, June 30). In string of strange robberies, thieves target expensive herbicides. *Chicago Tribune*, p. 12.

Snell, T. (1995). *Correctional populations in the United States, 1993* (Report for the Bureau of Justice Statistics). Washington, DC: U.S. Department of Justice.

Southern Poverty Law Center. (1998). Antigovernment rule: An Idaho county struggles with an insurgency. *Intelligence Report* (90), 21–23.

Staley, Sam (1992). *Bigger is not better: The virtues of decentralized local government* (Policy Analysis paper No. 166). Washington, DC: Cato Institute.

St. Clair, Jeffrey and Cockburn, Alexander (1997) Idaho's enemies: The National Guard counts environmentalists among them. *The Progressive, 61*(6), 18–20.

Stewart, Phil, & Sitaramiah, Gita (1997, November 13). America's heartland grapples with rise of dangerous drug. *Christian Science Monitor* [electronic edition]. Available: www.csmonitor.com/todays_paper/graphical/today/us/us.2.html

Stock, Catherine McNichol (1996). *Rural radicals: Righteous rage in the American grain*. Ithaca, NY: Cornell University Press.

Straus, Murray, & Gelles, Richard J. (Eds.). (1990). *Physical violence in American families: Risk factors and adaptations to violence in 8,145 families*. New Brunswick, NJ: Transaction.

Straus, Murray, Gelles, Richard J., & Steinmetz, Suzanne K. (1980). *Behind closed doors: Violence in the American family.* New York: Anchor Books.

Stull, Donald D. and Michael J. Broadway (1995). Killing them softly: Work in meatpacking plants and what it does to workers. In Donald D. Stull, Michael J. Broadway, & David Griffith (Eds.), *Any way you cut it: Meat processing and small-town America* (pp. 61–83). Lawrence: University of Kansas Press.

Swaim, Randall, Beauvais, Fred, Edwards, R. W., & Oetting, E. R. (1986). Adolescent drug use in three small rural communities in the Rocky Mountain region. *Journal of Drug Education, 16*(1), 57–73.

Swanson, Bert E., Cohen, Richard A., & Swanson, Edith P. (1979). *Small towns and small towners: A framework for survival and growth.* Beverly Hills: Sage.

Swanson, Charles R. (1981). Rural and agricultural crime. *Journal of Criminal Justice, 9*(1), 19–27.

Swanson, Charles R., & Territo, Leonard (1980). Agricultural crime: Its extent, prevention, and control. *FBI Law Enforcement Bulletin, 49*(5), 8–12.

Swanson, Louis E. (1990). Rethinking assumptions about farm and community. In Albert E. Luloff & Louis E. Swanson (Eds.), *American rural communities* (pp. 19–33). Boulder, CO: Westview Press.

Swindle, Howard (1993). *Deliberate indifference: A story of racial injustice and murder.* New York: Penguin.

Tabs, E. D. (1991). *Teacher survey on safe, disciplined, and drug-free schools* (Report No. NCES 91–091). Washington, DC: U.S. Department of Education, Office of Educational Research and Improvement.

Taylor, Bruce M. (1997). *Changes in criminal victimization, 1994–95* (Report for the Bureau of Justice Statistics). Washington, DC: U.S. Department of Justice.

Thorne, Gary E. (1976). The rural prosecutor and the exercise of discretion. *Criminal Law Bulletin, 12*(3), 301–316.

Thurman, Quint C., & McGarrell, Edmund F. (1997). *Community policing in a rural setting.* Cincinnati, OH: Anderson.

Thurman, Skip (1997, July 2). Saga unsettles small-town life. *Christian Science Monitor,* p. 3.

Tickamyer, Ann R., & Duncan, Cynthia M. (1990). Poverty and opportunity structure in rural America. In W. Richard Scott & Judith Blake (Eds.), *The annual review of sociology* , pp. 67–86. Palo Alto, CA: Annual Reviews.

Treaster, Joseph B. (1991, October 1). Study finds drug use isn't just urban problem. *New York Times,* p. A16.

Trojanowicz, Robert, & Bucqueroux, Bonnie (1990). *Community policing: A contemporary perspective.* Cincinnati: Anderson.

Tyson, Ann Scott (1996, September 16). Drug abuse is quiet scandal in America's countrysides. *Christian Science Monitor,* pp. 1, 14.

Unnithan, Prabha (1994). The processing of homicide cases with child victims: Systemic and situational contingencies. *Journal of Criminal Justice, 22*(1), 41–50.

U.S. Bureau of the Census (1990). *General population characteristics, 1990* (for each state). Washington, DC: U.S. Government Printing Office.

U.S. Bureau of the Census (1993a). *1990 Census of Housing: Detailed Housing Characteristics, United States* (Report #1990 CH–2–1). Washington, DC: U.S. Government Printing Office.

U.S. Bureau of the Census (1993b). *1990 Census of Housing: Detailed Housing Characteristics, Kentucky* (Report #1990 CH–2–19). Washington, DC: U.S. Government Printing Office.

U.S. Bureau of the Census (1993c). *Statistical abstract of the United States: 1993.* Washington, DC: U.S. Government Printing Office.

U.S. Department of Agriculture (1991). *Agricultural statistics, 1991.* Washington, DC: U.S. Government Printing Office.

U.S. Department of Commerce (1997). *American housing survey for the United States in 1995* (Current Housing Reports H150/95). Washington, D.C. U.S. Government Printing Office.

U.S. Department of the Interior (1991). *U.S. Fish & Wildlife Service Division of Law Enforcement: FY 1990 Annual report.* Washington, DC: U.S. Government Printing Office.

U.S. Department of Justice (1977). *Expenditure and employment data*, p. 428. Washington, DC: U.S. Government Printing Office.

U.S. General Accounting Office (1990). *Rural drug abuse: Prevalence, relation to crime and programs* (Report No. PEMD 90–24). Washington, DC: U.S. Government Printing Office.

Urschel, Joe (1995, May 16). Sentiments not held only by the fringe. *USA Today,* pp. 1A, 2A.

van Es, J. C., & Brown, J. E. (1974). The rural-urban variable once more: Some individual level observations. *Rural Sociology, 39*(3), 373–391.

Van, John (1998, February 16). Will new law mean selling the farm to afford rural communications? *Chicago Tribune,* Section 2, p. 2.

Verde, Tom (1998, February 2). 90's moonshiners add drugs and guns to the recipe. *New York Times,* p. A12.

Verhovek, Sam Howe (1994, April 25). 5 rural sheriffs are taking the Brady Law to court. *New York Times,* p. A8.

Victor, Jeffrey S. (1989). A rumor-panic about a dangerous satanic cult in western New York. *New York Folklore, 15,* 23–49.

Victor, Jeffrey S. (1990). Satanic cult rumors as contemporary legend. *Western Folklore, 49*(1), 51–81.

Victor, Jeffrey S. (1991). The dynamics of rumor-panics about satanic cults. In James T. Richardson, Joel Best, & David G. Bromley (Eds.), *The satanism scare* (pp. 221–236). New York: Aldine de Gruyter.

Victor, Jeffrey S. (1993). *Satanic panic: The creation of a contemporary legend.* Chicago: Open Court.

Walker, Samuel (1983). *The police in America: An introduction.* New York: McGraw-Hill.

Walker, Samuel (1992). *The police in America: An introduction* (2nd ed.) New York: McGraw-Hill.

Walsh, William F., & Donovan, Edwin J. (1984). Job stress in game conservation officers. *Journal of Police Science and Administration, 12*(3), 333–338.

Warner, W. Keith (1974). Rural society in a post-industrial age. *Rural Sociology, 39*(3), 306–317.

Websdale, Neil (1995). An ethnographic assessment of the policing of domestic violence in rural Eastern Kentucky. *Social Justice, 22*(1), 102–122.

Websdale, Neil (1998). *Rural woman battering and the justice system: An ethnography.* Thousand Oaks, CA: Sage.

Weinberg, D. (1987). Rural pockets of poverty. *Rural Sociology, 52*(3), 398–408.

Weingarten, Paul (1989, September 14). Profits, perils higher for today's bootleggers. *Chicago Tribune,* pp. 1, 8.

Weingarten, Paul, & Coates, James (1989a, September 12). Drugs blaze new paths: Interstates, backroads join courier system. *Chicago Tribune,* pp. 1, 8.

Weingarten, Paul, & Coates, James (1989b, September 10). Drugs find home in heartland: Crime, addictions destroying small-town way of life. *Chicago Tribune,* pp. 1, 11.

Weisheit, Ralph A. (1992). *Domestic marijuana: A neglected industry.* Westport, CT: Greenwood Press.

Weisheit, Ralph A. (1993). Studying drugs in rural areas: Notes from the field. *Journal of Research in Crime and Delinquency, 30*(2), 213–232.

Weisheit, Ralph A., & Kernes, Steven T. (1997). Future challenges: The urbanization of rural America. In Quint C. Thurman & Edmund F. McGarrell (Eds.), *Community policing in a rural setting* (pp. 123–133). Cincinnati, OH: Anderson.

Weisheit, Ralph A., & Klofas, John M. (1992). The social status of DUI offenders in jail. *The International Journal of the Addictions, 27*(7), 791–814.

Weisheit, Ralph A., & Wells, L. Edward (1996). Rural crime and justice: Implications for theory and research. *Crime & Delinquency, 42*(3), 379–397.

Weisheit, Ralph A., & Wells, L. Edward (forthcoming). The future of crime in rural America. *Journal of Criminal Justice.*

Weisheit, Ralph A., Wells, L. Edward, & Falcone, David N. (1994). Community policing in small town and rural America. *Crime & Delinquency, 40*(4), 549–567.

Wells, L. Edward, & Rankin, Joseph H. (1991). Families and delinquency: A meta-analysis of the impact of broken homes. *Social Problems, 38*(1), 71–93.

Wiers, P. (1939). Juvenile delinquency in rural Michigan. *Journal of Criminal Law and Criminology, 30,* 211–222.

Wilkinson, Kenneth P. (1984). A research note on homicide and rurality. *Social Forces, 63*(2), 445–452.

Wilkinson, Kenneth P. (1991). *The community in rural America.* New York: Greenwood Press.

Willits, Fern K., & Bealer, Robert C. (1967). An evaluation of a composite definition of rurality. *Rural Sociology, 32,* 165–177.

Willits, Fern K., Bealer, Robert C., & Timbers, Vincent L. (1990). Popular images of "rurality": Data from a Pennsylvania survey. *Rural Sociology, 55*(4), 559–578.

Willits, Fern K., Crider, Donald M., & Bealer, Robert C. (1973). Leveling of attitudes in mass society: Rurality and traditional morality in America. *Rural Sociology, 38*, 36–45.

Wilson, James Q., & Kelling, George L. (1989). Making neighborhoods safe. *Atlantic Monthly, 263*(2), pp. 46–52.

Wilson, Thomas C. (1991). Urbanism, migration, and tolerance: A reassessment. *American Sociological Review, 56*(1), 117–123.

Wolf, Daniel (1991). High risk methodology: Reflections on leaving an outlaw society. In William Shaffir & Robert Stebbins (Eds.), *Experiencing fieldwork: An inside view of qualitative research* (pp. 211–223). Newbury Park, CA: Sage.

Wolfner, Glenn D., & Gelles, Richard J. (1993). A profile of violence toward children: A national study. *Child Abuse and Neglect, 17*(2), 197–212.

Worldmark Encyclopedia of the United States (1986). New York: John Wiley & Sons.

Wray, Matt, & Newitz, Analee (1997). *White trash: Race and class in America.* New York: Routledge.

Wren, Christopher S. (1997, July 8). The illegal home business: "Speed" manufacture. *New York Times* [electronic edition]. Available: http://www.nytimes.com/yr/mo/day/news/national/crank-addict.html

Wright, James D., Rossi, Peter H., & Daly, Kathleen (1983). *Under the gun: Weapons, crime, and violence in America.* New York: Aldine.

Yetter, Deborah (1989, June 17). Bucolic "Mafia": Kentucky-based system of pot production called largest ever in the U.S. *Louisville Courier-Journal*, p. A1.

Zeskind, Leonard (1985). *Background report on racist and anti-Semitic organizational intervention in the farm protest movement.* Report prepared for the Center for Democratic Renewal. Atlanta, GA.

Index

Eisenstein, J., 113
Elderly, victimization of, 90-91. *See also* Senior citizens
Ellickson, R. C., 144, 145
Ellsworth, T., 154, 156
Emergency services, response time of, 8–9, 11, 67, 68, 133
Engel, D. M., 145
Environment
    crimes, unanswered questions about, 170–171
    ecology crimes and, 86–89
    fraudulent clean-up crimes, 87
    radical environmentalists and, 87
    rural vs. urban, 7–8
Erskine, H., 37
Esseks, J., 11
Ethnicity
    crime rates and, 23
    race vs., 23
    rural vs. urban crime and, 21–27
Expenditures, per officer, 106
Extremist groups. *See* Antigovernment attitudes,Christian Identity movement, Hate crimes, Survivalist groups
"Exurban" areas, 165

Fahnestock, K., 91, 145, 151, 152, 153
Falcone, D. N., 98, 105, 113, 115
Family violence. *See* Violence
Farm size, crime and, 81
Farmer, F. L., 185
Farmer's Home Administration, 189
Farms, 79, 189-190 . *See also* Agricultural crime
Federal Bureau of Investigation (FBI). *See* Uniform Crime Reports
Federal policing, cooperation with state and local agencies, 102–104, 178
Feld, B. C., 150
Felonious killings, of rural police, 175–176
Fields, G., 150, 168
Finn, L., 26

Firearms. *See* Guns
Fires. *See* Arson
Fischer, C. S., 42, 45, 68
Fish and Wildlife Service, 198
Fitch, S. D., 55
Flanagan, T. J., 110
Flynn, K., 30, 70
Focus groups, 200
Force
    deadly, use of, 121–122
    excessive, use of, 122–126
Forensic pathologists, vs. coroners, 67
Forest Service, 98, 198
Forsyth, C. J., 84
Fox, R. J., 48
Franchise, rural drug dealers and gangs, 52
Frankel, B., 125
Fraud
    credit card, 89
    environmental clean-up scams, 87
    telephone, 93
Freudenburg, W. R., 18, 19, 29
Friend, T., 25
Fringe groups. *See* Hate groups, Militia, Christian Identity movement, Survivalist movements
Frisch, S., 89
Fritchen, J. M., 86
Fuguitt, G. V., 18
Fundamentalism. *See* Christian Identity movement

Gagne, P. L., 63, 64
Gaines, L., 61, 62
Galpin, C. J., 165, 180
Gambling, 62, 160, 170
Game wardens. *See* Poaching
Ganey, R. E., 41
Gangs
    economic conditions for development of, 51
    in schools, 59
    movement into rural areas, 46–53
    National Youth Gang Crime Survey, 47–50

O'Brien, D., 25
O'Dea, P., 58
O'Donnell, P., 57
Occupational deviance, vs. abuse of
    authority, 124
Occupational information, defining
    "rural," 189–190
Oetting, E. R., 55
Offenders, police knowledge of, 28
Office of Juvenile Justice and Delin-
    quency Prevention (OJJDP), 47
Oklahoma City bombing, 30, 31
Ollenburger, J. C., 37
Organizations, crime-related docu-
    ments from, 198
Organized crime, vice and, 61–62
Orr, R., 88
Ostrom, E., 107, 108

Parker, L., 150
Pash, P., 83
Patrico, J., 158
Peek, C. W., 190
Perkins, C., 46
Personal crime, offending rate by
    community size, 23
Personal injury lawsuits, 145
Pesticide theft, 82
Peters, V. J., 55
Phillips, G. H., 41, 187
Photiadis, J. D., 191
Pimentel, D., 82
Pimentel, M., 82
Plea bargaining, in urban vs. rural
    courts, 151
Poaching, 83–85
Police
    brutality of, 112, 123–125
    community relations, 117
    concerns of rural, 110, 128–138
    consolidation vs. decentralization
        of departments, 107
    cooperation with, 32–33
    evaluation of performance, 113
    felonious killings of, 175–176
    job task analysis of rural, 174
    job task analysis of work, 174–175

misconduct of, 124–126
part-time departments, 174
range of noncrime services,
    110–111, 117
recruitment and retention of, 173
recruitment of rural, 173
relationship with community, 112,
    113, 116
relationship with rural prosecu-
    tors, 148
reserve, volunteer,and part-time,
    173
respect for, 103, 110, 111, 112
response to domestic violence,
    64–65
special problems of rural,
    128–130
training hardships of rural, 173
understaffing, poverty and, 17–18
urban-rural transition problems,
    174
violence and rural, 119–122
women and minorities as, 175
Police agencies
    definition of, 97–98
    department size, 104–107
    effect of regional poverty on, 17–18
    effectiveness by size, 108–109
    expenditures, 106
    in multijurisdictional task forces,
        103–104
    shrinking resources of, 105
Police brutality, rural vs. urban,
    123–124
Police-community relations, rural vs.
    urban, 112
Policies, urban vs. rural, 113–114
Policing
    community, 115–119
    nature of rural, 97–98
    rural styles of, 109–114
    rural vs. urban, 97–139
    small-town, 144
Pollution, environmental crime and,
    88
Pope, V., 57
Popper, F. J., 63

DATE DUE	
SEP 1 3 2000	